THE
SHAAR
PRESS

THE JUDAICA IMPRINT
FOR THOUGHTFUL PEOPLE

From Sinai

THE SHAAR PRESS

to Yerushalayim

Our Jewish Journey Continues

THE STORY OF
ROY AND LEAH NEUBERGER

RABBI NACHMAN SELTZER

Published by **SHAAR PRESS**
Distributed by MESORAH PUBLICATIONS, LTD.
313 Regina Avenue / Rahway, N.J. 07065 / (718) 921-9000

Distributed in Israel by SIFRIATI / A. GITLER
POB 2351 / Bnei Brak 51122

Distributed in Europe by LEHMANNS
Unit E, Viking Business Park, Rolling Mill Road
Jarrow, Tyne and Wear, NE32 3DP/ England

Distributed in Australia and New Zealand by GOLDS WORLD OF JUDAICA
3-13 William Street / Balaclava, Melbourne 3183 / Victoria Australia

Distributed in South Africa by KOLLEL BOOKSHOP
Northfield Centre / 17 Northfield Avenue / Glenhazel 2192, Johannesburg, South Africa

ISBN 10: 1-4226-3282-2 / ISBN 13: 978-1-4226-3282-6
ITEM CODE: STYH

Printed in the United States of America
Custom bound by Sefercraft, Inc. / 313 Regina Avenue / Rahway, N.J. 07065

Table of Contents

Foreword   7

Introduction   13

Prologue   15

PART 1

Chapter One: The Salant Connection   21

Chapter Two: The Wizard of Wall Street   31

Chapter Three: Jackson Pollock and Eastman Kodak   37

Chapter Four: A Chair for Edward R. Murrow   44

PART 2

Chapter Five: Climbing the Grand Teton   57

Chapter Six: Fieldston   63

Chapter Seven: A Honeymoon in Wyoming   70

Chapter Eight: Bear Jam   77

PART 3

Chapter Nine: The Turnaround   87

Chapter Ten: Getting Off the Merry-Go-Round   93

Chapter Eleven: The Rebbetzin   102

Chapter Twelve: A Jew With a Gun   112

Chapter Thirteen: Smashing Idols   120

Chapter Fourteen: The Train in Jamaica   131

Chapter Fifteen: The Rebbetzin's Diagnosis   140

PART 4

Chapter Sixteen: From Biker to Chaim Berliner   155
Chapter Seventeen: Growing With Hineni   164
Chapter Eighteen: Miniature Ambassadors of Torah   181
Chapter Nineteen: The Lives That Were Changed   189
Chapter Twenty: Serve Food and They Will Come   198

PART 5

Chapter Twenty-One: Yeshiva Ateres Yisroel   205
Chapter Twenty-Two: Life in Canarsie   212
Chapter Twenty-Three: A Stop on Wall Street   223
Chapter Twenty-Four: From Central Park to Sinai   230
Chapter Twenty-Five: A New Chapter   243
Chapter Twenty-Six: Ice Cream in the Snow   256
Chapter Twenty-Seven: A Bachur Named Benyamin   272
Chapter Twenty-Eight: From Tbilisi to Baku   280
Chapter Twenty-Nine: The Belarus Disco   295
Chapter Thirty: Flagpoles and Hurricanes   302

PART 6

Chapter Thirty-One: More Books   321
Chapter Thirty-Two: Acadia Man 1 and Acadia Man 2   329
Chapter Thirty-Three: The Movie   336
Chapter Thirty-Four: The NYPD and the NFL   341
Chapter Thirty-Five: Back on the Home Front   349

PART 7

Chapter Thirty-Six: The Journey of a Holy Soul   359
Chapter Thirty-Seven: Never Too Late   369
Chapter Thirty-Eight: A Meeting with the President   383
Chapter Thirty-Nine: Farewell in a Blizzard   389
Chapter Forty: The End of an Era   396
Afterword   402

Foreword

When Rabbi Nachman Seltzer told us that he wanted to write a book about us, we were flabbergasted. What! A book about us? We asked trusted rabbis whether we should go ahead with the project, and they said, "Yes, it will be a *kiddush Hashem.*"

That's how it began.

In the process, we became close friends and admirers of Rabbi Seltzer. He is one of those rare people who has an *ayin tovah*, a "generous eye." He's happy when he sees someone with a special attribute, and he isn't envious of the other person's good qualities, which is why he's so inspiring when he writes about other people. He looks inside the person, at the *neshamah*, and tries to understand the workings of the heart.

This is the essence of *ahavas chinam*, unconditional love for a fellow Jew, the *middah* that enabled us to receive the Torah at Har Sinai and that will eventually save us at the time of the final redemption.

You may know a little about our story, which is told

The Neubergers
with Rabbi Nachman Seltzer

in my first book, *From Central Park to Sinai: How I Found My Jewish Soul*. Parts of that story are recounted in this book because not everyone is familiar with it and it forms the background for the many recent stories that are told here for the first time.

As a child growing up without Torah, I was constantly filled with a deep-seated anxiety. I didn't realize that my anguish was rooted in a soul that couldn't live without Torah as I didn't know what this meant. Yet it is this sense that something was missing that spurred me to begin a lifelong search.

I believe that my wife and I were created to search together for Hashem. When, in His kindness, He opened the door to the Torah for us, we were so exhilarated that we wanted to share this gift with others. As King David said, "How can I repay Hashem for all His kindness to me? I will raise the cup of salvations and invoke the Name of Hashem" (*Tehillim* 116:12-13).

My wife has an ongoing job as an *ezer kenegdo* — a helpmate who molds me into a better person. She works with patience and wisdom to make me into a *mentch*. It is not, however, a one-way street. I help her, too. I try to provide the happiness that comes from the deepest kind of companionship. In the words of *Koheles*, "Enjoy life with the wife you love through all the fleeting days of your life He has granted you beneath the sun" (*Koheles* 9:9).

With that said, I believe that the greatest enjoyment in this world is spiritual enjoyment. The mutual satisfaction of a husband and wife who labor together in the fields of Torah is all anyone can ask for in this world. In aspiring to this endeavor, may we merit bringing honor to Hashem's Name, and with whatever talent He has given us, may we be His loyal servants and help bring to fruition His plan to restore the world to its original pristine state.

I wish to thank our children, Rabbi Dovid and Sarah Winer, Rabbi Osher and Yaffa Jungreis, Rabbi Avi and Miriam Hess, Rabbi Aharon Yaakov and Ariela Neuberger, and Rabbi Yaakov and Nechami Slatus for being our inspiration, with their exemplary *kibbud av va'eim*, wise insights, Torah leadership, and all the *chesed* they do for the *klal*. May they be blessed forever.

Throughout our life, *malachim* (yes, I think of them as angels) have come into our life to help us and guide us. There are many great people whom we have been fortunate to know, and many are named in this book. At the risk of offending others whom I have inadvertently omitted, I want to name a few:

- Our parents, who excelled in *derech eretz* and taught us the lessons of honesty and integrity.
- All the wonderful teachers who taught us how to express ourselves clearly. We have aimed to use this knowledge to be *mekadeish Shem Shamayim* with both the written and spoken word.
- The *malach* who came to Ann Arbor, Michigan, on January 10, 1966, and taught me that Hashem exists.
- Rabbi Meshulem HaLevi and Rebbetzin Esther Jungreis, who adopted us and taught us Torah and then became our *mechutanim*.
- The many rabbanim who took us under their wings, among them Rabbi Chaim Yisroel Belsky, Rabbi Aharon Brafman, Rabbi Avraham Pam, *zecher tzaddikim livrachah;* and *yblch"t* Rabbi Yaakov Bender, Rabbi Yitzchak Berkovits, Rabbi Shlomo Bussu, Rabbi Dovid Cohen, Rabbi Reuven Cohen, Rabbi Eytan Feiner, Rabbi Yaakov Feitman, Rabbi Yaakov Fleischman, Rabbi Binyamin Forst, Rabbi Yaakov Hillel, Rabbi Naftali Jaeger, Rabbi Yehoshua Kalish, Rabbi Shmuel Kamenetsky, Rabbi Yeshaya Klor, Rabbi Aryeh Malkiel Kotler, Rabbi Zev Leff, Rabbi Avigdor Nebenzahl, Rabbi Yechiel Perr, Rabbi Moshe Aharon Rosengarten, Rabbi Matisyahu Salomon, Rabbi Eliyahu Schneider, Rabbi Nate Segal, Rabbi Yechezkel Shraga Weinfeld, Rabbi Meir Weitman, Rabbi Elchonon Zohn.
- My wonderful *chavrusa*s who taught me Torah over the years: Rabbi Yaakov Jungreis, Rabbi Shlomo Gertzulin, Rabbi Moshe Grossman, Rabbi Shaul Geller, and Rabbi Yehuda Schiff. I learned Gemara for many years with our own brilliant son-in-law, Rabbi Osher Jungreis.
- I also want to express my admiration for Rabbi Pinchos Lipschutz, the publisher of *Yated Ne'eman*.

- I want to pay tribute to some of the great people at ArtScroll/Mesorah. Over the years, I had the honor to speak occasionally with Rabbi Meir Zlotowitz, *zt"l*, Rabbi Nosson Scherman, and Rabbi Gedaliah Zlotowitz. I am also honored to consider myself a friend of the *chashuve* Rabbi Yitzchok Hisiger, the "voice" of ArtScroll, who became my friend when he was my editor at *Yated Ne'eman*, in which my weekly column appeared for some twelve years. We are so grateful to Mrs. Miriam Zakon and Mrs. Suri Brand for their highly professional work, their kindness, and for the way they responded in such heartwarming fashion to the message of the book. It gave us a feeling of tremendous confidence to work with such *eidele* people!

   Once again, Reb Eli Kroen brought his unequaled graphic talents to the fore to create a striking cover design worthy of the book's message. My thanks to Mrs. Estie Dicker for her expert pagination, and Mrs. Esther Feierstein for her meticulous proofreading.

   ArtScroll has transformed the world of Torah in our generation. As a newcomer to that world, I wouldn't have begun to know how to swim in these deep waters were it not for the great achievements of this courageous publishing house. The beauty, clarity, and lucidity of their work is a *kiddush Hashem*.

- Over the years, Reb Tsemach Glenn has assisted us in many remarkable ways.

- Our family attorney of many generations, Jim Kaufman, has stood by our side with wisdom, integrity, and devotion.

- David Pedowitz and Mrs. Chani Gewirtz have gone beyond the call of duty to sustain and enhance our lives.

Now I want to touch on a delicate subject.

I grew up in an almost-Victorian world on the Upper East Side of Manhattan. Largely Jewish, it was a world of embarrassment at being Jewish, yet also a world of good manners and genteel people who carried themselves with an air of dignity. I was raised in a home where *derech eretz* and integrity were a way of life. No one ever thought of cheating, speaking crudely, or trying to earn a dishonest penny. Words themselves had to be enunciated properly. We were taught to say "twenty" and not "twenny," "February" and not "Febuary." There was a dignity about life that I learned from my parents and grandparents.

Although I grew up in a wealthy neighborhood, we didn't live an ostentatious life. We never focused on money in the family. My parents worked hard, but they were not crass or slaves to money. My father was a genius on Wall Street; he was successful, but he was never a grabber. He always said there is too much greed in the world, and he didn't want to contribute to that. He wanted partners in his firm who were "smarter" than he was. If they were more successful than he (and some were), he was happy for them. He earned his livelihood by honest and friendly endeavor and never begrudged anything to anyone else.

And my parents, appreciative of everything they had, gave generously to others. They gave back to the world that had given so much to them.

This is the setting in which I grew up and led me on the path I eventually took.

Several years ago I had the merit of being introduced to Rabbi Moshe Sternbuch, *shlita*, in Yerushalayim. Later that day we were scheduled to leave Israel and return to the United States. I was sad to be leaving the Holy Land, and I expressed this feeling, whereupon Rabbi Sternbuch told me something I will never forget: "Yisroel, you are a soldier, and soldiers have to go where the battle is!"

With those words ringing in my ears, I gained courage. I thought of King David, who said, "Hashem…illuminates my darkness. For with You I smash a troop, and with my G-d I leap over a wall…" (*Tehillim* 18:30). And I was able to return to the United States and continue carrying out my mission as a solder in Hashem's army.

There is a postscript to this story.

I was recently reading the ArtScroll biography of Rabbi Elchanan Wasserman, *zt"l*. In 1939, Rabbi Wasserman visited the

United States on behalf of his yeshivah in Baranovich, Poland. As he was preparing to return, his colleagues begged him to remain in the United States because they all knew of the almost-certain fate that awaited him in Europe, where the Nazi onslaught was just getting underway.

Rabbi Wasserman replied, "I am a soldier. I have to go to the front."

I was immediately struck by these words, which echoed the words I had heard spoken some seventy years later by Rabbi Moshe Sternbuch in Yerushalayim.

Then I noticed a footnote to this account: "Reb Elchanan repeated similar statements several times during those winter months, despite his premonition that the catastrophe was approaching. During Sivan 5699 (1939), he was among the guests of the Sternbuch family in London [where he expressed similar sentiments]."

No wonder these words were so powerful! These were the words of giants who toiled for Hashem every moment of their lives, of soldiers who were willing to sacrifice their lives if necessary to bring glory to His Name.

May Hashem have mercy on all of us and reveal the rebuilt Beis HaMikdash soon in our days.

Yisroel Neuberger
Yerushalayim
Chanukah 5783

PHOTO CREDITS

Beth Medrash Govoha
Cody Downard Photo, Vail, Colorado
EarthCaptured Photography courtesy of Bigstock Photos
Frances M. Roberts (New York Times)
Helen Stambler Neuberger, Florival Farm 2021
Howard Gordon Photography
Itzik Bellenitzki
Jens Lambert Photography
Ted Foxx/Alamy
Tsemach Glenn
Yeshiva University

Introduction

I'll be honest with you. The reason this book came to be written was because of Rebbetzin Jungreis. Let me explain.

When I was asked to write *The Rebbetzin*, I was given a long list of people to interview, people who had been close to her. Yisroel and Leah Neuberger were on that list. And not only did I meet with them, but I was also given a copy of Yisroel's first book, *From Central Park to Sinai*, because it would give me another perspective on the Rebbetzin.

I read *Central Park* and I really enjoyed it. It was honest and compelling writing, and I was touched by the passion and sincere authenticity portrayed by Yisroel Neuberger.

Of course, then I had to go ahead and write *The Rebbetzin*, which was, after all, the reason I had made the connection in the first place.

Then this thought popped into my head.

I had loved the story of *Central Park*, Yisroel and Leah Neuberger's story, and yet they had gone on to achieve many things since the book's publication so many years earlier. In the wake of *Central Park*, Yisroel and Leah began traveling the world to speak in so many communities, and people related to them as if they were their own *zeide* and *bubby*. Perhaps it was time to write the next part of the story?

One day Yisroel called me up with a book idea for me.

"I have a better idea," I told him.

"What's that?"

"I want to write the rest of your story."

And so our journey together began.

◆ ◆ ◆

I want to be very clear here: I have included quite a few of the original stories that were written in *From Central Park to Sinai*, rewriting them in my style yet doing my best to stay true to Yisroel and Leah's voice. I had a good reason for doing so. Those stories are precious and should be retold and shared anew with the next generation who never read them.

More, these are the stories that formed Yisroel and Leah and reveal the foundation of the people they later became. I wanted to weave a narrative of the old and the new — the beautiful stories that occurred when they were searching and first became *frum* and the tapestry of events that happened in the later years, after Yisroel's first book was published and they began addressing audiences around the globe.

If you read *Central Park*, you'll be familiar with part of this book while enjoying many new stories that you've never heard before. And if you've never read *Central Park*, you're in for a wild ride, so don't forget to fasten your seat belt...

It has been a true pleasure for me to embark on this journey alongside Reb Yisroel and Leah Neuberger. I can only wish the two of them immense *nachas* from their wonderful family and continued health for the rest of their lives.

Rabbi Nachman Seltzer
Ramat Beit Shemesh
2023

When fictitious names are used, an asterisk (*) will precede the first appearance of the name.

In general, the names "Roy" and "Linda" will be used when discussing their lives before they became observant; the names "Yisroel" and "Leah" will be used afterward.

Prologue

There was a time in Roy Neuberger's life when he published a weekly newspaper called *The Cornwall Local*. To promote and develop his newspaper, Roy joined the National Newspaper Association, the trade association of weekly newspapers around the country. At the time, the president of the NNA was a Jew by the name of Walter Grunfeld. Walter was a brilliant speaker and a wonderful human being, and he and Roy became friends.

One day Roy called Walter at home.

Roy at his desk at *The Cornwall Local*

"Walter, I wanted to know if Linda and I could come over and spend a day with you. I've never published a paper before, and I have a million questions."

"Sure, no problem," Walter said, and invited them to visit him one day that week.

A few days later, they drove two and a half hours to Binghamton, New York, where Walter owned three newspapers. Walter's advice was golden, and they spent the day enjoying hours of informative conversation. At the end of the day, they swung by the Grunfeld home before leaving town. It was six thirty, and Walter wanted to watch the news.

The reason Walter was so anxious to watch the news was because at that moment the State of Israel was fighting the Yom Kippur War. Until that point, the war had been going badly, but somehow the Israelis had suddenly turned the tide, and now the momentum was going in the opposite direction. For the first time, the attackers found themselves on the defensive.

Standing in front of the television, Walter Grunfeld broke down in tears.

Walter Grunfeld

"I can't believe it! I can't believe it!" he repeated over and over. "A week ago, Israel was finished! It was all over! And now look at this: General Sharon has crossed the Suez Canal, and he's got the Egyptian army surrounded. In the North, they're marching on Damascus. Israel is saved!"

Walter was overcome, his Jewish heartstrings getting a tug at seeing Israel's salvation.

Roy felt as if he needed to contribute something to the moment and made a comment like "Oh, yeah, I read something in the paper about a war in the Middle East. Sure, I know about this!"

But it was obvious that he didn't feel connected to the momentous events happening across the ocean, and this made Walter stop and take a new look at his visitors. Suddenly, Walter realized that the two Jews sitting with him in his living room were clueless about the fact that Israel was even involved in a war, never mind winning or losing.

Walter Grunfeld couldn't help it. With tears rolling down his cheeks, and every particle of passion he possessed, he began to shout.

"What kind of Jew are you? Are you made of stone? Don't you have a heart?!"

For Roy, it was a watershed moment.

Standing there in the living room of a man he respected but barely knew, Roy heard a question that he couldn't have answered for all the money in the world.

What kind of Jew are you, Roy?

And all Roy could think about was, *That's a great question because in truth, I have no idea what kind of a Jew I am. In fact, I have no idea what being a Jew even means in the first place.*

When he left Walter Grunfeld's home that night, that powerful question kept replaying itself in his mind.

What kind of Jew are you?

What kind of Jew are you?

I don't know, he said to himself. *I wish I knew the answer to that question. But the truth is, I just don't know.*

♦ ♦ ♦

As everyone knows, a person isn't born in a vacuum and every life is unique. In order to grasp how these two very special people became who they became, it's necessary for us to go back in time — back to life in the rarefied atmosphere of the Upper East Side of Manhattan in the 1940s and '50s.

PART 1

"It's a lot harder to lose a game while making it look like you're trying to win than it is to win..."

Roy Neuberger Senior,
describing a game of tennis he played against
the king of Sweden

Chapter One
The Salant Connection

Roy Neuberger was born in November 1942 and grew up in a home that was completely cut off from anything related to his heritage. His family was so far removed from Judaism that even days like Rosh Hashanah and Yom Kippur — days that garner recognition even in the non-Jewish universe — meant nothing to them. Yet the non-Jewish holidays were celebrated, along with all the tinsel. It wasn't that his parents had chosen to give up their heritage, but that they didn't know anything at all about that heritage. Even Roy's grandparents had long been living lives devoid of Jewish content.

When Roy was a child, the family celebrated American holidays, like Halloween and Easter. And with Irish maids in the house and the parade right there on Fifth Avenue, St. Patrick's Day was a big deal. But the biggest day of the year for Roy was December 25. Come December 25, the house saw lots of action. There was a tree, grandly decorated with lights, ornaments, and Anna the cook's gingerbread cookies. There was excitement and anticipation, but there was no *menuchas hanefesh*, no peace for his beleaguered soul.

For a while, Roy hoped the answer to his angst lay in great writers like Chaucer, Milton, Homer, and Shakespeare. If they were so widely read, they must have known the secret of life, he thought. This led him to study literature in high school and, later, at college and graduate school. Maybe by delving into classical literature, he'd find the solace he sought and his fears would recede.

Hamlet — a work of genius. The problem was, as Roy discovered, that one cannot live by *Hamlet*. Nor by any of the other works of literature he read.

Music soothed him as long as it was the right music and as long as the music was playing. He loved Beethoven's Ninth Symphony. When he listened to this piece, with all its complexities, he forgot his troubles. He also loved the music of Johann Sebastian Bach, hearing in it the sound of solar systems and galaxies revolving and orbiting in perfect, orderly rhythm. As a boy, Roy would sit on the floor next to the beautiful inlaid mahogany cabinet that housed the Victrola record player, inhaling the music like oxygen.

Eventually he learned to sing folk music and play the guitar. Music gave him a sense of purpose and comfort as a teenager. Camp Killooleet in Vermont, which he attended for five summers from the age of ten, was suffused with folk music. The owner's brother was the legendary Pete Seeger, a folk music icon at the time.

When Roy was ready to buy his own guitar, his friend Bob Stein took him to a music store in the Bowery. He became quite adept and eventually owned two guitars, one a six string, the other a twelve string. You need strong fingers for a twelve-string guitar.

The music took his mind off his churning thoughts, but they always returned. It was the balm that took his mind off of his troubles — until the music stopped and darkness returned. In his heart, the fears didn't go away.

"Later," Roy says, "I learned the words of Rav Shamshon Refael Hirsch, who wrote that when the peoples of the world turned away from Hashem, they lost the inner harmony that had been theirs in Gan Eden. Desiring to restore some feeling of peace, they turned to music and art. Rav Hirsch explains that music and art can achieve a high purpose when used to serve Hashem. Look, for example, at the music of the Levi'im in the Beis HaMikdash."

Roy with his guitar

In retrospect, the fear and ever-growing sense of desperation were a gift from Hashem because they made Roy increasingly determined to find something real, a dependable moral compass.

Shakespeare. Nature. Music. But when the symphony ended, the darkness returned, as it did when the hike was over and the last page of the book was read.

Clearly the answer lay somewhere else.

Roy's mother's maiden name was Salant, which became his middle name. Her father, Aaron B. Salant, was born in Europe, as was her mother, but by the 1880s the Salant family had immigrated to the States.

Roy's maternal grandfather arrived in the United States in 1878 as a child and grew up to become a professor of Greek and Roman history at City University in New York. All his children majored in economics, which he considered the wisdom of the future. Roy's mother herself attended Bryn Mawr, a prestigious women's college in Philadelphia.

Grandpa Aaron B. Salant eventually left the world of academia and went into business, eventually partnering with his brother in a company called Salant and Salant, which manufactured work

Roy's parents and grandfather, Aaron B. Salant, with Roy's brother, Jimmy, in the early 1950s

shirts. But he was an intellectual at heart and focused on economic reform and civic improvement. Grandma Salant was a dignified partner and a warm Old World grandmother. She was born in Czechoslovakia, spoke German (but not Yiddish), and loved *schnecken*, a sweet roll common in Germany. Roy inherited her sweet tooth.

You may recognize the name — Salant. Indeed, when Roy was a little boy, his grandfather told him that the family was descendants of a famous rabbi named "Israel Salanter." Roy never forgot this little fact, and while in his younger years that knowledge didn't mean anything to him, the older he got, the more significant it became. It's still not exactly clear whether he is actually a descendant of Rabbi Yisrael Salanter, but one thing Roy knows for sure is that his mother had a "Salanter *neshamah*."

"She was always working on her *middos*," he says, "never satisfied with herself as she was. She was respectful to everyone; she had no airs and she was a paragon of integrity. Because of her upbringing, she wasn't aware of the significance of the name

Salant, but she must have inherited Salanter genes, because she lived the life of a Salanter!"

Marie Salant Neuberger had a profound influence on her son, just by virtue of who she was as a person. He credits her influence for stimulating his own spiritual search. And when he was given a Hebrew name at the age of thirty-one, he chose the name Yisroel in honor of Rabbi Yisrael Salanter.

♦ ♦ ♦

On Roy's father's side, it was discovered that he was a direct descendant of Rabbi Yaakov Weil, famously known as the Mahariv, a German rabbi who lived during the fifteenth century and was considered an expert on *shechitah*. In 1549, a compilation of his *teshuvos* was published in Venice.

The story is told that the Mahariv was offered the position of chief rabbi of Nuremberg but refused to accept it because he wasn't willing to bring dishonor to the older rabbi who had served in that position for many years (despite halachic rulings that it would have been permissible). In another display of humility, Rabbi Weil generally signed his responsa as HaKatan (the small one) Yaakov Weil. Yet his *sefer*, *Shechitos U'Bedikos*, as well as his *She'eilos U'Teshuvos Mahariv*, has been reprinted more than seventy times.

But while the family could boast of a fine ancestry, they had lost their connection to Judaism. They lived in the vast "melting pot" of America, among German Jews whose attempt to erase the memory of their past had been very successful. The vestige of *Yiddishkeit* that remained was hidden deep inside their souls.

Roy's mother had gone to college with Janet Wise, the daughter of Steven Wise, the Reform clergyman who had advised President Roosevelt to essentially ignore the plight of the European Jews during the Holocaust and not to bomb the railroad tracks leading to Auschwitz. This was the distorted Jewish leadership and outlook of the Upper East Side.

What a miracle that anyone could emerge from that spiritual black hole!

All this may sound like just plain history, but it's much more than that. It's the psychological pain within each Jewish child who feels lost in this world, who is so far from the world of his or her ancestors. Many have managed to bury the ancient stirrings of their soul and adopt the ways of the surrounding culture in *galus*, but Roy could never do that, and as a result, he was constantly anguished.

Here is how he describes his childhood feelings: "I thought there was something wrong with me. Maybe I was insane. Maybe I was dangerous. I had frightening fantasies in which I would go out of control and do terrible things. So I began to think I wasn't normal. I was actually afraid of myself, as if my soul was bad. I had nowhere to turn to find solace because no one could possibly understand what was going on inside my head. And, even worse, when I realized that I was living in an environment that was apparently perfect, an affluent home with wonderful parents and everything I could possibly want on a material level, I could not reconcile this with the fact that I felt spiritually anguished. Something must be wrong with me!"

Roy's mother was empathetic but had no solutions. Though he was only a child, he said to her, "I think something called 'religion' might help me." But they didn't know where to look for that elusive thing that Roy was seeking. She initially sent him to the Ethical Culture Sunday School, hoping that there he would receive that thing called "religion," and this would cure him of his anxieties. Later, he attended the full-time program of the Ethical Culture School.

Focused on living life according to "ethical principles" rather than any specific religion, the Sunday school program exposed its students to varied theologies. One Sunday the teacher taught about Christianity, the next week Islam, then Greek mythology, Roman mythology, Buddhism, Hinduism, even something called Judaism. But it was all theory, empty words that were hard to take seriously and certainly not to be lived by either teacher or students. The school only left Roy feeling more empty.

When Sunday school flopped, Roy's mother did what everyone

in their social circles did: she sent him to a psychiatrist. The psychiatrist was a very renowned older woman — French, not Jewish — whom Roy consulted for six interminable years. He simply could not connect to her at all. He felt like a fugitive when he entered her apartment building, certain that everyone knew why he was there. (And there was another problem: his appointment always coincided with one of his favorite TV shows, *Highway Patrol!*)

The psychiatrist hardly said a word. She would sit next to Roy, scratching constantly with her pen on a white unlined pad as if he were the subject of a PhD thesis and not a person. She would write and write and write while he told her about his fears, his dreams, how he hated the foul language that his friends used, how he was afraid of crime and drugs and muggers. She listened and wrote, listened and wrote, but there was no balm for Roy's tortured soul.

She did nothing for Roy. By the time he stopped seeing her six years later, he was still worried about the same things that had been bothering him when he first began seeing her. He told himself that he was better than he was before, but he didn't really believe it.

He stopped seeing the doctor, but the fears didn't stop.

◆ ◆ ◆

Roy's mother was raised with a sense of responsibility. She was extremely civic-minded, working tirelessly for many causes. She was president of the Women's City Club of New York and chairman of the Board of Governors of the Ethical Culture Schools, which she herself had attended along with her brothers. Her children were also educated there, from the age of three to eighteen.

With no airs about her, Marie Neuberger never chose to ride in a limousine. Instead, she would travel on the Madison Avenue bus or the subway. That was the way she lived, not calling attention to herself.

While working for myriad causes, Marie made time to spend with her mother. The two of them often went out together for cake (maybe *schneken*!) and ice cream (Roy's mother's favorite flavors were coffee and peach) served on the highly polished square table tops at a Schrafft's restaurant. (The two ladies wore white gloves because that was what women wore on the Upper East Side in those days.)

As a part of Upper East Side society, Marie made sure that her children were taught what were considered the "social graces." Roy was sent for dance lessons at a local academy, where he was expected to wear white gloves and learn the art of graceful movement. Roy detested the place, especially since he seemed to have become quite the expert at treading on young ladies' toes.

Years later, after he became *frum* and started attending religious weddings, he suddenly knew how to dance. In fact, he was very good at it. It was all there, inside him. *Shelo asani goy!* he thought to himself at his discovery. *Thank G-d I am a Jew and live a Jewish life!*

It was also common in Upper East Side circles for meals to be served by a uniformed maid. The table setting included a silver

Leah lighting Shabbos candles using his parents' silver trays

napkin ring engraved with the initials of each member of the family. Yisroel and Leah use those napkin rings today, as well as beautiful crystal and silver pieces from their parents' homes, to sanctify Shabbos and Yom Tov. When they look at them, they remember a world of elegance. It wasn't a Jewish world, but there was a standard of dignity and proper behavior. They learned *derech eretz* in their parents' homes and "*derech eretz kadmah l'Torah*." A refined character and genteel upbringing makes a person more receptive to the gift of Torah, and this was certainly the case for Yisroel and Leah.

◆ ◆ ◆

When Roy was born, the family lived on the twelfth floor of 21 East 87th Street between Madison and Fifth Avenues. By the time he was fifteen, they had moved to 993 Fifth Avenue, which was located directly across from the massive Metropolitan Museum of Art and had a beautiful view of Central Park.

As a child growing up in the city, Roy thought that being an elevator man was very exciting. An elevator operator in those days didn't press buttons but controlled the elevator with a lever he

A festive meal at 993 Fifth Avenue; left to right:
Roy's father and his Salant grandparents

Elevator control panel
with the number 13 missing

turned one way for up and the other way for down. He had to be precise in order to line up the elevator cab perfectly with the floor when the elevator door opened. Then the door was opened manually by pulling down on another, long lever. You had to be a professional to operate an elevator in those days.

Roy thought maybe he'd like to be an elevator man someday.

He remembers when a telephone operator would answer the telephone and request the number you were calling by saying, "Number pleeez." Many phones were party lines, where several families shared the same phone line. He also remembers milkmen and even icemen, who delivered large chunks of ice for the icebox, before electric refrigerators. When Roy and Linda went to England to attend graduate school, they went by ship. True, they carried a lot of luggage and needed extra space, but transatlantic flight was still relatively new.

Here's another amazing fact about the Upper East Side: None of the elegant apartment buildings had a listing for a thirteenth floor!

How was that possible? Those buildings were certainly higher than thirteen stories.

Very simple: they *pretended* that they had no thirteenth floor.

The numbers simply skipped the number 13, because 13 was considered an "unlucky" number!

Chapter Two
The Wizard
of Wall Street

Two *roshei yeshivah*, each of whom has built a large and famous yeshivah, told Roy the same thing: "I owe it all to ADHD." In other words, if they were what we would call "normal" people, they couldn't have accomplished what they had, which required extraordinary abilities.

Roy's father — Roy R. Neuberger — could have said the same thing about himself.

(By the way, the middle initial stands for Rothschild. His mother was a descendant of the Basel branch of the famous banking family. It would appear that Roy's father inherited his business acumen from his mother's side.)

Roy Senior was both a dreamer and a legendary businessman, and it could be argued that part of the reason he became a legend was because he was a dreamer. He himself was the son of a successful businessman; his father had owned a haberdashery business in Marquette, in the upper peninsula of Michigan.

Michigan is a large state. Detroit sits at the bottom, but the Upper Peninsula is comprised of hundreds of miles that border the Great Lakes. This is cold country. The Neuberger haberdashery was there to outfit anyone who needed quality clothing, whether fisherman, trapper, lumberjack, or hiker. At some point Roy Senior's father sold the haberdashery and moved to Bridgeport, Connecticut, where he became the owner of the Connecticut Web and Buckle Company, which manufactured clothing accessories.

Sadly, both of Roy Senior's parents passed away and he became an orphan at the age of twelve, whereupon Roy Senior went to live with his sister, Ruth, and her husband, Aaron Potter. Until his last day, he never forgot their kindness to him. Their son, Billy, later became a partner in Roy Senior's investment firm Neuberger Berman, on the floor of the New York Stock Exchange, the one exception to Neuberger Berman's "no nepotism" rule.

Roy Senior had no patience for high school, being the kind of person who couldn't sit still. But he loved playing tennis and became the captain of Dewitt Clinton High School's tennis team.

Roy Senior playing tennis
as a young man

In 1921 he was the tennis champion of New York City. He enrolled in New York University, but he lasted there all of one year. Today he would have been diagnosed with ADHD. All he knew was that he lacked the patience to sit in a classroom.

Roy Senior decided that the time had come for him to pursue his dream, which was to develop his love of art, and in order to do that, he decided, he needed to move to Paris. Because when it came to art, well, Paris was the place to be. This was the way he was: he did what he thought was right for him without allowing himself to be derailed by other people's ideas.

And so he moved to Paris, where he lived for the next four years.

♦ ♦ ♦

He didn't remain in Paris but traveled extensively across the Continent. In Rome he enjoyed fettuccine alfredo prepared by the legendary Alfredo himself. You know how sometimes you hear people say, "I was there"? Well, he was there!

He kept up his tennis even while focusing on his art. While in Paris, he would meet and beat future world champion Fred Perry. He was so good at tennis that he was invited to play doubles against the king of Sweden. He would later recount that the king's handlers informed him that he would have to make sure he lost the match.

"It's a lot harder to lose than it is to win," he later commented, "especially if you want to make it look as if you're trying to win…" Still, challenging or not, he played against the king and succeeded in losing.

Yet there was something bigger happening for Roy Senior during those Paris years, because it was there that he found the courage to recognize that he didn't possess the talent necessary

Paris in the 1920s: Roy's father behind the wheel

to be a great artist. And if his skill level was merely mediocre, art wasn't for him.

This was a major turning point in his life.

I won't be a great artist, he told himself, *and the last thing I want is to become a mediocre artist. But I have a feeling that I have what it takes to become a great businessman.*

He decided to return to the United States and pursue a new dream.

He'd work on Wall Street, he decided, and make enough money to buy art and support unknown artists who are beginning to develop their careers. He'd still be able to fulfill his dream, even if he wasn't the one painting the pictures. He would become a patron of the arts, someone who would make a difference to struggling artists.

Today, when Yisroel Neuberger speaks to *yeshivah bachurim* or seminary girls, he likes to stress how amazing it is that every one of us is unique. No two *neshamos* have the same abilities or destiny. While it's true that very few people would have been able to do what his father did — to dive headfirst into Wall Street with very little formal education — everyone can succeed at whatever it is that they have been uniquely created to do. And part of the process of finding out what you are good at consists of first discovering what you're *not* good at.

At least, that's the way it was for the future Wizard of Wall Street.

◆ ◆ ◆

Roy Senior returned to New York in the spring of 1929, entering Wall Street six months before the Great Crash, which would leave millions of people destitute and send the world economy into a tailspin that would become known as the Great Depression.

It was arguably the worst time in history to embark on a career on Wall Street. But Roy Senior had an amazing sense of timing and had been blessed with an incredible sense of how the market works. He was able to do things that others were not.

Drawing on his intuitive understanding of business, Roy Senior made a series of decisions for reasons that only he comprehended. It would have been hard, if not impossible, for him to explain to an outsider (or maybe even to himself) why he was doing what he was doing, but it wasn't long before the smartest people on the Street began to realize that this young man knew what he was doing.

Somehow, he sensed the crash coming and made a move known as "selling short" — a trading strategy that involves selling a borrowed asset with the hope of buying it back at a lower price. He basically did the exact opposite of what the rest of Wall Street was doing. It was a risky move, because the potential losses from short selling are literally unlimited. With this move, Roy Senior became known as a trading genius. People realized that he was able to take the kind of risks that few others had the courage to take, but he had uncanny accuracy and was never reckless.

In fact, he proved to be almost prophetic.

While many previously wealthy people were literally jumping out of windows, unable to face life after having lost their fortunes, Roy Senior entered the Depression from a position of strength.

◆　◆　◆

In 1939, an investment firm called Neuberger Berman was founded with five partners, who included both Roy's father and mother. Bob Berman, one of the original founding partners and the one who gave his name to the company along with Roy Senior, died in the early 1950s, but by 1999, when the firm went public, there were over sixty partners. But even then, the original aura of the firm, its sense of responsibility and rock-solid integrity, were never compromised.

How was this accomplished?

Roy Senior was remarkably humble in a world of intense competition. He told his son that from the beginning, he brought in people who were smarter than he was. Now Roy Senior was plenty smart, but there are different kinds of smart. Roy Senior was brilliant in many ways, and one of them was finding other brilliant partners who excelled, each in his or her own way, to serve the company.

It is written on the tombstone of Roy Senior's grandfather, Eluzer Nieburger, in Winnweiler, Germany, that he was "a trustworthy man who died with a good name." This legacy, passed down from the Mahariv himself, was inherited by Roy Senior, whose unselfish idealism and integrity were at least as great as his brilliance on Wall Street.

Chapter Three
Jackson Pollock and Eastman Kodak

Neuberger Berman would become one of the most successful firms on Wall Street. In 1950, Neuberger Berman was one of the first firms to develop and market the concept of mutual funds.[1] One can say, in a sense, that Roy Senior was one of the inventors of the idea and the medium. His Guardian Mutual Fund is still going strong.

Many have noted that Roy Senior never removed the name Berman from the firm's name even though Robert Berman passed away in 1952. This is seen as a tribute to Roy Senior's integrity. He made sure that Robert Berman's family was well taken care of.

Neuberger Berman eventually moved to 120 Broadway, near Wall Street. Occasionally the young Roy would come to the office to spend the day with his father. At lunchtime, Roy Senior would take him up to the Banker's Club, an exclusive restaurant on the rooftop. Roy still remembers the very fast elevators operated by men in impressive uniforms that sped to the top floor.

One of young Roy's friends at the office was a kindly man

---

1. A mutual fund invests in many companies so a layman does not have to figure out how to invest. Instead, the layman simply buys shares in the mutual fund. It makes sophisticated investing available to a much wider segment of the public.

named Eddie Potter, a relative of his Aunt Ruth (the only other exception to the no-nepotism rule). Eddie shared one of young Roy's interests, photography. In those days, Wall Street was teeming with activity. There was a huge camera store where Eddie would take Roy to buy cameras, flash accessories, filters, camera bags, and all kinds of exciting paraphernalia. This was a safe and exciting corner of the world that the young Roy loved, and he still feels grateful to this man who was so kind to him.

(Some seventy years later, Yisroel and Leah were scheduled to speak at Heritage House in the Old City. The program was called off because of corona, and the students there were disappointed. One of them had very much wanted to meet them. It was Eddie Potter's granddaughter.)

◆ ◆ ◆

In 1950, someone told Roy Senior that there was an impoverished artist living on Long Island.

"What's his name?"

"Jackson Pollock."

"Never heard of him."

"Why don't you go meet him?"

Roy Senior had been a patron of the arts since the 1930s. He met many (later famous) artists when they were unknown and impoverished and bought their work, and some of them actually lived from day to day on the money he paid for their art. Because they were unknown, the price of their work was low. Later, when they became famous, the prices of their artwork skyrocketed, worth unimaginably more than they cost when he bought them from their then-unknown creators.

But Roy Senior never profited from the art he owned…because he never sold it! Instead, he donated the art he'd purchased to museums throughout the country and eventually gave his entire collection to the state of New York. (The collection resides today at the Neuberger Museum at the State University of New York campus in Purchase, where it also goes out on loan to other museums around the world.)

By the '50s, Roy Senior had amassed quite a collection of contemporary American art, including paintings by such artists as Milton Avery and Alexander Calder. They graced the walls of his home and the Neuberger Berman office, which was beautified by one of the world's first corporate art collections. So the news of another promising young American artist intrigued him.

Upon hearing about the promising young artist on Long Island, Roy Senior went to meet Jackson Pollock. He didn't leave the artist's home empty-handed: he purchased a painting that was displayed on the wall of his home for decades. It was a large canvas showcasing the "drip art" for which Pollock would become famous. Around that time, *Life Magazine* wrote an article ridiculing Pollock. But despite the criticism, he went on to become one of the most famous and successful American artists who ever lived.

Roy Senior paid eight hundred dollars for that painting, money that Pollock lived on for months. Another art collector purchased a similar painting from Pollock around the same time, also paying eight hundred dollars, but unlike Roy Senior, the other collector put up his Jackson Pollock for auction in the early nineties, some forty years after he had bought it for eight hundred dollars.

Roy's family in the 1950s with the Jackson Pollock painting
hanging on the wall to the left

It sold at auction for twenty-one million dollars.

For Roy's father, it was never about the money. It was a ful-fillment of the dream that he'd had back in Paris, a dream that came true, allowing him to develop and cultivate American art.

◆ ◆ ◆

Ironically, it was Roy Senior's eye for art that also made him such a successful investor.

Roy Senior was very visual, and in his line of work, this was a quality that made him unique, especially when one considers that virtually everyone working on Wall Street is a numbers whiz. These guys study company forecasts, what the company made per share last year, and what they are projected to make this year and the next year and the year after. They make their decisions based on the numbers and invest accordingly.

Roy Senior didn't operate that way.

Instead, every Friday, he would receive a big book filled with the stock charts of the previous week. The book contained graphs showing the movement of thousands of stocks. Roy Senior could look at the graphs and see where individual stocks and the market in general were headed. He had the ability to study those lines and predict where they were going to go in the future. This knowledge wasn't something he was able to explain. It was just something he could do.

That was how he made money back in 1929 when everyone else was going bankrupt. He saw the graph of the stocks heading up and up, and he knew that the whole house of cards was about to tumble.

It was the same when it came to art. He could look at a Jackson Pollock drip-art painting, a method Pollack created where the canvas was laid on the floor and the artist would drip paint all over it, and he knew that this artist was going to be great. And the market agreed with him, because the paintings people laughed at when they were first introduced are now selling for millions of dollars.

◆ ◆ ◆

In 1987, Roy Senior realized that the market was once more heading toward a major crash, and he began employing the same strategy he had used back in 1929. His decisions during the months leading up to the biggest ever one-day crash on Wall Street would help cement his reputation for all time. By then he was eighty-four years old, managing his family's finances with only one outside account.

One account, but it was huge.

The Eastman Kodak Corporation was the biggest name in photographic films and papers at the time. When digital cameras arrived, Kodak lost its prominence, but back in 1987, Kodak was still king, with the famous yellow and black film canisters holding a place of prominence in photography stores everywhere.

The Eastman Kodak Company entrusted Roy R. Neuberger with the management of its huge employee pension fund. It was the biggest single account at Neuberger Berman, and it belonged to Roy Senior.

◆　◆　◆

In 1987, when Roy Senior had a premonition that the bottom was going to drop out of the market, he turned his attention to the company's pension funds. Generally, pension funds are invested conservatively. A pension fund provides for the future welfare of longtime employees, after all, and no one wants to risk their retirement.

He asked the pension fund trustees for permission to go short — the same strategy he had used during the Great Depression, when he first started working on Wall Street. It was a risky business under any circumstance, but especially for a pension fund. Not only that, but he wanted to short S & P futures, a particularly volatile financial instrument. The market was doing incredibly well at that time, but Roy Senior felt the market was in for a big fall.

The trustees had confidence in his judgment, but the decisions he was making with the pension fund were risky, and the executive board of Neuberger Berman met — without his knowledge

— to discuss whether the Kodak account should be taken away from their founder. The market was up thirty-five percent during the summer of 1987, yet Roy Senior's Eastman Kodak account was performing the poorest of any account under NB management. Maybe he was just getting too old for such a responsibility.

The board met for two hours. In the end, they decided to do nothing. No one had the courage to challenge Roy Senior, and he was ultimately left alone to continue managing the Eastman Kodak account as he had been doing until then.

As the senior members of his firm watched anxiously, the founder of Neuberger Berman continued to maintain his short position in the pension fund, day in and day out. The account's value kept going down as the market continued to shoot upward — until October 17, 1987, when Wall Street experienced the greatest one-day crash in its history, tumbling some twenty-two percent. Roy Senior had foreseen it, and now his account was in the stratosphere, while people around him lost fortunes in a matter of a few hours.

He made no trades that day, which came to be known as Black Tuesday. The next morning, the market opened at nine thirty at absolute rock-bottom. Prices had dropped from the heights to the lowest of the lows in the kind of stunning reversal that can only occur on Wall Street. That morning, Roy Senior covered all his positions, buying back everything he'd been selling for months for a very low price and making hundreds of millions of dollars in the process for the Eastman Kodak pension fund.

Just moments after he covered his position, the market shot right back up into the stratosphere in yet another stunning reversal of the previous day's stunning reversal. By that time, Roy Neuberger had made his move. Then, having totally vindicated himself and his judgment, he marched into the office of Larry Zicklin — Neuberger Berman's managing director (whom Roy Senior had hired as a young man) — and told him that he was resigning from the Eastman Kodak account.

In the wake of his incredible victory, the *New York Times* ran a story headlined, "Lion in Winter on Wall Street," and chronicled the way Roy R. Neuberger had seen the future and maintained the courage to stick to his guns. The fascinating tale of the Eastman Kodak pension account serves as the pinnacle of Roy R. Neuberger's Wall Street career, cementing him as a legend for all time.

Chapter Four
A Chair
for Edward R. Murrow

L inda Villency Neuberger's grandparents were born in Poland to families that were deeply observant. On her mother's side, the family hailed from Lodz and Warsaw. Her grandfather was a weaver who immigrated to the United States in the early 1900s and made his way to Massachusetts, since he knew of a wool factory there where he'd be able to find work. It took him a year and a half to amass sufficient funds to bring his wife and child over to join him.

Eventually the family moved to Paterson, New Jersey, where her grandfather found a job at a silk mill. The family, five girls and one boy, still retained some Jewish practices and traditions. Linda's grandmother was strictly kosher, made her own gefilte fish, and kept separate dishes and pots for Pesach. She also kept Shabbos. Yet, despite the attention to Jewish tradition, it wasn't passed down intact to the next generation, and all their children left observance.

The children did speak Yiddish, but Yiddish does not a religious Jew make…

♦ ♦ ♦

Linda loved going to New Jersey for the Seder every Pesach and reading the Haggadah. Her grandfather davened at the shul of Rav Tzvi Hirsch Cohen, who was the maternal *zeide* of her future teacher and *machateineste*, Rebbetzin Esther Jungreis. The seeds were being planted already then, decades before the two would meet and the tree would bear fruit.

Linda loved hearing her grandparents conversing in Yiddish. She loved it when her grandmother called her "Linda'le." But since her grandparents hadn't succeeded in transmitting Torah observance to their children, Linda had to leave her *Yiddishkeit* at her grandparents' front door.

She attended the local public school where she lived in East Rockaway, Long Island, and sang patriotic songs such as "The Star-Spangled Banner" and where, every morning, she pledged allegiance to the flag of the United States. Come December 25, the regular songs were replaced by "holiday" songs.

When the Jewish boys in her class began celebrating their bar mitzvahs at the nearby Conservative synagogue, she made sure to attend, along with the rest of her class. Despite the fact that she was being raised in a secular home, when she heard the congregation reciting the *Shema Yisrael*, the words touched a chord inside her.

◆ ◆ ◆

Linda's family on her father's side was originally from Vilna. While generations of ancestors had been rabbis from the famed Rabinowitz family, her grandfather, who was orphaned at a young age, made his living as a cabinet maker and interior designer. Although he had severed his connection to *Yiddishkeit*, he was proud to refer to Vilna as the "Jerusalem of Lithuania."

He must have been very good at his trade, because the Russian government sent him to Glasgow to design and build cabinetry for their pavilion at the 1900 World's Fair. Once introduced to life in Scotland, where it was a lot easier to live as a Jew, he was in no rush to return to Russia. While there, he changed his family name to Vilensky to get the Russian government off his trail.

Linda's father in a Glasgow elementary school

So it was that Linda's father, Maurice, and his siblings were born and raised in Glasgow, and all his life, Maurice's English bore a trace of a Scottish burr.

When World War I broke out, the British began conscripting every eligible man for the army. Linda's father was in danger of being drafted, and for that matter, her father's father was also still young enough to be eligible. The family packed its bags once again. Destination: the US of A. The year was 1917.

In the middle of the transatlantic journey, the ship suddenly found itself in a fearsome plight as a German submarine surfaced and ordered their ship to stop. German sailors boarded and began searching for contraband that could conceivably be used against the Fatherland. When the German officers realized that the ship wasn't even a slight threat to Germany, the sailors returned to their submarine and allowed the ship to continue on its way.

This was an open miracle. The submarine could have easily blown them up without a second thought, just as German submarines had already done to countless civilian ships making their innocent way across the ocean.

And yet, that day they let them go.

Without question, a miracle.

♦ ♦ ♦

Linda's father went on to become famous. A talented artist, he parlayed his abilities into a career as a designer, manufacturer, and importer of the finest furniture from Denmark. While he'd been known as Morris Vilensky in Scotland, in America he changed his name to Maurice Villency. Villency was the kind of name that could be anything — French, Spanish, or Italian. Yet, even after he became famous and had left almost all Jewish tradition behind, Maurice Villency never forgot that he was a Levi who had been named Moshe at his bris.

He was very happy to have his furniture designs manufactured in Denmark because the king of Denmark and the Danish people had courageously protected their Jewish population from the Nazis, shuttling them to Sweden.

In the wake of Israel's victory in the Six-Day War, he took Linda's mother to Israel. That, however, was about the extent of his Jewish affiliation.

Maurice Villency specialized in contemporary furniture design. In the beginning, he built the furniture with his own hands, but as time passed and the business grew, he hired workers, always insisting on top quality. Later, he sent his designs to Denmark, where top-quality pieces were manufactured to his specifications and shipped to the United States. Some customers sought a particular piece, while others hired him to furnish an entire apartment or home. The

Maurice Villency: successful businessman but still an artist

A painting by
Maurice Villency

famous journalist and war correspondent Edward R. Murrow even commissioned him to create a specially designed chair that he used while delivering the news on TV. The youth from Scotland had come a long way.

Murrow had very specific demands before he was satisfied with his chair. He wanted one arm higher than the other so he could hold the hand in which he held his cigarettes at just the right height. He kept on sending the chair back to the shop so it could be adjusted, an inch taller or an inch shorter. Finally, after what seemed like the tenth attempt, Linda's father just left the chair in the warehouse for a couple of weeks. He didn't touch it. A few weeks later he sent it back to Murrow, who then pronounced it "perfect!"

It's hard to know how many orders streamed forth from Maurice Villency Furniture's flagship store on East Eighth Street to homes in Manhattan and across the country, but the mark he made on the furniture industry was undeniable. He had a reputation as a master craftsman, but he was equally known for his integrity. Every piece of furniture came with a lifetime guarantee. If anything went wrong, Maurice Villency wanted his customers to send their piece back to be repaired free of charge, whether it had been purchased five years or twenty years before.

He was also a painter and sculptor. Art was his true love, while furniture making was an outcome of the need to support his family.

♦ ♦ ♦

Linda's mother, Ruth (her Hebrew name was Rachel), grew up in Paterson, New Jersey. Although extremely bright, she never had the opportunity to go to college. She made up for this by reading everything she could get her hands on. She had a special love for Robert Frost's poems and enjoyed memorizing them. She was also a talented bookkeeper who was able to add long columns of sums in her head. She later used this talent to help manage her husband's business.

One afternoon Ruth had a first date to meet a young man at a museum and took the train into Manhattan from New Jersey. The train made a sudden stop between stations in the city of Passaic. A fire had broken out, and the firemen had been forced to stretch their hoses across the tracks, which meant that the train could go no further. She sat there, on the train, for hours, with no way to let her date know that she had been delayed. (This was way before the cell phone era.)

When the fire was brought under control, the train resumed its journey. Upon reaching the museum, Ruth approached the front desk and asked if the receptionist had seen a man waiting.

"Yes, I did," the woman replied. "He waited for a long time, but he finally left." Then she had a thought: "As long as you're here, there is a fascinating lecture taking place upstairs. Why not go and listen?"

Linda's mother, Ruth Villency

After the lecture, Ruth had a question for the lecturer. After a brief exchange, the lecturer said, gesturing to a nearby gentleman, "Let me introduce you to my friend, Maurice Villency."

And so they met…and so they married! Linda Neuberger considers the way her parents met as yet another example of this exquisitely designed world, where every detail is planned and executed exactly as Hashem wills it, from a fire hose stretched across a train track to a man who waited and left to a lecturer who moonlighted as a *shadchan*.

◆ ◆ ◆

Linda was born in March 1944. Growing up, her mother told her that had they still been in Europe, they would all have perished in the Holocaust. So although Linda's family wasn't religious, she was raised with some affinity for the Jewish people. As a child, Linda had to stay home from public school on Rosh Hashanah and Yom Kippur out of respect, unlike Roy, who didn't even know what Rosh Hashanah and Yom Kippur were. Linda's father told her that while his father had declared himself an atheist, he himself wasn't sure of the truth and identified as an agnostic.

Her Jewish education came in the form of a Reform Sunday school, and by the time she reached the third grade, she realized that whatever they were learning had nothing to do with her. A lesson about Succos had the same significance to her as if she had been taught about the customs of the Zulu tribespeople, because she didn't follow these practices at home.

So it was that Linda dropped out of Sunday school in the middle of the third grade.

◆ ◆ ◆

Linda never doubted that she was blessed with loving parents; there was never a question about that. Many times she would accompany her mother to meet her father at the train station when he returned from work. They would play a game on the way home. When Linda's father got into the car, she would hide behind the seat, wait a few minutes, and then jump up and say, "Surprise!" He always acted surprised.

"I could never go to sleep at night without Daddy coming in to tuck me in," Linda says. "He would sit with me every night, my little hand enveloped in his big warm hand. As I lay there, I felt secure, happy, and at peace with the world. The image of him holding my hand is a precious memory even now, so many years later, a reminder that the love we convey to our children is never forgotten."

Linda's parents lived prosperous lives, and along with that, they recognized that they had been blessed and wanted to repay the society that had given them so much. They were active in their community and went out of their way to teach their children to be kind and generous. It was natural that Linda would volunteer for an organization that served special-needs children well before such activities were in vogue. One of the neighbors had a special-needs child, and Linda would go to feed him on a regular basis.

It also wasn't a surprise to Linda and her brother when their paternal grandfather came to live with them in his old age. He remained in their home for years, Ruth devotedly looking after him even though he wasn't her father.

"I grew up watching my parents actively living lives of *chesed*," Linda says. "Of course, everyone knows that the best and most effective method of teaching children how to act is by example, and they were wonderful role models. This idea is something that I have made a point of bringing home to other *baalei teshuvah* after we became observant, reminding them that many of the qualities that made them who they are came from their parents. I stress that they should be grateful to their parents for all the wonderful qualities they so graciously bestowed upon them."

◆ ◆ ◆

Linda's parents were generous and provided her with everything they thought a young girl could need. She enjoyed piano, violin, and ballet lessons, and her father taught her to draw. She loved art and studied it when she was a student at Oxford many years later. Perhaps she would have been a professional artist, but when the children started arriving, Linda gave up that dream, recognizing that the job of child raising is the highest of callings.

It was as idyllic a childhood as anyone could want, but even then questions would surge through her mind from time to time — questions that demanded answers that she was never able to provide.

Both Roy and I were clueless when it came to matters of Judaism. Even though virtually all our friends were Jewish, that didn't make any difference, since none of them believed in anything. They were decidedly secular, assimilated Americans. No one we knew kept Shabbos or any other mitzvah. Nobody believed in G-d. I recall thinking many times during my youth that there just had to be more to life than the way we were living it.

This feeling tended to visit me on the occasions when I received a gift from my parents or purchased something nice that I had wanted for a while. Inevitably the enjoyment I had received from the new gift dissipated after a few days, and I was left asking myself, *Is this what life is all about?*

Yet while they hadn't given us religion, our parents did provide Roy and me with certain values that contributed to our eventually embarking on a search for the truth that had been missing from our lives until that point. I will never forget my mother sitting me down and having a deep talk with me about the sanctity of marriage, concepts that were more or less ignored by everyone around me. My mother didn't care what everyone else thought. If something was important to her, she lived that way, and she didn't bend her morals.

We used the foundation that we received from our parents and built on it, so that by the time we discovered the Torah, we were able to use that foundation to create a strong home. It took our parents time to comprehend why we had chosen the path that we did, but they eventually grasped the correctness of our choice, especially when they realized that they had grandchildren while many of their friends had none. Moreover, those grandchildren were respectful, treating them with love and *derech eretz*.

◆ ◆ ◆

Toward the end of her father's life, Linda was with him in the hospital, along with her husband, Roy. He was touched that it was so important to them to be with him at such a time. One night, as they parted from him, he used words that we as *frum* Yidden use every single day, but he never did:

"G-d bless you!"

For many people, that wouldn't have been a big deal, but for a man like Linda's father, uttering those words was big indeed. It was almost as if he was changing the way he had always identified himself. There was nothing random about his blessing. For Linda, that was tremendously significant.

Following her husband's death, Linda's mother came every week to spend Shabbos with Linda and Roy for years. Her greatest joy was spending time with her grandchildren and, eventually, great-grandchildren, either for an entire Shabbos at their home or even for Shabbos afternoon, even if it meant walking a mile in each direction at the age of eighty-nine.

PART 2

"I hope you didn't come here to proselytize!"

A former classmate at a school reunion

Chapter Five
Climbing the Grand Teton

Every summer, the Neuberger clan packed their bags, exchanging their apartment in the hot city for their summer house, Florival Farms, in northern Westchester, an estate originally established in the early 1900s by three families who were cousins. Each family built a large three-story stone home on a hill overlooking the Croton Reservoir. The Neubergers purchased one of these homes in 1946. The home had the kind of astounding view that leaves a person speechless at the sheer beauty to be found in Hashem's world. That was where Roy spent his summers until he was ten years old and ready to go to camp.

Roy went to Camp Killooleet in central Vermont for five summers from the age of ten. He was very homesick, but the camp director, John Seeger, was kind and patient. John sensed the angst in Roy's soul and went out of his way to talk to him every day.

"I was a supersensitive kid," Roy says. "One summer I was homesick for the entire eight weeks. When I finally returned home and was back in familiar surroundings, I found to my great shock and fear that I was still homesick, even though I was home! There was no way out!"

Roy felt deeply afraid of himself, as if something inside was truly wrong. People like John Seeger got him through some tough

View of Croton Reservoir from Florival Farms

moments, but he was still decades away from finding the Rock on which he could build the foundation of his life.

♦ ♦ ♦

There were usually a few weeks between the end of camp and the beginning of school when the family took a short vacation together. In 1954, they traveled to a hotel in Montauk on the far east end of Long Island. There was just one problem: Hurricane Carol, one of the most powerful hurricanes in recent memory, was headed right for them.

The hotel was cut off from the rest of Long Island during the storm. There was nothing to protect it. The owner tied down everything that could be tied down. Already the hotel was getting blasted by violent winds and the spray of the ever-growing waves.

It was all very frightening until, suddenly, everything changed. The sky turned blue, with nary a cloud in sight. In an instant, the wind ceased, and the ocean returned to the calmness of a placid summer day. That's when Roy learned the meaning of the phrase "eye of the storm." If you happen to see it on a weather map, you'll notice that the ten miles in the middle of a hurricane are perfectly calm, and that's where they were at that moment.

The eye of the hurricane is the most beautiful picnic day you can imagine, when the world is caressed by the gentlest of breezes. The hotel owner took advantage of the lull to rush outside and tie down more deck furniture, because he knew that in a few minutes the storm would turn around and come at them from the other direction.

When calm descended on their tiny corner of the globe, Roy went outside with the owner, who had asked him to help. When the job was done and the wind was howling again, the owner paid him by giving him...one glass of cola.

Roy's father was angry. "All that work and all he gives you is a Coke!"

The man's behavior went against Roy Senior's sense of fairness and generosity, which was legendary. All his employees were treated with respect and honor.

That storm taught Roy a lesson he would never forget. Many people go through life believing that everything is just fine. Little do they realize that the other half of the storm may be heading straight at them, from the opposite direction.

It was only later that he learned there is a Captain of the ship, Whom we trust to get us through to safety no matter what strikes at us.

◆ ◆ ◆

When he was sixteen, Roy went on a trip with a traveling camp to the western United States for the summer. Most of the group climbed the Grand Teton in Wyoming, a mountain whose summit is close to fourteen thousand feet above sea level. It turned out to be a frightening experience.

By the time the group reached the top, they discovered that there was only one way to get down: they had to use ropes to rappel down the cliff. The rappel began on a narrow ice-covered

Grand Teton from Jackson Hole

ledge. In order to get to the rappel point, they had to walk across another thin, icy ledge. There was a rope attached to the rock wall for people to hold, but one look over the edge of the cliff and Roy felt sheer terror. On top of that, it was freezing cold and he had a terrible stomachache.

Later he said that he couldn't believe he had survived the trip, mentally or physically. What frightened Roy most was the fear that he wasn't like those around him, that there was something intrinsically wrong with him. Why were others seemingly so carefree, while he was constantly battling the demons inside his head? It was a frightening inner existence that he never quite succeeded in pushing out of his mind. He was afraid of the interaction between boys and girls, the foul language he heard, afraid of the breakdown in morality (which today has mushroomed to cosmic proportions). He saw his contemporaries acting this way and couldn't take it, yet he thought that perhaps he was the crazy one.

◆　◆　◆

In the summer of 1961, the year Roy graduated from high school, he and a friend spent the summer hiking out West. The focal point of the trip was a seven-week trek from Cody, Wyoming, through the Teton Wilderness area to Grand Teton National Park.

The two friends flew from New York to Rapid City, South Dakota. Having nowhere to sleep that night (they had wanted to rough it), they finally went to the police station and asked the cops if they had any ideas.

"Well," they said, "we could put you up in one of the cells for the night..."

They accepted the kind offer and spent the night in the cell. (These were more relaxed times.) It wasn't so bad, especially since the cell was not locked.

They tried the same thing in a different city the next night, but there the sheriff told them that they would have to be charged with a crime in order to use the cell, so they slept in the park.

From Rapid City they tried hitching to Wyoming, but no one picked them up and they were forced to take a bus to Cody. From there they entered the wilderness. For the next seven weeks Roy and his friend literally saw more moose than people!

"We headed west from Cody," Roy said, "and headed on through the Teton Wilderness area until we approached Grand Teton National Park through Jackson Hole, a vast valley situated roughly at a seven-thousand-foot elevation. As you approach, you suddenly see the huge snowcapped mountain range, capped by the Grand Teton itself, rising an additional six thousand feet into the air."

Of course, for Roy, seeing that mountain brought back memories of the frightening climb he had survived just a few years earlier.

They had come prepared for the wilderness and were ready for the challenge, with plenty of dehydrated food and other necessary amenities. They had their maps and knew which trails they were going to use. They were in such good shape that nothing winded them, and they were practically able to run up and down

Roy on the saddle of the Grand Teton, Wyoming, in the summer of 1961

the mountain like mountain goats (although they shied away from actual mountain climbing, courtesy of Roy's past experiences).

"I remember standing on a ridge," Roy remembers, "probably about eleven thousand feet above sea level. It was a fantastic view, totally pure from a *gashmiyus* perspective, but I knew that I was still far from peace of mind. I could be in the most beautiful place in the world and it wouldn't matter. At the end of the day, it was still me with my fears."

What could he be afraid of in that pristine wilderness? But even there he had worries: *Maybe Congress will revoke the wilderness status of this pristine area.* He pictured endless rows of high-rise buildings being erected all over the mountains and valleys, ruining his paradise.

Actually, the fears went much deeper than the US Congress. What if he had answers to all his fears and yet was still afraid? Like the summer he came home from camp and was still homesick? Maybe there was no remedy for his fears. Maybe there was something intrinsically wrong with him, something with no cure.

This was all he could think about as he trudged through the Wyoming wilderness. Does this sound like paradise to you?

In truth, Roy needed to climb spiritual, not physical, trails, but he didn't know it at the time, and it would be quite a few years before he found them.

Chapter Six
Fieldston

There was never a question where Roy was going for high school. Fieldston was an elite private institution with a top-quality reputation, actually a continuation of the Ethical Culture elementary school he had attended for the past nine years. His mother and her brothers, as well as Roy's sister, had attended the school and his brother would follow him.

These schools are an offshoot of an organization called the Ethical Culture Society, which was founded in 1876 by a German Jew named Felix Adler, the son of a Reform rabbi. The institutions revolve around the concept of ethics without G-d. Based on this ideology, the society established the Ethical Culture schools, and the high school division became known as Fieldston since it was situated in the Fieldston section of the Bronx. These schools have succeeded, over many decades, in distancing a huge number of Jews from their roots. The student body, mainly children from well-to-do assimilated Jewish families, considered themselves sophisticated Americans first and foremost. Being Jewish was embarrassing.

Felix Adler considered even Reform too far to the right. He wanted to eliminate the knowledge of G-d and Torah altogether. In his mind, ethics was the key. But ethics based on what? Well, he would leave that up to the individual, which meant there could be as many systems of ethics as there are people.

"We used to have ethics classes in high school," Leah, who was in the year below Roy, relates, "where we discussed issues like 'How do you know what's right and what's wrong?' One person would say one thing, and another person would say the opposite. There were no absolutes at Ethical. If something was right for one person, it was wrong for the other. People acted very sophisticated about these discussions, but we were all hopelessly lost. This is why today, in our liberal society, there is no right and no wrong, just chaos."

"We were told that every person has the responsibility of making the world a better place," Yisroel says. "But it was never explained how one did that if one had no moral clarity. We felt guilty about being wealthy, so we volunteered at settlement houses in poor neighborhoods."

During high school, Roy and Linda demonstrated against businesses accused of racial segregation. In college, they joined the peace movement, protesting the war in Vietnam. Years later, when they would go around the world telling their story, Leah would say, "All those years when we worked for the peace movement, we never had a moment's peace — until we had Shabbos!"

In high school, she was invited to join the cheerleading squad. But after one year, she'd had enough. To her, it was an obvious waste of time.

"I was feeling empty," Leah says, "and I didn't know why. I wanted to be a good person, but I didn't even know what that meant, since being a 'good person' meant something else to every person. There was no right and no wrong, no clarity regarding the purpose of life."

Like Roy, Linda struggled with thoughts like these for years.

Two teenagers trying to swim against the tide in an ocean of atheism and ignorance, searching, always searching.

◆ ◆ ◆

The head of the English department at Fieldston was a brilliant Jew named Elbert Lenrow. Everyone in his Advanced English class was way ahead when they entered college, even if it was Harvard or Yale.

Mr. Lenrow was a highly cultured individual and spoke like an Oxford don. He had so many books in his apartment that the floor had to be reinforced with steel beams to support the weight. He taught his students how to read and analyze a book. More than that, he taught them how to write. Writing would become Roy's preferred method of expressing himself. Both Roy and Linda credit him and other great teachers, like Spencer Brown (whose poems appeared in the *New Yorker*), for teaching them a command of the English language, skills that they would use for the rest of their lives.

Despite the darkness of those years and the spiritual dangers to which they were exposed, Roy and Linda were able to take precious gems out of this dark environment, just as the children of Israel left ancient Egypt with great wealth.

It would have been very easy to have become totally lost at Ethical. Most of their classmates not only drowned in the sea of assimilation but later, after Roy and Linda became religious, refused even to speak to them. Roy came to the conclusion that it's because they're afraid of confronting their own Jewishness. Years later, when Roy registered at the University of Michigan, his adviser was a religious Catholic professor of history who looked at his transcript and said, "Oh, the Ethical Culture Society. That's for the Jews who are too embarrassed for Reform."

Roy and Linda emerged from their childhood by a miracle, just as the Jews who left Egypt emerged through miracles. To this day, Roy marvels when he sees young Jewish boys who are so much more fluent in Torah than he. It's clear to him that one can't truly make up the learning of one's youth in later life. But he is also grateful for those years of darkness, because he appreciates the light so much more.

"For years," he says, "we lived without spiritual air and water. Our souls were starving. That is why, to me, every *berachah* and every *tefillah* is so precious. I approach davening and learning as a starving man approaches a loaf of bread. I lived in darkness for so long, and now I'm able to dwell in the land of the living."

♦ ♦ ♦

Roy played soccer at Fieldston and starred as a halfback on the varsity team. Less skilled at basketball, he served as manager of the junior varsity team, making sure that everything ran smoothly. He ran the clock during the games and made sure there were enough towels in the locker room. Being JV manager proved to be pivotal in Roy's life.

The year he was manager the team had a phenomenal season, which is why, at the end of the season, they had a huge party

Roy and his friend Alan Borut racing on the Fieldston track

that took place at fellow classmate Bob Kheel's mansion-like home in Riverdale. Bob's father was the labor lawyer Theodore W. Kheel, the man who broke the New York subway strike and who was at one time suggested as a New York mayoral candidate.

Roy decided to ask Linda to go with him to the party at the Kheels' house, an act of courage on his part. Why was this courageous? Linda was very popular at Fieldston. She was a

The soccer player

grade below him (unusual for a social relationship at the time) and Roy had just met her. Their date was big news in the Fieldston world, especially since it was shy Roy and not one of the athletes or social "celebrities" who was going out with Linda.

Roy felt the hand of destiny at work.

During their date, Roy and Linda had a long conversation for the first time. They spoke about University Settlement Camp, the camp for inner-city kids where Roy had worked the previous summer. They spoke about taking responsibility for themselves and others. And Linda had never met a more interesting person. One thing she knew: with Roy she would never be bored.

As the conversation ensued, they realized that they had common goals. Sometimes people know instantly that they've found the other half of their *neshamah*, and that was exactly what happened for Roy and Linda.

For many years, Roy and Linda attended the annual Fieldston reunions even after becoming religious, hoping their presence would lead to the return of some of their old friends to the world of their forefathers. Since the reunions were inevitably scheduled on a Saturday, usually in June, Roy and Linda were unable to show up until around ten at night, and only a few people whom they knew were still there. Sometimes there was a follow-up event on Sunday morning, and then they were able to see all their old friends.

In 2011, Roy's class celebrated their fiftieth high school reunion. For the big event, he had a carton of his first book, *From Central Park to Sinai*, delivered to a classmate's town house where the festivities were taking place over the weekend. He hoped that reading about his journey might strike a chord.

When Roy and Linda arrived at the reunion, they were accosted by someone Roy had grown up with his entire life. "I hope you didn't come here to proselytize!" were his words of greeting.

Welcome to the fiftieth reunion!

Ignoring the opening salvo, they began making the rounds, greeting old friends. They received some brief hellos, and then their old friends turned away. No one wanted to speak to them. Maybe they had seen the book at the townhouse. Roy and Linda had become like lepers, and they didn't want to contract the disease.

Some of them had been Yisroel's friends from the age of three.

Roy understood their reaction. "They were afraid to confront their own souls. They pushed us away, afraid to come close."

The vast majority of Roy and Linda's former friends and classmates had cut themselves off from anything remotely connected to Judaism. Some of their lives became terribly twisted and even tragic. Roy recalls one girl from his class as sweet, quiet, and refined. After Fieldston, she went to college, where she met and married a non-Jew. The couple became radicals.

Somehow, this sweet, quiet, refined girl ended up on the FBI's Ten Most Wanted list. She was later convicted of attempting, along with her husband, to blow up the ROTC building at the University of Washington in Seattle and sentenced to a federal penitentiary for her crime.

Chapter Seven
A Honeymoon in Wyoming

Linda was nineteen years old and Roy was twenty when they married. They were both in college, and it was the beginning of summer vacation. The wedding was held at Florival Farms, the Neubergers' estate in upper Westchester. It was a magnificent day in June 1963. Of course, everyone was happy that Roy was marrying such a wonderful girl, not because she was Jewish but because she was a great person. Had Linda married a non-Jew, it would have troubled her parents, but they wouldn't have said a word. On the Neuberger side, no one would have objected had Roy chosen to marry a non-Jew. But Hashem was watching over them, and they were both Jewish.

Roy's family wanted an Ethical Culture leader (Ethical Culture is legally considered a religion in the state of New York) to officiate, but Linda's grandfather couldn't accept that.

"You have to have a rabbi at my granddaughter's wedding," he insisted.

A compromise was needed. A rabbi was hired, but at Roy's insistence, he was as Reform as could be. For the wedding, the rabbi donned a long black robe and draped a tallis-like scarf around his neck. He looked more like a priest than a rabbi. Roy also insisted that no Hebrew be used during the ceremony, but here the rabbi put his foot down and refused to omit the timeless words *"Harei at mekudeshes li..."*

Left with no choice, Roy gave in and repeated the eternal words connecting himself with his bride for the rest of their lives.

Linda (rear right) and her cousin Roni with their maternal grandparents

While the rabbi insisted that the *chassan* say, *"Harei at...,"* he wasn't as concerned with the matter of a *chuppah*, explaining that nearby tree branches were covering them like a *chuppah*. In truth, the trees weren't even close.

So no, there was no *chuppah*.

No *kesubah*.

No kosher witnesses.

The rabbi did present them with a piece of paper on which was written, "I am my beloved's and my beloved is mine." There were two spaces underneath for witnesses to sign, but he didn't bother to have anyone fill them in.

◆ ◆ ◆

After the wedding, the young couple left for their honeymoon in Wyoming. This involved a very long drive in the new Land Rover that Roy's parents had given them as a wedding present. The reason they bought a Land Rover was because Roy loved roughing it, and the Land Rover was the perfect car for off-road adventures. This was a car built to drive through a desert or forest, perfect for a safari. But it wasn't built for the highway.

The Land Rover at that time was one of the worst cars for driving across a country the size of the United States. At highway speeds, the engine sounded like a garbage truck rumbling down the street, and that sound accompanied them for thousands of miles.

Just before the young couple pulled out of Florival Farms, someone had placed a bottle of champagne into the back of the car. That bottle bumped along the highways with them for some eight hundred miles. The temperature in the rear of the car was brutal — this was during a long heat wave, with temperatures exceeding one hundred degrees — which meant that the bottle of champagne was being primed to go off like a rocket if someone would be foolish enough to attempt to open it.

Lee Bromberg was one of Roy's best friends. Since he hadn't been able to make it to the wedding, the young couple planned to stop off at his home in Skokie, Illinois, on their way to Wyoming. Where better to open the champagne?

So Roy opened the bottle in Lee Bromberg's dining room.
Boom!

It exploded like Old Faithful. The cork shot out like a rocket and embedded itself in the ceiling. The champagne gushed out like a geyser, and the only one who drank champagne that evening was Lee's dog, who lapped it up before passing out drunk on the floor.

So began a honeymoon for the books.

◆ ◆ ◆

They spent those weeks hiking in the wilderness during the day and sleeping in the tent they had brought with them at night. Though it was June, they were seven thousand feet above sea level in the mountains of Wyoming, and the nighttime temperatures plunged to twenty-eight degrees.

They hiked up mountains and through valleys. At night they listened to the howling of the coyotes, who seemed to have come from far and near to keep them company.

"At four in the morning we would suddenly hear them," Roy says. "When you're in the middle of nowhere and you hear the bloodcurdling sound of what seems like thousands of coyotes, it's more than unnerving."

The Alaska Basin

The howling seemed to wash over the mountains, so that even if the creatures weren't close, it felt as if they were right outside the tent.

One day they started hiking the trail that would take them all around the base of the Grand Teton. Since the mountain is so big, it's a three-day hike, and you could walk for miles without seeing a soul. Occasionally a ranger or hiker passed by, but they were few and far between.

On the western side of the mountain is a valley called Alaska Basin, which is covered with wildflowers for miles. At night, you can see countless stars. Yet even with all that beauty and majesty, part of them understood that nature on its own was not enough to satisfy them. The more time they spent in the wilderness, the more they came to grasp the depth of the vacuum. It was perfect, yet it was empty.

♦ ♦ ♦

After roughing it for a few weeks, the couple decided the time had arrived to return to civilization. They drove the Land Rover into Jackson, a small town in Wyoming. Back then, Jackson was

Res Clute

so laid back that if the police were needed, they weren't called on the police radio frequencies (radio frequencies: so New York!). There was a traffic light in the center of town, and if the red light went on above it, the cop would call headquarters and the dispatcher would tell him where to go.

Since they had a few weeks left before they had to be back in college, they decided to stay in town for a while. To tell the truth, they were getting a bit bored.

Roy found gainful employment as a busboy at Ed Hodgkins Old Wyoming Chuck Wagon, a restaurant that served hearty western fare, and became friends with a retired cowboy who worked with him at the restaurant. His name was Res Clute, and he was powerful and rugged from years spent in the great outdoors.

One day at work Roy suddenly felt a searing pain in his thumb. Looking down, he saw a splinter sticking out of his finger. Realizing that he needed a professional, he and Linda went straight to Jackson Hospital. The doctor gave Roy a local anesthetic and removed the splinter, and for the next three days he was out of commission, exhausted, in bed, and unable to move. From his body's reaction to the most minor surgery, Roy grasped the utter fragility of the human body and realized how even the slightest invasive procedure is enough to throw a person's body off, even if he is young and strong. Life is full of shocks, and this was a memorable one for an otherwise healthy young man.

◆   ◆   ◆

The weeks passed, and it was time to return to Ann Arbor and their little apartment on campus.

Goodbye, honeymoon.

Welcome to a new term.

Linda was a sophomore and Roy was a junior at the University of Michigan. It wasn't long before the newlyweds ran into trouble. They knew that they belonged together and that their marriage was meant to be, but they didn't know how to make it work.

"Western society tells us that you're supposed to tell the other person how you feel," Linda says. "If you're angry, then you should vent. Let your spouse know your feelings!"

This doesn't work if a person wants to have a good marriage. Communication requires self-control. The Torah tells us that when one speaks out of anger, not only is it ineffective, but it's actually akin to *avodah zarah*. Harsh words are like knives. Why would anyone want to hurt the person they are closest with?

Years later, when Roy and Linda met Rebbetzin Jungreis, one lesson that resonated was the account of how Sarah Imeinu learned that she was going to have a child at the age of ninety. She laughed, saying, "I am old and my husband is old. How is it possible that we will have a baby?!"

Hashem changed the words when He repeated this message to Avraham. He told Avraham that Sarah had said *she* was old, leaving out any reference to Avraham's age.

"Hashem was teaching us a lesson for all time," the Rebbetzin explained. "Our words should promote *shalom bayis*."

Her husband, Rabbi Meshulem HaLevi Jungreis, used to say, "You do not have to see everything. You do not have to hear everything."

But this would only come years later. Now, lacking guidance in the art of marriage, it was tough going for the young couple.

In addition, Roy was still struggling with his old anxieties. Of course, he had never heard of the *yetzer hara*, but some inner part of him was always walking around frightened that he would end up making decisions that he didn't want to follow and would regret, decisions "forced" upon him by the same powerful angst that he had feared from his earliest childhood. Roy had been fighting these demons his whole life, and nothing seemed to get rid of them.

Linda was different. She also felt the emptiness, but she was also happy, upbeat, and optimistic — "normal," in Roy's words. Roy felt the emptiness as a threat, and it permeated his mind until he was constantly focusing on his perception of the downward path of civilization and wondering where he could find an anchor for his soul, like the dove that left the Ark and couldn't find a resting place.

Chapter Eight
Bear Jam

After spending their first summer as a couple in Wyoming, Roy and Linda were ready for another adventure the following summer. This time they found jobs with the National Park Service, employed as fire lookouts in Crater Lake National Park, Oregon, one of the most beautiful places in the world. The job entailed keeping a sharp lookout for forest fires, and they would be living in a cabin perched on a mountaintop with a 150-mile

Fire lookout cabin on Mount Scott in Crater Lake National Park

Looking across Crater Lake. Our lookout cabin was on top of Mount Scott, the highest point on the horizon.

view in every direction. The lake below was situated in a caldera (the bowl remaining after a volcano has erupted), and its deep waters were always bluer than the sky.

Since park visitors would often hike up the mountain, Roy and Linda became a popular tourist attraction. They had to purchase their food outside the park, and on their days off, they would drive to the closest city, Fort Klamath or Klamath Falls. Shopping would be followed by shlepping, where everything they bought was lugged up the mountain on their young and strong backs. They cooked on a wood-burning stove and obtained drinking water by shoveling snow (which could be found at that elevation until August 10!) into ten-gallon milk cans and letting it melt. If they wanted a shower, they hiked down the mountain to the home of their boss, District Ranger Roy Allen. (By the time they returned, they would have appreciated another shower...)

Roy Allen, a redheaded career park ranger, treated the young couple like family and was happy to help them in any way he could. They remained friends for years after Crater Lake, even after the Allens had moved on to other parks.

When the snow ran out on the summit, rangers had to bring them water using a motorized buggy. One day a hiker arrived whom they welcomed with a glass of their precious water. He asked where they were from.

"New York."

"I don't like New York," he said. "Too many Jews."

Roy and Linda felt very uncomfortable, but kept their thoughts to themselves. They were happy when he left. This incident stayed with them until today, and yet, ironically, Roy himself was also allergic to Jewishness!

Maybe that's why it made such a deep impression.

Roy didn't like this man.

Maybe he also didn't like the man inside himself.

◆ ◆ ◆

There's nothing quite like living through a thunderstorm while sitting on the top of a mountain at 8,934 feet above sea level. Lightning always heads to the highest point, and they were right in the thick of it. It was a relatively quiet summer, but all you need is one storm.

"During a thunderstorm," Roy says, "we had to sit on our beds. High-voltage power lines were originally constructed using glass insulators. Well, our beds were also outfitted with glass insulators to protect us from the lighting. Sitting on the beds during one of those storms, we were protected from the intense current surging around our cabin."

The cabin had been built in the thirties by the civilian conservation corps — it was constructed from solid timber and stones — built with the intention of keeping the fire lookouts safe and protected. But there were metal shutters over the windows. When there was a lightning storm, blue fire danced around the shutters, and the entire cabin buzzed with electricity, as if a million wasps were trapped inside. While the entire world seemed to be exploding around them, Linda and Roy sat on their beds, theoretically safe in a scene reminiscent of Avraham Avinu entering Nimrod's fiery furnace.

The following summer, Roy worked as a ranger-naturalist in Great Smoky Mountains National Park in Tennessee, guiding visitors on hikes and delivering nature talks. Roy's father, who loved nature, was excited about this development. A man who thought big, he dreamed that his son would one day become secretary of the interior. Roy actually took graduate-level courses in botany at the University of Michigan and was considering a career in conservation.

This job was at a much lower elevation but held its own dangers. One part of Roy's job was to patrol the campgrounds in the evening, making sure everyone was safe and protecting campers from the many bears in the vicinity who enjoyed raiding campers' food stashes. There are no grizzly bears in that park (they are extremely dangerous), but plenty of black bears who were also capable of getting annoyed with humans if they felt threatened. Roy was assigned a long metal flashlight (he could smack an unruly bear on the nose) and a ranger uniform and hat, and when confronting a bear he made sure to speak with the voice of authority. The rangers themselves were convinced that the bears recognized their uniforms, and that they would leave if a uniformed ranger would demand that they take a hike.

Roy the Ranger in Great Smoky Mountains National Park

"I was very impressed with my own courage!" Roy remarks, remembering how he'd yelled at bears to move away.

So it went until the day that Linda's parents came to visit. Roy and Linda were driving them around the park on his day off, when they happened upon what is popularly referred to as a "bear jam'"— a bunch of bears hanging out at the side of the road, causing cars to stop and people to get out to take pictures. This wasn't only dangerous but created serious traffic problems on park roads.

For some reason, although people would normally shy away from bears unless they are safely behind bars, when it comes to a National Park, people walk right up to them in complete disregard for their own safety. This has led to serious injuries. Bears can go from docile and cute to aggressive and deadly in an instant. Adult black bears can weigh over six hundred pounds. That's a lot of bear, and they can move fast. So it's never a good idea to get on the wrong side of a bear.

Roy found that out the hard way.

Whenever there is a "bear jam" and cars are stopping, it's park policy for the ranger to move the people back into their cars and move the cars along the road. Roy had seen plenty of bear jams

A black bear in Great Smoky Mountains National Park

and had done what was necessary, but on the day Linda's parents were visiting, he forgot one thing: he was out of uniform.

When they came upon a bear jam, with Linda and her parents in the car, Roy decided to show his talents and move things along. He began by yelling at the nearest bear, who merely turned and looked at him.

Suddenly Mrs. Bear (who had her cubs with her, and it's a bad, bad idea to get between a Momma Bear and her cubs) started chasing Roy. It didn't last long, but every moment is ingrained in Roy's memory.

In the car, his family was screaming as Roy ran for his life. The bear was gaining on him fast. This was getting dangerous.

Suddenly Roy rounded the front of his car and put the car between himself and the bear. As soon as Roy reached the other side of the car, Mrs. Bear turned around and left with her cubs. But it had been too close for comfort. And just as he never forgot the incident, neither did his wife or his in-laws.

It was an embarrassment for years to come.

A similar scene actually occurred years later in Israel.

Roy and Linda were visiting Tel Dan National Park, a rugged place on the border of Lebanon known for a huge, old olive tree, ancient ruins, and a tributary to the Jordan River. Since the visit took place in the spring, the river was rushing, swollen with the snowmelt from Mount Hermon. It was an altogether beautiful scene, made especially so by the fact that there were very few people in the park at the time. For all practical purposes, they were alone in the middle of the vast reserve.

There they were, walking down the trail, heavy underbrush on both sides, when suddenly they heard a guttural growling sound emanating from the underbrush only a few feet away. It was the kind of sound that made the hair on your arms stand up, the kind of sound that meant "Danger! Beware!"

It was as if they were hiking in Africa and had just been warned off by a lion telling them that they were entering its territory. The growling was loud and close. There was something very scary and very big in those bushes.

The ancient, majestic olive tree in Tel Dan National Park

Roy looked at Linda. Linda looked at Roy. Then, with communication born of decades of marriage, they turned and slowly — very slowly — began backing up the trail, reversing course, away from the vicious growl. A few minutes later they exited the danger zone. To their relief, the growling stopped.

A year later they were courageous (or foolish) enough to return to the same spot at the same time of year. They even chose to walk the same trail. ("Lightning would not strike twice!")

As they neared the danger zone, they saw a park ranger and told him about their experience the previous year.

"I know exactly what happened," he said. "If you stand here, you can see her."

"Her?"

"Just wait."

About ten seconds later, they saw a gigantic wild boar — she must have weighed several hundred pounds.

"That's who you heard last year," the ranger said. "She had her babies with her, and you passed too close. She gives birth at that spot every year."

They realized that a miracle had happened to them in that very spot the previous year and Hashem had saved them from an angry mother boar.

Hashem saves us every day, every minute, even when we don't realize it!

PART 3

"Even the pope wears a yarmulke. If he can do it, what are you embarrassed about?!"

Rabbi Meshulem Jungreis

Chapter Nine
The Turnaround

The day: January 10, 1966.

The time: two o'clock in the morning.

The place: 606 East Ann Street, Ann Arbor, Michigan.

The biggest turnaround in Roy Neuberger's life happened when he was a graduate student at the University of Michigan.[2] That night Roy felt like his entire life was exploding, with no hope of redemption. Humpty Dumpty was about to fall and all the king's horses…

Well, you know the rest, but it wasn't a nursery rhyme. It was reality.

He was twenty-three years old, and everything seemed hopeless. For the last few years, he and Linda had tried numerous paths, searching for the formula that constantly seemed to elude them. More, their marriage was falling apart, and Roy's brain was worn out and frazzled.

Our Sages tell us that a marriage without Hashem is like fire. Roy says, "We can attest to that. Every couple has an occasional argument where a little fire starts burning. But when you don't have Hashem there to help you put out the fire, then it starts to get out of control. After a while, the blaze can consume the entire

---

2. Linda was then still an undergraduate.

marriage. Torah is compared to water, and we had no water with which to extinguish the conflagration.

"The panic I was feeling at that moment is almost indescribable. I had been able to survive until that point only because I had become adept at convincing myself that there was something else out there and I would find it one day. But I had run out of options, and there seemed to be nothing left."

♦ ♦ ♦

Roy was studying for his master's degree in English language and literature at the time. A final exam was fast approaching in Old English, a subject that he was unable to wrap his mind around no matter how he tried. He'd been cramming all night for the final, which was scheduled for 9:30 Friday morning. He finally went to sleep in the small hours of the night and didn't hear the alarm. He awoke at 9:20. The test was in ten minutes.

He flung himself out of bed and out the front door and flew through the streets of Ann Arbor on his bike. He arrived for the final fifteen minutes late, not even knowing the material to begin with.

Roy felt like he was cracking up.

That was Friday, January 7.

♦ ♦ ♦

At 2 a.m. Monday, January 10, Roy woke up crying, the knowledge that his life was falling apart hitting him in the gut. He felt like Alice in Wonderland falling down a bottomless rabbit hole, hurtling through endless space, and all around him was utter blackness. He had no idea what was his purpose in the world, and he didn't know how to figure it out — or even if there was a purpose at all (terrifying thought...). He felt like he was going to end up in a padded cell, locked away in a mental institution forever.

That was when the miracle happened.

Suddenly a feather floated down with him as he dropped down the rabbit hole: it was the flash of an idea, that maybe, just maybe, there is a G-d in the world. Until that moment he had never even considered such a concept. He was a student of the Ethical Culture Schools. He came from a sophisticated, affluent Upper East Side background. G-d had no place in such a life.

But suddenly, it hit him.

He was being confronted with a choice: It was either G-d or death.

Roy didn't want to die.

"G-d," he called out, "if You're there, help me!"

A cry from the deepest inner recesses of Roy's soul.

That night, Roy chose the thing he had never believed existed. The only reason he chose it was because there was no other option left — and yet it was the biggest breakthrough of his entire life. To many people, this may be laughable.

After all, what really happened here?

Did he suddenly begin believing in G-d?

No. All he did was recognize the possibility that maybe there is a G-d in the world.

Why was that such a big deal?

And yet it was the biggest deal in the world for Roy because it allowed him to internalize the possibility of a Larger Force, and if such a Force existed, then maybe there was a reason to live.

Maybe this Force was bigger than his problems. And if so, then maybe he wasn't crazy, after all.

And wasn't that a reason to celebrate?

Suddenly, a fascinating thing happened.

The moment Roy Salant Neuberger acknowledged the possibility that maybe there is a G-d in the world, it was like a light turned on in his brain. For the first time in forever, he suddenly had hope that there was a chance that he could figure out the giant mystery called life. Just the possibility of a maybe was enough to turn everything around.

And so it was that for the first time in his twenty-three years on earth, Roy Neuberger had hope.

◆ ◆ ◆

The next thing he knew he was writing furiously, his natural mode of expression. He wrote for hours, laying down his life

Years later, Yisroel and Leah in front of 606 East Ann Street

of agony and hopelessness on paper. Until that night, he hadn't even been able to acknowledge that this was what it really was. But now that he suddenly felt the possibility of hope, he was able to recognize how wrong he had been in his thinking up until that point. As he wrote, torrents of tears gushed out until his eyes were red from weeping.

So it went through the night until morning came and the sun rose above Ann Arbor.

Even today, whenever Roy and Leah find themselves in the vicinity of 606 East Ann Street (and this happens every time Roy and Linda go to speak in Ann Arbor), they feel that there should be a giant billboard stating, "This is the place where Yisroel Neuberger was born."

♦ ♦ ♦

Did Roy and Linda become religious the next day?

Not at all. They were just emerging from the shell at that point.

Take-off would only happen in 1974 — eight years later. But after that experience in Ann Arbor, Roy began believing in G-d. He still didn't want to be religious, having an intuitive feeling that once he would admit that Hashem is G-d, he would have to obey His commands, and Roy wasn't ready yet to obey anyone.

But Roy and Linda now embarked on a journey to discover the truth, which is how they ended up investigating Buddhism, Hinduism, and eventually Christianity. Both he and Linda didn't even consider looking into Judaism. After all, they had never met a Jew who believed in his own religion, so clearly there was nothing there.

♦ ♦ ♦

Years later, after they became religious and Roy found out that there is something called a Jewish calendar, he looked up the Hebrew date of January 10, 1966. After a little research, he figured out that it coincided with the eighteenth of Teves. After that, he couldn't help noticing that numerous important things kept on happening to them in the month of Teves.

Linda's father passed away on the tenth of Teves.

Roy's father passed away many years later on the seventeenth of Teves.

Roy and Linda's first child, Susan, was born on the fifteenth of Teves.

On the eighteenth of Teves, decades later, their first grandson who is a Kohen, Yaakov Moshe HaKohen Hess, was born in Jerusalem.

There was just something about that month.

In 2006, they attended the *vort* of Rebbetzin Jungreis's grandson in Monsey. By midnight they were on the Major Deegan Expressway in the Bronx, heading back to Long Island. Roy was driving in the middle lane. Linda was sleeping in the passenger seat. Suddenly a car passed on the left at around one hundred miles an hour. In front of Roy's eyes, the driver lost control, and his car careened to the right, cutting across three lanes before hitting the high stone barrier over the Harlem River. The car started going up and over the barrier but didn't quite make it before falling back onto the highway. Then it spun around and now was heading directly toward Roy and Linda in what would clearly be a head-on collision. At that moment, Leah awoke to see a car bearing down on them at high speed.

Roy slammed on the brakes. As he did so, the car behind them smashed them from the rear, and at the same moment the other car smashed them from the front. They had been crushed at high speed between two cars. The entire world was spinning around like some crazy amusement park ride that had come off its moorings and sent its riders sailing off into the wild blue yonder.

And yet...

Seconds later, Yisroel realized that they were still alive and somehow parked on the grassy median by the side of the road. They would never know how they survived. The car was totaled.

The police arrived. The fire department showed up with five trucks. There were ambulances all around. One police officer looked at them and said, "How on earth are you both alive? I've seen way too many accidents on this stretch of road. But I've never seen such a terrible accident where people walked away without an injury."

The car had been turned into an accordion and yet, somehow, they had walked out without a scratch.

The date was the fourteenth of Teves.

Many times Yisroel wondered to himself, Why did all these miraculous events take place particularly in the month of Teves and not in one of the "big" months, like Adar, Nissan, or Kislev?

Why Teves?

One year. he was davening Hallel on Rosh Chodesh Teves when he suddenly had an astonishing thought.

Everything is planned; nothing is haphazard. There is only one Rosh Chodesh during the year when the Jewish people recite the entire Hallel, and that is for the month of Teves. That is because Rosh Chodesh Teves always falls during Chanukah, during which we say full Hallel. In full Hallel, we recite two additional chapters of *Tehillim*.

There he was, reciting the second of the two chapters, and he uttered the words "*Tzarah v'yagon emtza u'vesheim Hashem ekra... Ana Hashem malta nafshi* — The pains of death encircled me; the confines of the grave have found me... Then I would invoke the Name of Hashem. 'Please Hashem, save my soul!'"

At that moment, Roy realized that he had never been able to describe fully the events that occurred at the moment of the Great Breakthrough in Ann Arbor on January 10, 1966. But here David HaMelech had written the perfect words to describe exactly what Roy Neuberger felt when he called out to Hashem on that long ago night on a college campus in Michigan.

Hashem answered him, and life was never the same.

Chapter Ten

Getting Off
the Merry-Go-Round

Finally a breakthrough. A ray of sunlight in the midst of what seemed to be endless hopelessness and agony. For the first time, Roy and Linda were willing to consider that maybe there actually was a G-d in the universe. But just because they had come to this realization, it didn't mean that they knew the path to travel.

Not yet.

They were going to find it, but they weren't there yet.

While they were now open to the concept of G-d and were even willing to start searching for Him, it was going to take them some time before they would connect the existence of G-d to the Torah. Their search for G-d first took them to the cathedrals of other faiths. The idea of Judaism being the correct path was so remote that it didn't even enter into the realm of possibility. In Linda's experience, being a Jew was just a material thing. She could hardly be blamed for thinking this, since everyone she knew who celebrated a bar mitzvah never seemed to return to shul again.

Roy and Linda's "Jewish experience" at that point included attending a few friends' bar mitzvahs, at which an expensive meal was served and a lot of generous checks were handed over to the young man or his proud parents. So they associated Jewish observance with roast beef and money. No one ever mentioned Hashem!

No, it seemed clear that Judaism didn't have much to offer.

Roy had an inkling that G-d and the Torah were intricately connected, but he didn't want to accept orders from anyone, even G-d. Though he had come to the realization that he had been suffering because of his estrangement from Hashem — he felt as if he were hurtling through outer space with no connection to anything solid — and that there had to be Truth somewhere, he pushed away the knowledge that this truth had to be rooted in the Torah. Subconsciously he knew that once he acknowledged the existence of G-d, he would have to subordinate his entire life to Him, and he wasn't willing to give up his "freedom." He wanted to be the boss of his world.

Well, as we know, the Jewish nation are a stubborn people. Only one thing could alter this stalemate: Life would have to become so intolerable that without Hashem, it would all just fall apart. Only after everything else crashed would he be able to admit that there was no other viable path than Hashem and His Torah.

So they began studying other religions. Since they were academically minded, they weren't fazed by having to master vast quantities of new information they were confronted with. If anything, the opposite was true: they loved diving into new worlds. Among other things, they were given in-depth instruction into Hinduism by an Indian professor at the University of Michigan.

This odyssey continued for the next eight years.

♦ ♦ ♦

In June 1966, six months after Roy's breakthrough, Linda received her bachelor's degree and Roy was awarded his master's in English Language and Literature (despite the disastrous Old English final) from the University of Michigan. They left soon afterward for Oxford University in England, where they studied for the next fourteen months. The plan was for Linda to study painting and drawing in the historic Ashmolean Museum and for Roy to further his studies in English literature at Balliol College, hoping eventually to become a college professor.

At Oxford, the year is broken up into three eight-week terms — eight weeks of learning followed by six weeks off. The time off is supposed to be for studying and preparing for the eight weeks to come, but Roy and Linda used the free time for traveling. They traveled all over England, then went further afield, to Scotland, Ireland, France, Italy, and Switzerland.

Europe is filled with Christian art and architecture — frescoes, paintings, and sculptures in ancient cathedrals, monasteries, and the Vatican itself, the seat of Catholicism and residence of the pope. For Roy and Linda, the Vatican was a cultural treasure of history and art. Only later would they realize that the Vatican represents the antithesis of Judaism, the legacy of Esav, the enemy of Yaakov. It was a slippery slope that could easily have led into the dark waters of idolatry. Hashem mercifully rescued them, but that was still in the future.

It was during this time that they made the decision to pursue the study of Christianity. They approached their research with seriousness and diligence. But their initial excitement soon turned into disappointment as their Jewish souls kept niggling at them: *This isn't it, guys. You're barking up the wrong tree...*

One thing that turned them off from Christianity was their desire to live a spiritual life as normal, married people who were also part of a community. The more they read about Christianity, the more it seemed to them that there was no way for regular Christians to attain a high level of spirituality. They wanted to raise their children alongside other people. They wanted to live a meaningful spiritual life, but not as monks. And somehow they knew that it couldn't be true, that a person should be able to pursue a fulfilling spiritual life while having a family.

As much as they had initially hoped that the answer lay in the gospels, the more they learned, the more the truth seemed to be slipping away.

Roy and Linda returned to the States from England in October 1967. Roy found a job as New York City's first (and only) director of conservation in the Department of Parks, Recreation, and Cultural Affairs. One of his successes was the creation of the Staten Island's Greenbelt, a network of parks and nature trails in the heart of Staten Island that was saved from the fate of urban development. He instituted self-guiding nature trails so that New Yorkers could go for informative walks among the greenery. He was also instrumental in saving Jamaica Bay, which was incorporated into the Gateway National Seashore.

Roy's "extracurricular" responsibility was to write speeches for his boss, Commissioner August Heckscher. Mr. Heckscher had previously been an editor at the *New York Herald Tribune*, so he was a writer himself and could appreciate how Roy was able to capture his voice on paper.

Roy worked for the city for several years but eventually became

Department of Parks, Recreation, and Cultural Affairs farewell party for Roy
(Commissioner Heckscher is the one wearing a bow tie)

restless. Somehow he felt that he still wasn't doing what he was meant to do with his life. The question was, what to do next?

His former boss, August Heckscher, made a call to the editorial-page editor of the *Times*, who offered Roy a job. But it didn't work out. Roy and the editor didn't see eye to eye. It wasn't the place for him.

With the job at the *Times* a bust, Roy and Linda were ready for a change of scenery. Their first child, Susan Eve (later Sarah), had just been born[3] and they wanted to get away from the pollution and noise of the city to raise their family in a more peaceful environment.[4] Their first stop was the Neuberger country house in Westchester, but soon afterward they moved across the Hudson River and a bit north to the town of Cornwall.

Cornwall is situated at the base of Storm King Mountain, between Newburgh and West Point Military Academy, with incredible views overlooking the Hudson River. They saw the town as a lovely and peaceful environment in which to raise their children, and they pictured themselves entering small-town life where everyone is kind and friendly.

Moving to Cornwall seemed like the answer to all their doubts and confusion. They were seeking a more pure and holy life, and while they really had no idea how to find it, they figured this was a step in the right direction.

In the meantime, Roy needed an occupation. His fingers were itching to put words down on paper. He could picture himself as an author, sitting for hours every day and writing. But he had no idea what to write about. Somehow he had never managed to figure out what it was exactly that he wanted to say. He thought that being surrounded by nature would help him find his voice.

After moving into their new home on Hilltop Road, he made an attempt at writing, but he still couldn't find his direction. He'd get up every morning, make a coffee, eat some breakfast, and then settle himself at his desk with a pristine pad of paper, which remained empty of meaningful content. It was terribly frustrating.

---

3. January 1969.
4. Juliet Rose (later Yaffa) was born in September 1971.

Roy compares their life in Cornwall to a merry-go-round: One rides the horse as the music plays, round and round. When the music stops, you get off the horse, but you're exactly where you had been two minutes before. Every Friday night Roy and Linda would go to one of the local pubs for food and music, just the two of them riding the merry-go-round. Life was going nowhere.

One day Roy heard that *The Cornwall Local* was for sale. Roy could picture himself as the publisher of a small-town paper. *The Local* had been in existence since 1885 and was a fixture, respected and trusted. He discussed his vision with his lawyer, Steve Duggan III.

Steve also lived in Cornwall, and the two men went way back, Roy's parents having known Steve's parents in the city. Now the friendship took a more serious turn when the two of them decided to go into business together as partners at *The Local*. Roy would manage the operation, while Steve would remain in the background. Roy's parents helped make the purchase, and within a short time Roy and Linda, along with Steve, were the new owners of a weekly small-town paper and printing business.

◆ ◆ ◆

Roy had big dreams. He wanted to increase circulation and turn the paper into a prize winner, as well as make the business profitable. One of the first things Roy did was to begin using the latest technology to print the newspaper. This made the paper more aesthetically pleasing and easier to put together. Before Roy took over, the paper was still using the venerable Linotype machine. Roy made the brave (and rather costly) decision to take the paper into the computer age. They started preparing the articles for the paper on the computer, and the quality of the pictures was taken to a whole different level.

Roy threw himself into his new job. Since he was the editor, he ended up writing many of the paper's articles. Although he did hire a reporter, he edited everything, and the quality of the articles improved noticeably. There were national prizes to be won for layout, graphics, and articles, as well as for best newspaper, and Roy was ambitious. He rose early and rushed out to cover every local story, from car crashes to fires to storms. The second he got the call, he was out the door and in his Chevy sedan heading to the scene. Roy was also a member of the local ambulance corps (he had trained as an EMT), and since he went on calls, he was usually one of the first people to know about anything traffic-related. If there was news, Roy was there.

It didn't take long for everyone in town to find out about their new editor and publisher. In a small town, an editor occupies a prominent role. The local newspaper reflects the town's personality and lets everyone know what's going on. Roy's prominence also highlighted the fact that he was a Jew in a town largely inhabited by non-Jews. He didn't mention it or even think about it, but somehow everyone knew. And one day he received an anonymous letter from someone who threatened to kidnap his children!

This wasn't pleasant, to say the least. Roy's reaction was to head right over to see his friend at the Cornwall police station, Chief Mike Triolo. This was a lot of excitement for the small-town police officer, and it ended with Roy and Chief Mike proceeding to the local FBI headquarters about an hour's drive from Cornwall.

The FBI showed remarkably little interest in the case. Meaning that they did nothing. Thankfully, Roy never received another letter nor was he the object of any overt hatred. Yet the situation revealed an important truth: a Jew can never hide his identity. As Rashi reminds us, "It is known that Esav hates Yaakov."

Despite these bumps on the road, life went well for the next few years. Roy immersed himself in his new career, determined to build a paper that would be journalistically and financially successful.

◆ ◆ ◆

The Jewish families living in Cornwall were either Reform or unaffiliated. To Roy and Linda, who knew nothing about Judaism, the Reform lifestyle appeared extremely religious. They formed a relationship with one family, who invited them to their Pesach Seder. The family didn't use a classic Haggadah, but rather one they had written themselves. Roy and Linda were impressed.

"That was very informative and inspiring," they told one another when they left their new friends' home. But in their hearts, they knew somehow that it wasn't the real thing.

It was around this time that Roy joined the National Newspaper Association, the trade association of the country's weekly newspapers, to promote *The Cornwall Local*. That's when he met and befriended its president, Walter Grunfeld. After a visit to Walter's home to pick his brain on developing the paper, when Walter uttered those unforgettable words — "What kind of Jew are you? Are you made of stone? Don't you have a heart?" — Roy's Jewish soul shifted into high gear.

Walter's question wouldn't go away. It was there when he went to sleep at night, and it was there when he rose in the morning.

What kind of Jew are you, Roy?

A better question would have been, "What is a Jew in the first place?" And this question reverberated continually in Roy's and Linda's minds.

Six months after this emotional outburst, Roy was speaking with one of his friends and main advertisers, a gentle and thoughtful Jew from Newburgh (about five miles north of Cornwall) named Bob Ushman. Bob, who owned a hardware store in Cornwall, was a member of the local shul. Still bothered by Walter's question, Roy opened up.

"I'm thirty-one years old," he said, "and I've completely exhausted every option that I thought might lead me to the truth. There is absolutely nothing left."

Bob listened sympathetically.

"Bob," Roy said, "I really don't know what it means to be a Jew. I was never even in a synagogue! What do people do there?"

"Do you want to come to our synagogue and find out?"

Still, Roy remained noncommittal. "Maybe."

◆ ◆ ◆

Bob called Roy that evening.

"I checked out the program at my shul and there's this woman, a 'Rebbetzin,' coming to speak this Thursday night. They're billing her as the 'Jewish Billy Graham.' Maybe you'd like to come over and hear what she has to say."

Roy and Linda decided to go and hear this "Rebbetzin" speak. ("What's a 'Rebbetzin' anyway?") By this point they really wanted to know what it means to be a Jew. Maybe this woman had the answers they were seeking.

The fact was that they had run out of options. They had tried everything, without exaggeration. Nothing had made the grade. There was now, at this fateful moment, nothing left that they hadn't investigated.

One of Roy's favorite quotes comes from *Sherlock Holmes*: "When you have eliminated all which is impossible, then whatever remains, however improbable, must be the truth."

Maybe the "Jewish Billy Graham" had the answer.

Chapter Eleven
The Rebbetzin

Having no idea what a rebbetzin was, Roy and Linda didn't know what to expect. But since he was entering a synagogue for almost the first time in his life, Roy decided to show respect and put a yarmulke on his head. It felt strange, but he did it.

The Neubergers would never forget the moment Rebbetzin Esther Jungreis[5] entered the room. They had been expecting a religious lady who looked two hundred years out of date. But the woman who entered the room was extremely put together and well-dressed. They were hard-pressed to reconcile their expectations with the reality that stood before them.

From one moment to the next, all their preconceived notions were shot. The GPS had to be recalibrated.

---

5. Rebbetzin Jungreis was born in Hungary, the descendant of a long line of distinguished rabbis. She, her parents and two brothers miraculously survived the war and found their way to the United States. Even as a young girl she found she had an unusual gift for communication. She began to speak publicly about the greatness of the Torah way of life. Her father brought her to *gedolim* like Rabbi Moshe Feinstein *zt"l* and Rabbi Yosef Eliyahu Henkin *zt"l* for *berachos*. As a young rebbetzin she was encouraged to use her talents for the *klal*, and this culminated in the groundbreaking Madison Square Garden *kiruv* rally of November 1973. Her husband, Rabbi Meshulem HaLevi Jungreis *zt"l*, was her biggest supporter. She founded an organization called "Hineni" that became the vehicle for a worldwide *teshuvah* campaign.

The woman began to speak, and it was as if she were talking directly to them.

"You are a Jew. You have created civilizations. You have given birth to every ideal that has shaped mankind. Justice, peace, love, and the innate dignity of man have all had their genesis in your Torah. But above all, you have been given the unique mission of proclaiming the Oneness of G-d."

The Rebbetzin was incredibly emotional. Though she spoke quietly, every word packed a punch. Her demeanor reminded Roy of a teacher at Fieldston who held her class in the palm of her hand because she taught in a whisper. The Rebbetzin told them about the patriarchs and the matriarchs and how it was the Jewish people who taught the world that there is a G-d.

"Not only did we teach the world about G-d," she said, "it was the Jewish people who introduced the concept of morality as well. And where does that come from? From the Torah, which the Jewish people have studied day and night for thousands of years."

♦ ♦ ♦

It was a revelation.

They didn't know why, but suddenly Roy and Linda found themselves crying. They had grown up attending the Ethical Culture Schools, traveled the world, and seen it all. They had been honor students at the University of Michigan and graduate students at Oxford University, but when it came to Torah, they were still in nursery school.

Suddenly they comprehended how little they knew. A bolt of lightning had struck their *neshamos*: There was a world out there that they had never known existed, one that was inviting them inside. It was as if they had been living in an alternate reality their whole lives, and the two worlds — the one in which they had been living and the unknown world to which they were being introduced — had suddenly collided with a fantastic explosion.

Roy and Linda were so overwhelmed by what the Rebbetzin had said, were so out of their depth, that they couldn't even speak to her after the lecture. Roy would have loved to have gone over to the Rebbetzin, to introduce himself and his wife and tell her of the impact her words had made on them, but they lacked the words to articulate their feelings. That's how he was. When Roy found himself overwhelmed, he wasn't able to find the words to describe his emotions. Instead, he needed to sleep on it and would find greater clarity in the morning.

Before leaving, they purchased a recording of the Rebbetzin's famous speech at Madison Square Garden and then left the shul awestruck and speechless. It took them both a long time to fall asleep that night. When they awoke the next day, they knew one thing: they needed to investigate what they had heard the night before. Something huge had occurred, but they had no idea what to do with it. They needed to figure it out and follow where it led.

Roy wasted no time. He wrote a letter to the Rebbetzin and mailed it to the address on the back of the recording they had bought the night before. Today he might have communicated with her through one of the endless choices afforded by modern technology, but back then, in 1974, people still wrote letters. It was a good medium for Roy. He always felt that if he had something complex or important to say, he must put it into writing. When he put his thoughts on paper, he could survey them and discern whether they made sense. He could figure out how those words fit together. While his father focused on paintings and stock charts, Roy focused on words.

Here is what Roy wrote to the Rebbetzin:

> Dear Rebbetzin Jungreis,
>
> I'm thirty-one years old and I am the publisher and editor of a weekly newspaper in Cornwall, New York. I was raised in New York City and attended the Ethical Culture Schools, the University of Michigan, and Balliol College, Oxford. The time my wife and I heard you speak in Newburgh was the first time I had been in a synagogue in my life (with the exception of friends' weddings and bar mitzvahs).
>
> Ever since January 1966, when I had a spiritual "turn-around," I have begun to believe that G-d exists. Up to that point, I scorned the idea. Since then, I have examined

various oriental religions and Christianity, but I have recently begun to realize that I was overlooking the thing that was most obvious: my own heritage.

I cannot say that I really believe in G-d or that I *feel* that He exists, but I think that, as I come to know my heritage, I will feel the truth.

I do not know a word of Hebrew. I know almost nothing about Jewish law, services, life, or tradition. I do know parts of the Bible, in English. I want to learn Hebrew, but more than that, I am seriously considering getting out of the newspaper business and becoming a rabbi. I feel that the amount of time and energy I now have to devote to my business, to pushing a pencil and hustling in the world of business, to pushing someone else down in order to get ahead, creates a cleavage in my life because my mind longs to be on the things that I truly care about.

I agree with most of what you say and write; I feel it to be true. (Some of it sounds like my editorials.) I feel as if you could give me some good advice. I'd like to hear what you think and, if you're willing, come with my wife and have a talk with you.

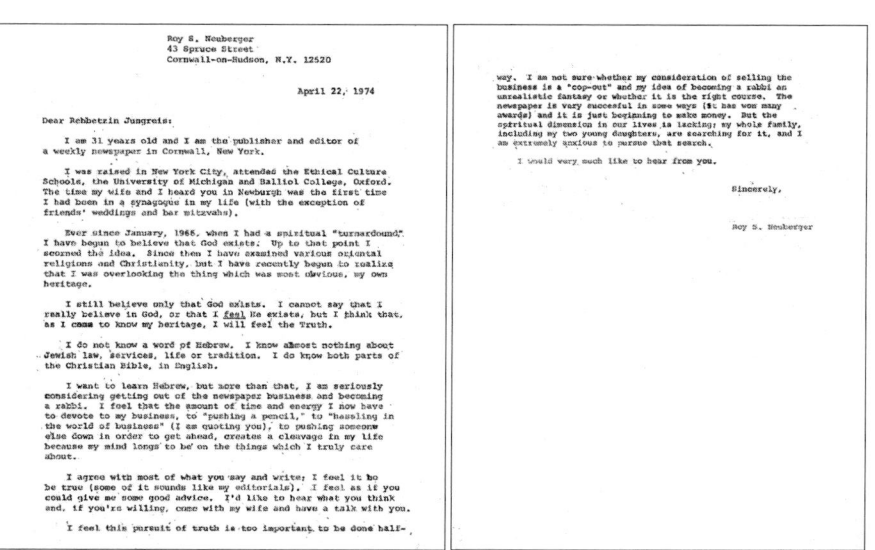

Roy's original letter to the Rebbetzin written in April 1974

I feel this pursuit of truth is too important to be done halfway. I am not sure whether my consideration of selling the business is a cop-out, and my idea of becoming a rabbi an unrealistic fantasy or whether it is the right course. The newspaper is very successful in some ways, but the spiritual dimension is lacking in our lives. My whole family, including our two young daughters, are searching for it, and I am extremely anxious to pursue that search.

I would very much like to hear from you.

Sincerely,

Roy S. Neuberger

To his utter amazement, the Rebbetzin wrote back, explaining that she wanted Roy and Linda to be in touch and that more than anything else they needed to learn Torah.

Dear Mr. Neuberger,

I am very happy to hear [about] your interest in learning about Judaism… If you are ever going to be in the Brooklyn, N.Y., area, I would like to invite you to an adult Bible class, which is held every Tuesday night, which would be great for your entire family. If that is impossible for you, then maybe you and your wife could meet with me for a talk. I have a very tight schedule, but if you will be willing to call, then we can arrange something. Also enclosed is information on our trip to Israel. Your whole family is invited to come. Please keep in touch.

Sincerely,

Rebbetzin Esther Jungreis

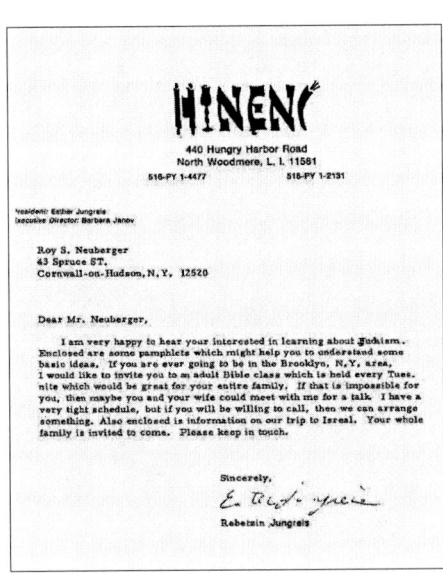

The Rebbetzin's reply

♦ ♦ ♦

It happened to be that their meeting with the Rebbetzin came at a very auspicious time, a moment in time that was eerily similar to the night of Roy's breakthrough in college. For the first time in his life, his *neshamah* recognized that it was finally hearing truth.

Besides, he had totally run out of all other options. It was now or never, like the Children of Israel in Egypt who fell to the forty-ninth level of impurity and faced a situation in which they would either lose all connection to spirituality or be redeemed and elevated to the most sublime level, that of Har Sinai.

As Roy himself puts it:

> By the time I met Rebbetzin Esther Jungreis, I had spent years studying at the most advanced educational institutions. I had traveled extensively and seen the world, and after trying so many things, I had come to the conclusion that they were all empty, filled with contradictions and untruths. Even after I had come to Cornwall, I was still busy tinkering with Christianity and experimenting with other foreign ideas.
>
> It happened to be that the headmaster of a private school in Cornwall was a Christian missionary. He spent a lot of time trying to convince me that his way was the best and most truthful approach. He even brought in one of the bigger guns to meet me, and both of them devoted a lot of attention to the cause of trying to convert me, which only left me with a bad taste.
>
> Not only that, but while we were trying to figure out whether Christianity was for us, our eldest daughter, Susan, was constantly bombarded by her friends, who loved talking about their religion. It wasn't long before she was coming home and asking some pretty difficult questions about G-d and the world and how everything worked. We didn't really know what to tell her.
>
> Ironically, I had no problem writing a book that I titled *Why the Jews Are Wrong and the Christians Are Right.* Though I was an *am ha'aretz*, I didn't allow my lack of knowledge

to stop me from writing as if I were the biggest expert on religion in the world.

It didn't matter, because nobody wanted to publish the book! I guess the reason was because the central thesis made no sense, even if you were Christian and happy that a Jew was writing such a book. I sent a copy of the manuscript to every publisher I could think of, and they all turned me down. I was, of course, devastated that no one wanted to publish my work, but in retrospect, it was an immense kindness from the Master of the World, Who saved me from having my name attached to such a piece of utter falsehood and nonsense.

Roy still had his newspaper, but he wasn't feeling as much of a sense of accomplishment from it as he'd imagined he would. The rejection of his book was the final nail in the coffin.

Rebbetzin Esther Jungreis came along at just the right time, the exact instant Roy and Linda needed to hear what she had to say, like a flash of lightning in the midst of darkness. When she spoke, Roy suddenly realized how remote they were from G-d. Suddenly he knew that they had been floating just above rock bottom, especially considering the falsehoods Roy had spent so much time writing (and which nobody wanted to publish).

Walter Grunfeld had questioned what kind of Jew Roy was, and he hadn't known what to answer.

Their daughter was asking questions about G-d that they couldn't answer.

They had tried every religion they encountered and hadn't found the answers.

Without question, their meeting with the Rebbetzin had saved their lives, because there was nowhere else for them to go.

◆ ◆ ◆

Later they would learn that the Rebbetzin wasn't even supposed to come to speak at the shul that night. She had been scheduled to speak there in December, but she had contracted the flu and the speech had been postponed.

Barbara Janov, the director of the outreach organization that Rebbetzin Jungreis and her husband had founded, Hineni, hadn't been keen on rescheduling the Newburgh speech at all. "Why do we need to go to Newburgh?" she'd asked the Rebbetzin. "To speak to two cows and a chicken?"

But Rebbetzin Jungreis wouldn't budge. If Jews wanted to hear her speak in Newburgh, she would go to Newburgh.

Had the speech taken place when planned — before Roy's conversation with Bob Ushman — he and Linda wouldn't have met the Rebbetzin. It became crystal clear that their meeting with Rebbetzin Jungreis had been orchestrated by Heaven to the millisecond. A day before or after, and it probably wouldn't have occurred.

◆ ◆ ◆

The Neubergers began driving to Brooklyn every Tuesday to hear Rebbetzin Jungreis speak. At the time, she was giving the class at Shaare Zion, a synagogue on Ocean Parkway affiliated with the Syrian community, to a modest group of twelve people. Attending the *shiur* meant a two-hour drive in each direction. It was a huge act of *mesirus nefesh* on their part, yet they did it willingly and happily.

The classes were a challenge on many fronts. Besides the amount of time it took them to get there and back, their decision to make a weekly drive to Flatbush happened during the energy crisis of 1974. Gas was being rationed; people were allowed to fill up only every other day, and this meant waiting in line at the gas station to fill up the tank of their blue Chevy (four doors, tail fins, and about twenty feet long). They also needed to find a babysitter for their two little girls.

The newspaper was another challenge, because it needed to be put to bed Tuesday night in order to reach the printer early Wednesday morning. Back then, Roy had to do everything manually: cut the articles to size, paste them in place with hot wax, and make sure the layout was attractive and readable. He did a beautiful job, but it was painstaking and took him hours. It was literally an all-night job.

When they found out when the classes took place, they knew they needed to go — they viewed it as a matter of life and death — but Roy also needed to put the paper to bed.

He solved the problem by getting up at 2 a.m. Tuesday morning so the paper would be ready for the printer first thing Wednesday. He would finish the layout just in time for them to make the two-hour drive to Brooklyn.

Roy and Linda were juggling a lot of balls, but they didn't mind, because they had to find the answer to the core question: "Who are we and how should we live?"

◆ ◆ ◆

Roy and Linda were veteran students. They knew how to read and analyze. They knew how to research and discover the depth in great literature. It took them no time to figure out that all the literature in the world couldn't compare to the Torah. The Torah was totally different from anything they had studied in the past. There were layers here that were loftier than the stars and deeper than the sea. Their previous studies had nothing on the treasures they were discovering on a weekly basis.

Rebbetzin Jungreis's classes became the highlight of their week. She warmed them with her intensity and comforted them with words that emanated from *Shamayim*.

For the first time, Roy and Linda were learning the secrets to a happy marriage, how to raise their children, and how to understand and relate to the world around them. It was as if Moshe Rabbeinu himself had come down from the mountain and was speaking to them directly.

They'd been searching for so long for meaning and purpose. The search had begun when Roy was a little boy and intensified when he met Linda at Fieldston. Now here they were, at the age of thirty and thirty-one, and it was finally happening. When they heard the Rebbetzin teaching Torah, all the literature they used to spend so much time analyzing became empty and irrelevant.

More than that, they realized that a person doesn't have to exile himself to a mountaintop or monastery to live a spiritual life. It's possible and even preferable to live among like-minded people in a Torah community. That was the best — really the only way — to live a life of genuine spirituality.

Within a short period, the allure of life in Cornwall, a place devoid of religious Jews, began to fade. The Neubergers sold the newspaper and moved to North Woodmere, only a block away from the Jungreises on Hungry Harbor Road. By Rosh Hashanah of 1974, only a few months after traveling with the Rebbetzin to Israel, they were established in the Jungreises' community.

Chapter Twelve
A Jew With a Gun

L et's back up a few months.

In May 1974, having attended Torah classes for about eight weeks, Roy and Linda found themselves preparing for a trip to Israel with the Rebbetzin. The decision to go wasn't simple. It wasn't easy for Roy to abandon the paper for longer than a day, especially since their staff was skeletal at best. It seemed impossible for a while, and the staff was upset at Roy for going.

But this wasn't negotiable. Roy and Linda had to go.

What to do with their girls, Susan, age five, and Juliet, almost three, was another major question. But a solution was found: Linda's mother kindly moved into their house for the duration of their trip to take care of them.

Roy and Linda weren't the only ones who were unsure about the trip. The Rebbetzin herself didn't know what to expect. She had been invited by the IDF to come and speak at several army bases, but people kept warning her that the whole thing was a mistake and that the soldiers were going to throw tomatoes at her when she stood up on an army stage and gave Torah classes.

In a way, the naysayers were correct: It turned out that the army had misunderstood who the Rebbetzin was. They had thought she was a singer! It was another example of Hashem making the most incredible things happen, even if that meant having an openly religious woman like Rebbetzin Esther Jungreis being invited to speak at military bases by the IDF itself. The Rebbetzin had her doubts, but the army kept calling (assuming she was a singer). And so the tickets were booked, and the Rebbetzin brought along with her a small group of close people, including Roy and Linda.

♦ ♦ ♦

They took the El Al midnight flight. At JFK Airport, the Rebbetzin's mother (everyone called her "Mama") gave yarmulkes to all the men going on the trip. They were light blue with the Hineni logo prominently displayed on them. Roy accepted the yarmulke and promptly stowed it in his pocket. Where else should he put it?

The Rebbetzin noticed. "Excuse me, Roy," she said, "but it goes on your head."

Linda, for her part, trying to be respectful, had left her pants at home and had come equipped with skirts and dresses. Little did she know about skirt or sleeve lengths, but her learning experience was only just beginning, after all.

The plane took off after midnight, and it wasn't long before the travelers were all sleeping. A few hours into the flight, Roy and Linda were awakened when they heard rustling noises all around them. Men were rising from their seats like celestial beings who needed no sleep. Before their disbelieving eyes, the men wrapped themselves in white prayer shawls, which was followed by the placement of boxes on their heads and arms.

It was surreal. They had never seen talleisim or tefillin. But by the end of the trip, Roy would be putting on those boxes as well. What is life if not filled with surprises?

When they finally landed in Israel, the Rebbetzin walked down the staircase from the airplane to the tarmac, then bent down and kissed the ground.

Roy and Linda had never seen anything like it in their lives.

(Just add it to the list...)

♦ ♦ ♦

It was a trip of many firsts. Before their departure, someone donated a pair of tefillin to Yanky Jungreis[6] to give as a gift to someone in need of them. Roy ended up being the recipient, and Rabbi Yanky helped him don tefillin for the first time in his life.

The two of them, Roy and the Rebbetzin's brother, really connected, particularly after the rabbi shared a personal story with him.

The story had occurred many years earlier, when he was a young man traveling to Eretz Yisrael to learn. Since it was the fifties, he didn't fly but went by boat, which docked along the way in Naples, Italy. Yanky took the opportunity to disembark and stretch his legs.

As he walked along the quay, he spotted something that made his heart soar with pride: a navy ship flying the Israeli flag. For a boy who had survived Bergen-Belsen, it was a heartening image.

A sailor stood guard at the gangplank. Yanky stopped and asked, "Excuse me, can I please come aboard?"

"No," the Israeli sailor replied.

Yanky tried again. "I'm a Holocaust survivor, and being able to see your ship, a ship from Israel, would mean a lot to me."

"Not possible."

Then Yanky saw something half hidden in the sailor's shirt. It looked like a medallion hanging on a chain.

"What's that?" he asked the sailor, pointing.

The man softened. "This?" He reached into his shirt and showed Yanky a coin hanging on a chain. The coin had a hole in the middle so that the chain could go through the hole.

"I received this coin from a holy man back in Hungary," he said. "A rabbi and his young son came to see us off before we were taken away to the labor camp where I was incarcerated along with many other Jewish boys. He did his best to give hope and comfort to all of us. He gave every boy a coin like this one

---

6. This is Rebbetzin Jungreis's older brother, who joined the trip. (Rebbetzin Jungreis's married and maiden name are identical; she married a cousin with the same last name.)

and told us that we should hold on to the coin, that it would serve as a *segulah* to protect us. I wear it wherever I go."

"I have to tell you something," Yanky said when he heard the sailor's story.

"What is it?"

"The man who gave you the coin? That was my father. And the young boy — well, the young boy was me."

Yanky's father had gone out of his way to visit the Jewish boys who had been taken away by the Nazi-controlled Hungarian wartime government. Giving them coins was his way of providing them with a source of *chizuk* that was tangible, something physical for them to hold on to.

"Wait here," the sailor said suddenly. "I'll ask the captain whether I can take you aboard."

"It's not necessary," Yanky responded. "I've seen enough."

"What do you mean?"

"Well, this is the first time I ever heard a Jew say no. When I was growing up in Europe, no Jew ever dared to say no. We lived in fear, and you could be shot for that. Now I've heard a Jew say no, and I see that this is a new world.

Rabbi Yanky Jungreis with his father at a *simchah* in the early days of Hineni

"And I can see that you're holding a gun. For a child who survived the Holocaust, seeing a Jew with a gun is an outright miracle! What more do I need to see?"

After hearing Rabbi Yanky Jungreis's incredible story, everything he told Roy meant that much more. The two of them were a study in contrasts — the newly religious Roy Neuberger, who had been raised across the street from Central Park and whose father was a legend on Wall Street, and the European-born Rabbi Yanky Jungreis, who had grown up in a concentration camp and whose father had been an illustrious rabbi in prewar Europe.

A study in contrasts, but it worked.

◆ ◆ ◆

Suddenly, Roy and Linda were making *berachos* on food for the first time, using unfamiliar words that, oddly enough, felt natural flowing off their tongues. The days were a never-ending mix of spirituality and adventure as the Rebbetzin introduced them to the wonders of Torah and mitzvos, to their heritage and the holy Land of Israel.

And then it was time for their first Shabbos.

The first Shabbos of their lives took place on the rolling hills of picturesque Kibbutz Lavi not far from the city of Tiveria. The kibbutz, always a peaceful place, became even more peaceful on Shabbos. There were no cars on the roads. All one saw were magnificent views of mountains in the majestic Golan Heights, the world of nature at its most beautiful, and all one heard were the sounds of birds chirping.

The peace of mind that Shabbos presented to Roy and Linda was irresistible. Though they had been born into a world of material comfort, Roy and Linda had never had a moment's peace in their lives. From a young age they had tried different lifestyles, searching constantly for a truth and peace of mind that had only eluded them. But no more. Shabbos had arrived, and for the first time ever they experienced the peace they had never known but always longed for.

It was 1974, and the hotel at Kibbutz Lavi was relatively new.

Everyone davened in the kibbutz shul, guests and locals alike. After Maariv on Friday night, Roy and Reb Yanky walked back to the hotel together, meandering down flower-lined paths, their heady fragrance wafting through the air.

"You know," Reb Yanky said, "since you've made the gigantic leap to becoming a *frum* Yid, you're going to need a Jewish name."

Roy was listening.

"Rabbi Yisrael Salanter was your *zeide*."

"I think so."

"I know that your *zeide* has been davening for you, turning over the heavens, so your name has to be Yisroel."

On Shabbos morning, Roy stood at the *bimah* and was given the name Yisroel in honor of the famous tzaddik who forever changed the way *Klal Yisrael* approached their spiritual development.

And so the young man who had been given the name Roy thirty years earlier on the Upper East Side of Manhattan finally became the proud bearer of a Jewish name in the mountains of the Galil in the Holy Land.

When it came to Linda's Jewish name, Zeide, the Rebbetzin's father, made the decision and chose the name Leah. Now this is fascinating, because Linda's mother had called her Linda in memory of Linda's maternal great-grandmother, whose name was Lyla and with whom Linda's mother was very close. Years later, Leah realized that Lyla must have been the Polish way of saying Leah. And so it turned out that Leah was named for the great-grandmother who had been so dear to her own mother.

♦ ♦ ♦

For the second Shabbos of their trip, Yisroel and Leah stayed in Jerusalem and davened at a big shul in the center of the city. Roy was honored with *galilah* (rolling up the Torah scroll), which threw him for a loop, since he had no idea what *galilah* was and imagined that perhaps one had to be a learned individual to perform it. Maybe it was a speech in Hebrew!

He did fine, and no one realized how nervous he was. Later

that day they returned for Minchah, and Yisroel being Yisroel was drawn into the davening in a big way. That Shabbos afternoon, he was *shuckling* away. It was the second Shabbos of his life and he was into it.

A well-dressed man approached, and from the look on his face, he wasn't a huge *shuckling* fan.

"You know," he said, "you're not in Meah Shearim right now. We don't do that here."

Roy was extremely taken aback and had no words. The man would never know how close he had come to turning off a fellow Jew.

◆ ◆ ◆

Since that incredible first Shabbos, Yisroel and Leah have been back to Kibbutz Lavi on numerous occasions. Just setting foot on the property brings back the memory of that first Shabbos, and it was there that they spent many memorable Shabbosos with their family.

There is a beautiful garden on the kibbutz, a perfect spot for taking a stroll. The lighting is soft, and nighttime shadows add an air of mystery. At the eastern end of the garden there is a viewing area that looks out over the Golan Heights. Part of the garden is dedicated to herbs and plants that are cultivated for their distinctive aromas. One of Leah's favorites is a small flowering tree called Queen of the Night. This plant's flowers close during the

Queen of the Night flowers open at night...   ...and close during the day

day, but at night they open and emit an amazing perfume into the air. Leah never forgot that plant. Years later, she planted one in their own garden in Jerusalem. The aroma is magical.

Every time Yisroel inhales this fragrance he has the same thought: the Queen of the Night flower is the perfect analogy for how a person can merit smelling the aroma of Gan Eden even while struggling through the hardships of *galus*.

Chapter Thirteen
Smashing Idols

Whereas many people take their time when making major changes in their lives, Roy and Linda's decision to relocate to North Woodmere happened almost immediately after they returned from Israel and decided that they must live a Jewish life. North Woodmere was the Jungreises' community. The Rebbetzin was their trusted guide and teacher, and there was no question in their minds that they needed to live in her vicinity. This way they would be able to raise their children as Jews, a goal that had suddenly become very important.

When they told their friends about their plan, the reactions were many and varied. Their non-Jewish friends thought it was the most wonderful thing in the world, but some of their Jewish friends told them that it was time to see a psychiatrist.

The power of guilt is prodigious. Their Jewish neighbors knew deep inside that Yisroel and Leah were doing the right thing, but they were unwilling to do it themselves and could not face the dissonance in their own lives. The non-Jewish neighbors didn't have the same imperative and so had only praise for the courageous young couple.

It made no difference in any case. Having met the Rebbetzin and seen the beauty of Torah for themselves, they were determined to follow the new path on which they found themselves. They packed their belongings and left Cornwall without seeing a psychiatrist. After all, they had a doctor of the heart waiting for them in North Woodmere.

Before leaving Cornwall, they made a very important decision: Since they were moving to North Woodmere to start living a Torah life, their plan was to do everything the Torah way. It was a case of "*Na'aseh v'nishma* — We will do and we will hear," and they trusted the Rebbetzin, whom Hashem had sent to teach them.

Yisroel and Leah moved to North Woodmere about two weeks before Rosh Hashanah in 1974. Over that summer, before moving to North Woodmere, they had been unable to keep every mitzvah simply because they weren't sure exactly what to do and how to do it. But after their move, they were determined to keep Shabbos, kashrus, *taharas hamishpachah*, and everything else they learned about.

It was as if they were standing on the edge of a gigantic and very deep pool, the kind where you can't even see the bottom, and they were ready to take the leap and dive in.

And that's exactly what they did.

Torah goggles on. Take position on edge. And jump!

♦ ♦ ♦

Roy's brother, Jimmy, recalls well that time and the shock he felt when Roy and Linda informed their family that they were making some major lifestyle changes:

> Forty-seven years after the day, I still remember it almost perfectly. It was June 16, 1974. Gathered around the dining room table at our family house in Westchester County, New York, were my brother Roy, his wife Linda, their two children, myself, and our parents. I remember exactly where I was sitting.
>
> Roy explained that he and his wife had met Rebbetzin Jungreis in April, after hearing her speak. Her message had resonated with them in a big way. They had started going to her Bible study classes in Brooklyn, a long drive from

their home in Orange County. They had gone to Israel with her in May. And now, barely two months after meeting her, they had made a decision that would change the course of their lives: they would henceforth follow a strictly Orthodox Jewish way of life. This decision entailed a number of major actions: moving to the Rebbetzin's community in Long Island, selling Roy's business and their home upstate, and uprooting his wife and children. I also couldn't help but notice that Roy was talking and Linda was not. It appeared to me that the decision was his and she was following him.

I was very upset. *Here we go again!* I thought. *Roy is going off on another of his fixations, and he's dragging his wife and children with him.*

This wasn't the first time that Roy had devoted himself fully to an ideology. In high school, he was enchanted with the outdoors. He spent a summer with a friend hiking in Wyoming. Another summer he was a Ranger in the Smokies. After Roy and Linda were married, they spent their honeymoon in Grand Teton National Park. And yet another summer they were fire lookouts living on top of a mountain at Crater Lake National Park.

Another obsession was Buddhism. Roy studied it for months. I don't remember whether he practiced it in any meaningful way, or whether Linda shared his feelings, but it totally engulfed him. Until it didn't. Another was vegetarianism. He was a rabid vegetarian for a number of months. Then he suddenly gave it up.

There was a clear pattern here.

So on that day in 1974, I was sure that this was just another temporary obsession. It would last for a month or a year and then it would be over. I felt that he was being selfish, and I was angry and upset.

But over the next few years, I visited Roy and Linda many times in Long Island, spent the Sabbath with them, and accompanied Roy to the synagogue. I even traveled to Israel with Roy, Linda, and a group led by Rebbetzin

Jungreis. Roy tried to get me to follow his course, but I was steadfast and unmovable. In fact, I considered myself an atheist. But although we disagreed about religious observance, in other respects we remained and remain close.

But the critical point was the extent to which Roy and Linda became involved in their community. They visited people in the hospital. They called people to wish them a good Sabbath. They brought food or other supplies to people. They invited people to their home for Sabbath. And I realized that Linda was as equally active and zealous as Roy; they were in this way of life as equals. Together they were devoted to their community, and in their devotion, they flourished as people and as a family.

As for me, while I didn't change my way of life, I did change my perspective. I realized that Roy and Linda loved what they were doing. They believed wholeheartedly in its righteousness. And it wasn't in the least bit selfish. In fact, it was the opposite: selfless. I came to the realization that this way of life was an expression of their true selves, a fruition, an apotheosis.

Roy Senior with his children (l to r) Jimmy, Ann, and Yisroel

So I look back at that day forty-seven years ago and realize how wrong I was.

And I am very glad.

◆ ◆ ◆

Once in their new home, Yisroel joined Rabbi Jungreis's minyan at Congregation Ohr Torah and began studying Torah with Reb Yanky and the Rebbetzin's son-in-law, Rabbi Shlomo Gertzulin. Leah began wearing skirts and covering her hair. The Rebbetzin hadn't said a word about modest dress but gave Leah the freedom to figure it out on her own. Meanwhile, Yisroel and Leah continued attending the Rebbetzin's classes and studying as much as they could.

To their great joy, becoming religious didn't mean that they had to give up the things they enjoyed. Yisroel continued singing. The difference was that now he was singing Jewish songs and *zemiros* and leading the singing at Hineni Shabbatons. His dancing was vastly different from that of the white-gloved dance academy of his childhood. When it came to Jewish weddings, Yisroel found that he was in his element.

Since they had been brought into the Torah way of life through the Rebbetzin's non-pressuring approach, Yisroel and Leah themselves would adopt the same *derech* when they themselves began guiding others in the years to come.

Looking at their story from the outside, it seems like Yisroel and Leah made a hasty decision and moved too fast. But that wasn't the reality. They had been searching for so long that when the truth finally showed up, there were no questions at all. They felt within themselves the fulfillment of the words of the prophet Amos, who says, "Behold, days are coming, says Hashem Elokim, and I will send hunger into the land, not a hunger for bread nor a thirst for water, but to hear the word of Hashem" (*Amos* 8:11). That was the way it was with them. In their minds, they had been dead for so many years, and now they were alive. Now they were ready to truly start living.

Among other things, they were determined to learn how to

read and write Hebrew. Rabbi Meshulem taught Yisroel and Leah the skills. He gave a course over ten weeks, and at its conclusion, they had acquired the basics.

Once Yisroel had inhaled the aroma of Torah, he knew he had a lot to catch up on. He had to make up for missing out on more than thirty years of Torah education. How could he even learn to put his foot in the water — the ocean of Torah?

It wasn't simple. He wasn't a child sitting in a first-grade class-room and he had a growing family. But there was no question: he had to learn!

In the early years, he loved attending Reb Yanky's Gemara *shiur* in Canarsie, and soon he had a regular *chavrusa*: Rebbetzin Jun-greis's brilliant son-in-law, Rabbi Shlomo Gertzulin. Rabbi Gertzulin became the protégé of the legendary Rabbi Moshe Sherer at Agudath Israel of America (and later, one of the administrators of that great organization), but in the late 1970s, when Yisroel was just entering the world of Torah, he would drive to the home of the newly married Rabbi Shlomo and Rebbetzin Chaya Sora Gertzulin on Foster Avenue in Flatbush for a learning session.

It was Yisroel's first real experience in one-on-one learning. He and Rabbi Gertzulin learned *Shulchan Aruch* together, and Yisroel's eyes were opened to the world of Torah. When Rabbi Gertzulin moved on to the Agudah and Yisroel moved on to the next stage in his own life, he had many more wonderful *chavrusa*s. For several years he learned with the great *talmid chacham*, *posek*, and *rosh kollel* Rabbi Binyamin Forst, who over the years has been a great friend and source of wisdom to the Neuberger family.

Then, for a total of nine-teen amazing years, he learned with Rabbi Moshe Grossman, a man who over

Rabbi Shlomo Gertzulin (left) with Yisroel and Leah's son Aharon Yaakov

Rabbi Moshe Grossman (left)
with Rabbi Naftali Jaeger

Rabbi Shaul Geller (right)
with Rabbi Shlomo Bussu

a lifetime has taught and inspired hundreds, perhaps thousands, of elementary school *talmidim* at two great yeshivos, Chaim Berlin and Darchei Torah. Among Rabbi Grossman's students would be Yisroel and Leah's own son, Aharon Yaakov, and their future son-in-law, Osher Anshil Jungreis.

When Rabbi Grossman moved to Lakewood, Yisroel was privileged to learn with Rabbi Yehuda Schiff, the highly respected rebbi of many serious young *talmidei chachamim*. Yisroel would say that he always needed oxygen when learning with Rabbi Schiff. Why? Because at the heights to which Rabbi Schiff rose in his learning, the air was very thin!

He also enjoyed learning Gemara at Hineni over the years with Rabbi Osher Anshil Jungreis. Later, when Yisroel and Leah would move to Israel, Yisroel would be fortunate to learn regularly with a young, brilliant *talmid chacham* named Rabbi Shaul Geller, a yeshivah rebbi who learns Torah literally day and night.

"What a privilege," Yisroel says, "to be close to such brilliant *talmidei chachamim*, who have given their heart and soul to teach me to swim in the deep waters of Torah."

◆ ◆ ◆

The Jungreises soon became like a second family to Yisroel and Leah. The Rebbetzin adopted them as her younger brother and sister, and her parents, Zeide and Mama, took them in as grandchildren. Rabbi Shlomo and Chaya Sora Gertzulin, the

Yisroel speaking at a Chanukah party at the home of Rabbi Yehuda Schiff

Rebbetzin's eldest child, gave them a standing invitation to their home, and Yisroel spent hours learning with Reb Shlomo. Leah became very close with Chaya Sora.

For their first Pesach after becoming *frum*, Yisroel and Leah were guests of the Jungreis family at the Sedarim. Rabbi Meshulem Jungreis had prepared a tape for them on which he recorded all the key components of the Seder, from *Mah Nishtanah* to *Dayeinu*. Before Pesach, they listened to the tape over and over to familiarize themselves with the songs and rituals. The rabbi also conducted a model Seder for the members of Congregation Ohr Torah. There was no reason for them to rush into making their own Seder. There would be plenty of time for that in the years to come.

Yisroel and Leah felt fortunate to have been granted such a special family to guide them. The fact that such amazing people had become their mentors, teachers, friends, and, indeed, family was something that Yisroel and Leah would never take for granted. It made perfect sense, then, that the Jungreises would host a bris milah ceremony for Yisroel.

Yisroel had had a medical circumcision as a baby, but since there was no way it could be termed a bris, he was informed that he would have to have what is called a "*hatafas dam bris.*" And while a *hatafah* is not a painful procedure, he was still extremely nervous.

The truth is that a *hatafah* is really not that big a deal — unless it's being done on you! "When you're eight days old," Yisroel says, "you're not aware of what's happening. When you're thirty-one years old, it's a little different."

The ceremony was held at the home of Rebbetzin Jungreis's parents, Zeide and Mama. Rabbi Meshulem, of course, was in attendance.

Zeide saw how nervous Yisroel was. "Here, Yisroel," he said. "Read this."

It seems safe to say that Yisroel Neuberger was the only person in Jewish history to have had a bris while reading the *Daily News*!

Not only did Yisroel need to have a bris, but Yisroel and Leah needed to remarry. There was nothing kosher about their first wedding, and now that they were finally ready to live a Jewish life, having an authentic *kiddushin* was imperative. The wedding took place at the Jungreis home in the presence of a minyan, and so it was that the couple who had been married for so many years finally had a real *chuppah*.

◆ ◆ ◆

At the start of their journey, Yisroel and Leah used to enjoy the occasional Motza'ei Shabbos movie with their children. They particularly enjoyed the old-time Disney films. At one point, Yisroel decided that they might as well buy a bigger screen. One day, he walked into an electronics store in Boro Park, and a salesman with long *peyos* asked what he needed.

"I want to buy a big screen," he told the man.

"Do you know what size?"

"Not really. I just want something bigger than what I have at home."

The salesman looked at him, then asked him a question.

"How big do you want the *yetzer hara* to be when he's dancing across your screen?"

The moment he grasped what the man was saying, Yisroel practically ran out of the store, all thoughts of purchasing a new screen forgotten. It turned out that the salesman wasn't much of a salesman, but there's no question that he was very much a caring Yid.

◆ ◆ ◆

A few weeks after Yisroel and Leah first moved to North Woodmere, seventeen-year-old Yisroel Jungreis, the older son of Rabbi and Rebbetzin Jungreis, came to visit.

"What's that on the shelf?" he asked.

"We bought it a few years ago. It's pre-Columbian art."

The art in question was a clay sculpture of a human head, a smiling youth, which had been purchased from an art dealer in Manhattan.

Yisroel Jungreis studied the piece. Finally he gave his opinion.

"I think this looks like *avodah zarah*. Maybe you should find out."

"What do you mean?"

"That piece looks like an idol. It might be a good idea to call the art dealer and find out what it represents."

Yisroel called the art dealer, who knew exactly what piece Yisroel was referring to.

"Can you tell me what this piece represents?"

"Sure," the dealer replied. "It's a sculpture of the head of a young Mexican boy who is about to be thrown into the fire and sacrificed to his parents' idols. Before they threw their children into the fire, they would drug them so that they would go to their deaths with a smile. That's why the head you bought has a smile on it."

Yisroel Jungreis had hit the bull's-eye. How had he known?

"It was shocking to realize that what we had imagined was an innocent sculpture of a happy child was really a boy who was about to be offered on the altar of idol worship," Leah says.

Yisroel called Yisroel Jungreis to tell him what they had learned.

"What should we do now?"

"It's a mitzvah to smash it. I'm coming over to the house. We're going to destroy an idol!"

Yisroel brought the sculpture out onto the driveway, and, using a hammer, he smashed it into dust. Yisroel would always remember that moment as a huge *zechus*. How many people can say that they were able to pulverize an actual idol?

After he smashed the idol, Yisroel swept up the fragments and carried them across the street to Doxy Pond — the place where Rabbi Jungreis's shul recited *Tashlich* every Rosh Hashanah — and scattered them across the water.

He watched in reflective silence as they sank to the bottom. Then he turned around and went home, knowing that he had just been part of something much bigger than himself.

Chapter Fourteen
The Train in Jamaica

Leaving Cornwall meant that Yisroel would need to find a new job since there was no way he would be able to commute from North Woodmere to upstate New York on a daily basis. Besides, he had sold *The Cornwall Local*.

Yisroel arranged a meeting with David Starr, the father-in-law of one of his best friends, Lee Bromberg from Skokie, Illinois. David Starr was the editor of the *Long Island Press*, a daily newspaper published in Jamaica, a neighborhood in Queens, that in its heyday boasted a circulation of 750,000. They hit it off, and David gave Yisroel a job as an editor.

Afternoon papers go to press at about six in the morning so they can arrive at newsstands at around one in the afternoon. Yisroel would arrive at the office at 3 a.m. every morning and was done by noon, with a "lunchbreak" at 6 a.m.! (During his break, Yisroel would daven Shacharis. Knowing his editor would not approve, he would conceal himself behind the giant printing presses that were turning out the paper!) It was a half-hour drive from North Woodmere to the paper, and it was an insane schedule, but that was the job that had allowed them to relocate, and Yisroel made the best of the situation.

♦ ♦ ♦

When he first started working at the *Long Island Press*, Yisroel didn't have the courage to wear a yarmulke outside the house or shul. Having never worn a yarmulke in his life, he was embarrassed to wear it at work. But it wasn't long before he felt like a hypocrite, so he began leaving it on for longer and longer amounts of time, usually removing it as he approached the office.

That year, on Yom Kippur, Rabbi Meshulem Jungreis devoted his *derashah* to the idea of wearing a yarmulke in public. "Even the pope wears a head covering," he stressed. "If he can do it, why should you be embarrassed to wear one?"

His words made an impression on Yisroel. On the day after Yom Kippur, when Yisroel returned to his job at the *Long Island Press*, he was determined to show up with a yarmulke on his head.

You wore the yarmulke in the car, he told himself, *and you will continue wearing it when you get to work. What are you afraid of?*

When he walked into the *Long Island Press* with a yarmulke on his head after having worked there for a month, everyone had something to say. Since they were mainly non-Jews, their comments were along the lines of "Well done!" and "Good for you!"

Roy's immediate boss was a different story. A Conservative Jew, he was considered the "religious" Jewish presence at the paper.

He had plenty to say.

"Why are you wearing that on your head?"

"On Yom Kippur my rabbi spoke about how a person should make sure to keep his head covered all the time. Even the pope wears a yarmulke! And I decided to listen."

Yisroel's boss looked at him and said, "That's disgusting!" Then he turned and walked away.

There was no question that Yisroel had succeeded in poking the proverbial hornet's nest.

It was a little bit of a rough welcome to the job.

◆ ◆ ◆

Growing up, Yisroel had always been fearful that he would be attacked on the street or subway. Those fears had never material-ized. He had never been attacked and never been in any danger.

Until he was.

One morning Yisroel drove his car to the garage for an oil change during his 6 a.m. "lunch break." Leaving the car at the garage, he took the train back to the paper. When he clocked out at twelve noon, he walked back to the train station (literally the end of the line) for the short ride to the garage. During rush hour, this line was packed with people, but this was the end of the line and the middle of the day, and the train was empty. Yisroel found a seat and waited for the short journey to begin. He didn't expect it to be anything but peaceful.

As soon as the train left the station, the doors at the end of the car opened, and two very large young men walked in. An alarm went off inside Yisroel's head. He felt the way he had as a fire watcher at the top of the mountain: he could feel the lightning buzzing in every fiber of his being.

But this was worse than an electrical storm. Then at least he had been able to take refuge on the insulated bed. Here there was no place to hide.

He was maybe half the size of the guys who were heading his way. And he was wearing a yarmulke on his head. As they moved closer, they started singing. He was unable to make out the words amid the clatter of the train, but something told him the lyrics had been specially composed for him. Then these two gentlemen sat themselves down on the seats across from Yisroel.

Somehow Yisroel wasn't at all surprised at their choice of seats. He'd had a premonition that this was where they'd been headed. He looked away, pretending that he didn't see them and silently cried out to Hashem, "Please get me out of this!"

Sitting across from his fellow passengers, Yisroel davened his heart out while keeping his gaze averted. Suddenly there was a lull in the noise of the subway, and he was able to hear the words they were singing: "Hitler killed six million Jews," they serenaded, obviously quite proud of their original composition. "Why didn't he kill them all?"

Meanwhile, Yisroel was begging Hashem to save him. One of the young men, perhaps frustrated by the fact that they were being ignored, called out, "Hey, mister!"

Yisroel couldn't pretend anymore that he didn't notice them. Turning in their direction, he said, "Oh, hi!"

"Hey, mister. Why did Hitler kill six million Jews?"

At first, Yisroel had nothing to say. And then a surge of strength swept through his soul. Suddenly he knew that everything was going to be fine. He understood intuitively that he was completely protected, and there was nothing the two men could do to him.

He didn't know how he knew it. He just knew it.

Yisroel stood up from his seat and walked across the car until he was standing directly in front of his two potential attackers. Then he bent down until his face was mere inches from the face of the man who had been speaking to him. The man recoiled, almost jumping back in the seat, a look of fear crossing his face. For some reason, he was shaking, as if Yisroel Neuberger, a man half his size, had managed to frighten him beyond all description.

"You want to know why Hitler killed six million Jews?" Yisroel asked softly.

Softly, yet with an undercurrent of steel in his voice.

The men could barely get out a reply, but they mumbled something about Jewish bankers stealing everyone's money.

"You don't know what you're talking about," Yisroel told them. "You never met a Jew in your life. You don't even know what a Jew is!"

Somehow all the fear was gone, and he felt an indescribable feeling of power coursing through him.

"I'll tell you why Hitler killed six million Jews."

He paused.

"He killed them because he was sick. You have to be sick to kill a Jew!"

The men were literally shaking, unable to meet his gaze, experiencing some sort of unfathomable fear that left them speechless. At that moment, the train came to a halt and the doors opened. Yisroel saw that they had arrived at his station.

"Guys, I'd love to talk to you some more, but this is my station. Sorry, but I have to go. See you around."

He walked off the train and onto the platform, knowing beyond a doubt that he had just been granted a glimpse into the way Heaven protects the Jewish people. Glancing over to the side of the elevated platform, Yisroel felt that if he had to jump over the wall at that moment, he would unquestionably have been able to fly. He knew that he had been protected from all harm during the encounter, as if Hashem had sent angels to stand at his side and watch over him.

◆ ◆ ◆

By 1974, Jamaica, where the *Long Island Press* was published, was no longer the neighborhood it had once been. Yisroel seldom walked around there, usually getting around in his car. One day, as he drove down Jamaica Avenue, he glanced out the window and, to his surprise, caught sight of a store that boasted a sign that read "House of Israel."

He parked the car and walked over to the store, which sat on one side of a park-filled square. As he walked, he suddenly realized that he was looking at the remnant of a world that once was: the square he was passing through contained the Yeshiva of Central Queens (the yeshiva and bookstore both moved to new locations about a year later) and across from it was the House of Israel *sefarim* store.

Yisroel had never been in a *sefarim* store in his life; he had never purchased a yarmulke or pair of tzitzis, nor had he ever bought a *sefer*. He had only recently become religious and everything was new.

He walked into the store and met the two *tzaddikim* who owned it: Reb Avrohom Gross and Reb Menashe Weissman. Though their store was located in Queens, they themselves lived in Far Rockaway, and it wasn't long before Yisroel became very close to both of them.

Yisroel's decision to stop at the store proved auspicious. After that, whenever he needed a *sefer*, he bought it at the House of

Israel. Reb Avrohom and Reb Menashe were always there for him, able and ready to guide him as he entered the world of Torah learning and Jewish books. If Yisroel needed his tefillin checked, his friends at House of Israel were there to do it. If the strings on his tallis had become tangled and he didn't know how to untangle them, they were there. They understood Yisroel's needs and made sure he was looked after every step of the way until the bookstore felt like home. Time there meant time in the company of friends.

This was taking place "BA" — before ArtScroll. *The Birnbaum Siddur* — perhaps the first Hebrew-English siddur — was available, as well as the Hertz *Chumash*, and Soncino's English version of *Shas*. Had it been a few years earlier, Yisroel would have found himself even more hard-pressed, but as it was, the English-language *sefarim* industry was beginning to find its feet, and the House of Israel had an array of helpful items to offer. *To Be a Jew* by Rabbi Hayim Donin was a particular favorite, especially during the Neubergers' first year of observance. And Rebbetzin Jungreis recommended Rabbi Avigdor Miller's *Rejoice O Youth*. It was truly fortunate that their return to Judaism coincided with the blossoming of English Torah literature.

Reb Avrohom Gross making his
Erev Shabbos *l'chaim*

Avrohom Gross had a *minhag*. Every Erev Shabbos he'd make a *l'chaim* at his house on Beach Ninth Street in Far Rockaway. Yisroel would try to attend as often as his schedule allowed. Mrs. Gross was a beloved teacher at TAG, and the two of them were a wonderful couple. Later Yisroel also became close with their late son, Reb Shmuel (for years the *gabbai* of Agudath Israel of

Far Rockaway and fabled *cholent macher* for the Shabbos *kiddush*).

It's now decades later, but Yisroel sometimes makes a *l'chaim* on Erev Shabbos even today. When he holds a little glass cup filled with golden liquid up to the light, he recalls his dear friend Reb Avrohom and the unique relationship they shared during the period when he was taking his spiritual baby steps.

Yisroel would never forget his last conversation with Reb Avrohom.

He was in Mount Sinai Hospital. Yisroel didn't know how sick his friend actually was, and he called Reb Avrohom on Friday afternoon to wish him a good Shabbos. If he closes his eyes and retreats into the mists of time, he can still hear Avrohom's voice:

"Hello, *tattele*."

The words are seared into Yisroel's soul for eternity.

There was no way for Yisroel to know how sick he was, not from the love and warmth in his voice. The conversation was as normal as possible under the circumstances, and even though Reb Avrohom was hovering at the brink of death, his focus was solely on Yisroel as he asked how things were going and if there was anything he, Avrohom, could do for his friend.

Reb Avrohom, the holy bookstore Yid, passed away that Motza'ei Shabbos.

♦ ♦ ♦

Years later, Yisroel also came to meet another special Yid in Jamaica, this time in the New York Supreme Court building for the Borough of Queens.

For many years, Judge Moshe (Martin) Ritholtz[7] presided at the Queens County courthouse, dispensing wisdom, justice, and common sense to the people who passed before him. Judge Ritholtz wore a yarmulke while on the bench and was treated with great respect by all who knew him. He was also extremely funny, though he usually kept his sense of humor in check when court was in session.

---

7. Yisroel knew Judge Ritholtz from Yeshiva Sh'or Yoshuv, where they both davened.

"He told me that he had studied at the 'Pun-ovitch' Yeshiva in Bnei Brak," Yisroel says, which is typical of Moshe's sense of humor. Ironically, in the case of Moshe (or "Shofet Moshe" as Yisroel came to call him), he actually did learn at Ponevezh!

Upon his retirement, Shofet Moshe made aliyah and can now be found every morning at the Kosel. Just before he left his chambers for the last time, Yisroel visited the courthouse to see him in action. It also afforded him the opportunity to take part in the daily Minchah minyan that Judge Ritholtz held every day in his chambers, which was attended by many lawyers and other judges, some of whom had never davened in their lives before meeting His Honor Reb Moshe Ritholtz.

As Yisroel walked out of the courthouse, he remembered all the experiences he'd had through the years on Jamaica Avenue, from working at the *Long Island Press* to meeting the Jewish booksellers who held his hand as he took those early wobbling steps. And he recalled the frightening moment on the train when he had begun wearing his yarmulke for the first time.

Davening Minchah at Queens Supreme Court with Judge Moshe Ritholtz
in the foreground

Now, looking around at a Jamaica Avenue that had virtually nothing in common with the place he recalled from so long before, he had to smile. He had just left a Minchah minyan, an oasis in the desert. To Yisroel's way of thinking, it was just another indication that no matter where a person goes, he will be able to find pockets of light in the darkness. One just has to be willing to open his eyes and look for it.

When Yisroel was called up for jury duty by the County of Nassau, he showed up at the courthouse with a briefcase large enough to hold all the *sefarim* he might need while he waited for the opportunity to fulfill his civic responsibility. When he arrived at the courthouse security check, there was a burly policeman standing there — a gentleman with an Irish name like O'Flaherty — and, as Yisroel began opening his briefcase to show the cop what was inside, the policeman stopped him.

"You don't have to open your briefcase," he told Yisroel, and then he said words that Yisroel never forgot...

"You...we are not worried about."

With that, the police officer took Yisroel's arm and walked him into the jurors' waiting room. As the officer turned to leave, Yisroel understood that, no matter what happens in life, when a Jew stands proudly with G-d, the world respects him. Then he thanked the policeman, gave him a *berachah,* and wished him good day.

Chapter Fifteen
The Rebbetzin's Diagnosis

*Z*eide chose Hebrew names for the entire family. Susan Eve became Sarah and Juliet Rose became Yaffa.

Yaffa was normally the picture of health. One night, in February 1975, three-year-old Yaffa developed an earache. Leah took her around the corner to the doctor, while Yisroel stayed home with Sarah, who was then about six years old. He went to sleep, getting his much-needed hours of sleep before his early-morning trip to the *Long Island Press*, not thinking very much about the doctor's visit. He assumed that his wife and daughter would be home soon with a prescription and some calming words.

He couldn't have known that in the middle of the examination, Leah suddenly felt unwell and fainted.

It was 11 o'clock when the phone rang.

"Mr. Neuberger," said Dr. Schwartz,* "your wife just fainted. She's lying on the floor of my office, and I'm finding it hard to get a pulse. She may have had a heart attack. I am a pediatrician and don't have the equipment to treat her. You'd better come over immediately. We have to get her to the hospital!"

This was before the days of Hatzolah, and an ambulance was available only by calling the 911 police number.

Yisroel didn't know what to do first. Should he call an ambulance? Should he rush to the doctor's office? What about Sarah sleeping in her bedroom? How could he leave a young child all by herself?

Suddenly he had clarity. He knew what he had to do.

Call the Rebbetzin.

◆ ◆ ◆

At that very moment, the Rebbetzin and Barbara were walking through the door of the Jungreis home after returning from a speaking event. Barbara answered the phone. Yisroel told her what had happened.

"Stay where you are with Sarah," Barbara said. "I'm going over to the doctor right now."

Yisroel heard a voice in the background. It was the Rebbetzin.

"Barbara, give me the phone."

Seconds later, Yisroel heard the Rebbetzin's voice. The words she was about to say would be played and replayed in Yisroel's mind for the rest of his life. He would never know how she knew what to say, but it was as if an angel was speaking to him over the phone.

"Yisroel, Yisroel."

She uttered his name twice.

"Mazel tov! Your Leah is expecting. She's going to have a beautiful baby!"

From her tone and words, there was no question that Rebbetzin Esther Jungreis was completely confident in her diagnosis.

"Yisroel, Barbara is going to the doctor's office to get Leah. You stay with Sarah. Don't worry, everything is going to be just fine."

The Rebbetzin turned out to be one hundred percent correct. By the time Barbara got there, Leah's pulse had normalized and she was sitting up.

Somehow, the Rebbetzin knew that Leah was expecting a baby — even before Leah did.

When Barbara and the doctor arrived at the Neuberger home

with Leah and Yaffa, Yisroel had calmed down. The next day Leah went for a test, and, sure enough, she was expecting.

In due course, a beautiful baby girl was born. The proud parents called her Miriam Basya. Now they had three little girls.

The Rebbetzin wasn't the only one who had extraordinary intuition. Years later, Yisroel walked into shul one Shabbos morning. Davening hadn't started yet, and very few people were there. Almost as soon as Yisroel walked in, Rabbi Meshulem Jungreis approached him.

"Good Shabbos, Yisroel," he said.

"Good Shabbos, Rabbi."

"Yisroel, I had a dream last night. I dreamt that you have another baby on the way."

Rabbi Jungreis's dream was accurate. Leah went to the doctor a few days later, where she learned that she was indeed expecting another child. So it was that Yisroel and Leah found out about the impending birth of their son Aharon Yaakov, whom they call Ari. He is their fourth child and only son. Rabbi Shlomo and Chaya Sora Gertzulin were the *kvatterin* at the bris, which was the prelude to their own *simchah*, since their first child, Yosef Dov, was born ten months later!

◆ ◆ ◆

Several years later, the Rebbetzin came through for Leah again.

It all began when Leah went to the doctor for what she imagined was a routine checkup, only to learn that he wanted her to take some tests. When the results came in, she was informed that she had a tumor.

"You need to see a surgeon," said the doctor.

This is not something that anyone wants to hear. Leah was, understandably, frightened. She made an appointment with a surgeon. He examined her, studied the results, and concluded that she needed surgery. Of course, Leah and Yisroel went to visit the Rebbetzin and told her everything.

"Okay, this is what we have to do," came the Rebbetzin's reply. "Yisroel, you, Leah, I, my husband and all of our children are going to say the twentieth *kapittel* of *Tehillim* seven times every single day, starting today."

Later Leah found out that this was a *segulah* that the Rebbetzin had received from the Czengerer Zeide,[8] but at the time she started reciting that chapter of *Tehillim* seven times every day with heartfelt *kavanah* simply because the Rebbetzin had recommended it.

A few weeks later, she returned to the surgeon, who wanted to confirm his initial diagnosis, and give her another, more detailed test before they proceeded with the surgery.

When the surgeon examined the test results, he was in shock.

There was nothing there!

The tumor had disappeared.

Ever since then, some forty years ago, Leah Neuberger recites the twentieth chapter of *Tehillim* seven times every single day. She has never stopped.

◆ ◆ ◆

By the spring of 1975 Yisroel and Leah had been immersed in the sea of Torah for over half a year. They felt the consoling Hand of Heaven over their home and the flow of their lives. The emptiness of their past was beginning to dissipate.

But every life has tests. All those tests are *l'tovah*, for the good, but along the way, in the midst of them, they can be very frightening. Yisroel and Leah were about to face a frightening test.

One afternoon, just as Yisroel was returning from his job at the *Long Island Press*, the Neubergers' phone rang. Yaffa's school was on the line.

"Mrs. Neuberger?"

"Yes?"

"Yaffa fell off the jungle gym and got hurt."

"How badly?"

"It's pretty serious. Please come now. She needs to go to the hospital."

---

8. The Czengerer Zeide, Rabbi Osher Anshil Jungreis, was the great-great-grandfather of both Rabbi and Rebbetzin Jungreis. He lived in Czenger, Hungary, from 5567 (1806) to 5634 (1873).

The monkey bars in the schoolyard weren't intended for three-year-olds. Yaffa, who was quick and agile and loved to climb, had been high up when she lost her grip and fell to the ground, breaking her arm just above the elbow.

◆ ◆ ◆

It's common for children to get sick or injured, and they usually recover quickly. Sometimes doctors misdiagnose. One time a doctor had diagnosed one of the Neuberger children with something serious. Frantic with worry, Leah took the child to a different doctor, a beloved old-timer in the neighborhood, and asked for a second opinion.

The doctor examined the child and turned to Leah.

"This is a case of GMG."

"What is GMG?" she asked, the panic welling up.

"*Gurnisht mit gurnisht!* Nothing at all!"

He was right and everything turned out fine.

But there are other times when injuries are as serious as they seem to be and maybe even worse.

This was one of those times.

When Yisroel and Leah arrived at the school, they found Yaffa in terrible pain. Yisroel had experience as an EMT in Cornwall, and he knew exactly what to do. He secured her to a wooden board and laid it down on the back seat of the car for the drive to the hospital.

When the doctors examined Yaffa in the emergency room, she was unable to move that hand at all and they couldn't feel a pulse in that wrist. The doctors quickly concluded that putting her arm in a cast wasn't going to work. Surgery was needed, but they weren't able to operate because little Yaffale had been given apple juice after the fall and they couldn't administer anesthesia until the juice had been digested.

The Neubergers had arrived at the hospital at two in the afternoon. The operation didn't begin until nine that night. Seeing their three-year-old daughter in such agony was heart-wrenching. They didn't know whether the doctors would be able to repair the nerves in her arm and whether she would be able to use her fingers again.

Yisroel called Rabbi Meshulem to update him. When the rabbi grasped what Yaffa was going through, there was silence on the line. Yisroel thought maybe they had been cut off or he was preoccupied with something else.

Then Yisroel heard crying.

The rabbi had broken down.

Of course, the moment Yisroel heard his rabbi crying, he couldn't hold back his own tears, and he broke down as well. And so Yisroel and the rabbi cried together, one in the hospital, the other at home.

♦ ♦ ♦

Yaffa's pediatrician managed to assemble some of the top orthopedic surgeons in the New York area to perform the operation. The operation took four hours, from nine at night until one in the morning, and Dr. Wallace Lehman and Dr. Stephen Borkow did a magnificent job. Joining Yisroel and Leah at the hospital were Rabbi Meshulem and Rabbi Yanky Jungreis. The two rabbis sat and recited *Tehillim* for the entire duration of the surgery.

It's difficult to describe the emotion that Yisroel and Leah witnessed on the rabbis' faces. It was as if they were praying for their own daughter and not just the daughter of their dear friends.

And they davened that way for four hours straight.

Witnessing such a scene made a huge impression on Yisroel and Leah. They had never seen anyone pray like that before. Yisroel felt as if he could see the air rippling above the rabbis from the intensity of their prayers. Since they themselves were still fresh to *Yiddishkeit*, they weren't able to read the words of *Tehillim* with the fluency needed to sustain such davening for a long period of time. The fact that the two rabbis had come to daven for them was a source of strength, comfort, and hope when they needed it most.

When the doctors emerged from the operating room at 1 a.m.,

they told the anxious parents that this had been the most challenging surgery of its type that they had ever performed.

"Your daughter's arm is so tiny that it was like operating on a watch," they said.

The bone had splintered, leaving razor-sharp exposed edges. Every one of those shards had to be reconnected. Arteries and nerves were wrapped around the bone fragments, and it had been a tedious and painstaking process. More than once, the doctors hadn't known whether they would succeed.

"It was a miracle that the broken bone didn't cut any arteries or nerves," the doctors said, "which would have been a disaster."

Then they said one more line:

"We attribute the success of this operation only to the prayers of the rabbis."

◆ ◆ ◆

"Why did a child have to suffer so much?" Leah later asked Rabbi Jungreis.

That question led to a lengthy conversation on the topic of faith in the Ribbono shel Olam. One line the rabbi said would reverberate within their hearts and minds for decades to come.

"Hashem wants our *tefillos*," he told them.

Had the concepts they were hearing on faith and trust in Hashem been given to them by someone who had lived a charmed life growing up in America, they might never have been able to accept them. But the answers were coming from Rabbi Meshulem Jungreis, who had gone through the war and lost his entire family. He had miraculously survived but had suffered more than they could fathom. While they had grown up in the safety of the United States, Rabbi Meshulem had been starving in the camps. Despite these conditions, he gave *chizuk* to his fellow Yidden, refused to eat non-kosher food, and somehow managed to hold on to his faith in the face of the kind of adversity that had destroyed so many others.

When a person like Rabbi Jungreis talked about accepting that everything that happens in the world is orchestrated by Hashem, one couldn't help but accept his words. When the rabbi said, "Hashem wants our prayers," Yisroel and Leah knew that those words came from a place that had been forged in fires ignited in one of the darkest moments of our history.

After this traumatic event and its miraculous conclusion, Yisroel and Leah's faith only grew stronger.

◆ ◆ ◆

Yaffa had to remain in the hospital for a week.

This wasn't a simple situation since hospital policy dictated that no one was allowed to remain with a child — not even parents — from 8 p.m. to 11 a.m. This meant that she was all alone throughout the night without the comfort of a familiar face.

The hospital was very strict about enforcing their policy. But every rule has an exception. In this case, the exception was Rabbi Meshulem Jungreis.

The morning after Yaffa's surgery, Yisroel went to daven Shacharis at Ohr Torah, where he met the rabbi.

"Do you know where I just came from?" Rabbi Jungreis asked him.

Yisroel had no idea.

"I made sure to be at the hospital with Yaffa when she woke up."

As a clergyman, Rabbi Jungreis was allowed unlimited access.

"I didn't want Yaffa to wake up all by herself," he explained. "I knew that she would be frightened, so I made sure to be there when she opened her eyes. Then I said 'Modeh Ani' with her before I drove to shul for Shacharis."

Rabbi Jungreis visited Yaffa every morning until she was released. Little did anyone dream of the connection that would come to exist between them, the rabbi and the three-year-old girl, in years to come...when she became his beloved daughter-in-law!

◆ ◆ ◆

Even after she was released, Yaffa's broken arm would remain part of her life for a long time. The doctors warned Yisroel and

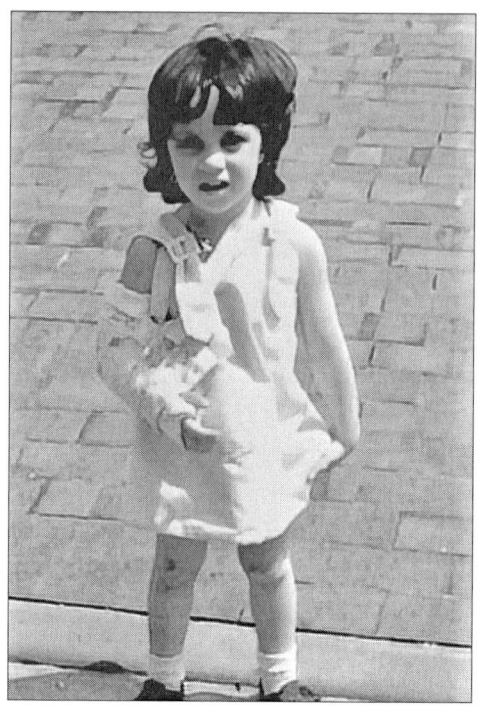
Little Yaffale and her broken arm

Leah that there was a risk her arm wouldn't grow normally, and her progress would have to be monitored every six months.

Shortly after Yaffa returned home, she had a visitor. The Rebbetzin had just stepped off the plane from a visit to Eretz Yisrael, and she came straight from the airport to see her beloved Yaffa.

The Rebbetzin gave Yaffa a huge hug and showered her with kisses. "I'm giving you a hug and a *berachah* with the air of Eretz Yisrael still on my coat!" she said.

Yisroel and Leah had been planning to join the Rebbetzin on yet another Eretz Yisrael adventure several weeks after the surgery.[9] But now, because of Yaffa's injury, they were sure they would have to cancel.

"No, you will come to Eretz Yisrael," the Rebbetzin told them, "and you will see that Yaffale will do great things there!"

So it was that the Neubergers booked tickets and got ready for the trip.

♦ ♦ ♦

The Rebbetzin and her entourage toured many army and air force bases as well as military hospitals around the country, visiting wounded soldiers to bring them cheer and *chizuk*. Yisroel will never forget one hospital visit where he met a soldier who had been shot above the elbow.

---

9. The Rebbetzin would always take a small group with her on her speaking tours in Israel. They visited holy sites as well as the many venues where she spoke.

It was the exact spot where Yaffa had broken her arm. I remember how the Rebbetzin called up Yaffa to stand next to her on the stage. She explained to the crowd that Yaffa had broken her arm near the elbow and that it had been a very serious operation.

"Yaffa," she said to the little girl, "can you lift up your arm and wiggle your fingers?"

Yaffa lifted up her arm — which was still in a cast — and wiggled her fingers, just as the Rebbetzin had asked.

At that moment there was a shout from the audience. The soldier who had been shot above the elbow, who hadn't been able to move his fingers in over a year, had cried out. Seeing Yaffa move her fingers after her serious accident convinced him to try and move his as well.

"I've just moved my fingers for the first time since being injured!" he exclaimed.

Utter pandemonium erupted. The crying, the sheer happiness — it's impossible to describe. It was incredible! The soldier had seen a three-year-old wiggle her fingers and that had given him hope that he would be able to do it, too.

Yisroel and Leah held Yaffa in their arms and thanked Hashem over and over for the miracles that He had done for them. They recalled the words of Rabbi Meshulem Jungreis — "Hashem wants our *tefillos*" — and they understood at that moment how their daughter's injury and recovery had given someone else the power to recover as well. And that many times what a person can see is not the end of the story.

Not at all.

Yisroel and Leah followed the doctors' instructions and brought Yaffa for her checkups. The first few times she was examined they were told that she was making wonderful progress.

Yes, against all odds.

Then one day she arrived at the hospital and the doctor was unable to tell the difference between her arms. The break had healed so well that there was so sign of it at all.

♦ ♦ ♦

In 1980, the Neubergers joined Rebbetzin Jungreis for their third trip to Eretz Yisrael. Accompanying them were their five children: Sarah, Yaffa, Miriam, Aharon Yaakov (Ari), and Nechami. Ari was turning three and Nechami was one. It was no simple matter making sure that all the children were ready to leave the hotel by nine every morning for the day's activities, especially since they were suffering from jet lag.

"I don't recall ever being so exhausted," Leah says. "None of us was sleeping much at night, but we were all still getting on the bus every day for hours of traveling. I was so tired at times that I thought I might not survive the trip."

The Rebbetzin took them to the Kosel, to Chevron and Kever Rachel, as well as to Tzefas and Meron. Glancing at the itinerary, Leah noticed that they were scheduled to be in Meron on the second day of Elul, which happened to be Ari's Hebrew birthday. She mentioned this bit of information to the Rebbetzin without realizing that there was any special significance to a little boy's third birthday.

"His third birthday," the Rebbetzin remarked. "That's a special day!"

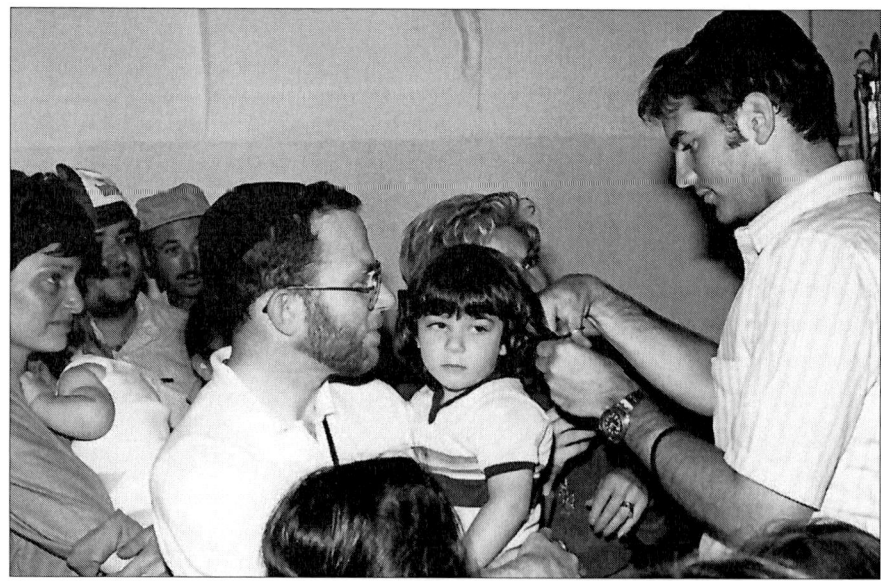

Ari's *upsherin* at Kever Rashbi in Meron. Yisroel Jungreis is cutting his hair.

The Rebbetzin made sure to bring a pair of scissors to Meron, and suddenly they found themselves in the middle of a beautiful *upsherin* for the first time in their lives. The Rebbetzin gave a speech, and everyone on the tour was given the *zechus* of cutting a few locks of Ari's hair. Emotions ran high as people marveled at how incredible it was that Hashem had arranged for them to be in Meron of all places on Ari's third birthday.

◆ ◆ ◆

On a different trip, they were crossing into Israeli air space and the "fasten seat belt" sign had already been turned on when the Rebbetzin gave Yisroel a mission.

One of the people on the trip was a young man named Josh,* who had been living with a cult on the West Coast. Yisroel knew his family, and Yisroel had not only convinced Josh to meet the Rebbetzin, but also to join the Hineni trip, which is why he was sitting about ten rows from Yisroel, Leah, and the Rebbetzin.

Though Josh had agreed to come, the Rebbetzin knew he was still wavering about giving up his attachment to the cult and everything it represented. The Rebbetzin motioned to Yisroel to get out of his seat and speak with Josh.

"But we're not allowed to stand up," he protested. "The seat belt sign is on."

"Yisroel, you need to go over to Josh right now and tell him something for me."

"What?"

"Tell him that he can't enter Eretz Yisrael if he is still faithful to *avodah zarah*."

"But I'm not allowed to get up," Yisroel insisted.

"Yisroel, go now!"

He didn't know what to do. He wanted to comply, but everyone on the plane was already sitting and the crew was checking to make sure seat belts were fastened.

"Yisroel, go now!"

Yisroel unbuckled his seat belt. The plane was rapidly descending. He heard a stewardess yelling, "Sit down, sir! Sit down!"

But he was on a mission. He made his way over to Josh, who looked at him, puzzled.

"The Rebbetzin told me to let you know that you need to do *teshuvah* before entering Eretz Yisrael. You can't enter the Holy Land if you are still on the fence regarding the cult. Do you understand? You have to give up everything other than Hashem right now!"

Message delivered, Yisroel returned to his seat.

The Rebbetzin's message penetrated and Josh did *teshuvah*. He entered Eretz Yisrael with a pure heart and went on to live a *frum* life. It wasn't easy for him to make the change. The Rebbetzin spoke to him at length during the course of the trip, and Yisroel spent many hours with him as well. In the end, he turned his life around.

PART 4

Chapter Sixteen
From Biker
to Chaim Berliner

Yisroel and Leah had just moved to North Woodmere. There were boxes everywhere, and they were still unpacking their belongings when the phone rang.

It was Rebbetzin Jungreis calling to tell them that she was sending them three guests for Shabbos. They said yes even though they had never before kept Shabbos in their own home and barely knew what keeping Shabbos meant. At that point, they still didn't even know how to read the *alef-beis*.

Leah voiced her doubts, and the Rebbetzin said, "It's true that you know very little. But these people know even less. Remember, you are going to inspire them to become better and more connected because they will think to themselves, *If Yisroel and Leah can do it, so can we.*

"And don't worry," she continued, "the guests are going to feel really comfortable with you. If you have any questions, just walk down the street and ask the rabbi what to do."

Since their new home was just two blocks from the Jungreis home and only one block from Congregation Ohr Torah, receiving an answer to any one of their thousands of questions was the easiest thing in the world, just as the Rebbetzin had said.

Their guests — a man, his wife, and their teenage son — were from Georgia. The man had served in the US Army twenty years before. Somehow he had crossed paths with missionaries who had convinced him to convert to Christianity. As if that were not enough, the man had gone on to become a minister himself and was actively trying to convert Jewish people.

Here is how this came about. The previous summer, this "minister" had decided it was his mission to convert Rebbetzin Jungreis! So he and his young disciple, Danny, also Jewish, traveled to the Pineview Hotel in the Catskills, where the Rebbetzin was the featured speaker the entire summer. They arrived on Friday and immediately tried to engage the Rebbetzin in a debate. But she said to them — pure Rebbetzin style! — "It's almost Shabbos. Let's first have Shabbos and then we will speak."

One thing the Rebbetzin had learned early on and taught her students in turn was never to argue. It's not an effective way to change people, especially when it comes to the beauty of Torah and mitzvos.

"We don't want to argue with another Jew," she would say. "We want the Jew to keep a Shabbos, hear a Torah class, or do a mitzvah."

The Rebbetzin insisted that anyone who wanted to meet with her had to attend a Torah class first. This would soften the callus around their soul. Once the beauty of Torah had been imbibed, the Rebbetzin knew she had a better chance of getting her message through.

That Shabbos with the Rebbetzin — her parents were also at the hotel — turned the minister's world upside down! By the time Shabbos was over, he was ready to burn his idolatrous books (literally). His disciple moved in with Yisroel and Leah (for years, it turned out) and the minister himself showed up with his family a few weeks later at Yisroel and Leah's house for Shabbos, after the Rebbetzin had told him that was what he needed to do.

After that first Shabbos, Yisroel and Leah understood that even though they themselves were still completely fresh to *Yiddishkeit* and knew very little, they could still host their fellow Jews for

Shabbos. If they had been concerned that they wouldn't be able to answer the questions posed to them, they quickly learned that their years of searching for their purpose in life were now coming in handy, since they were familiar with other lifestyles and could discuss them knowledgeably. It wasn't long before they became official Hineni Shabbos hosts.

Twenty-six years after the minister and his wife came to the Neubergers that first Shabbos, he sent the Rebbetzin a letter:

"Dear Rebbetzin Jungreis, I just want to let you know I have finally become completely *shomer Torah u'mitzvos.*"

It had taken him a long time. But he had gotten there at last.

After reading that letter, Yisroel and Leah looked at one another and recalled that memorable Shabbos — their first Shabbos in North Woodmere — and how at first they couldn't understand why the Rebbetzin would want people like themselves to host other Jews. Yet the Rebbetzin's intuition had proven to be correct.

◆ ◆ ◆

Sometimes the Rebbetzin would ask the Neubergers to have people come and live with them, and the visits could last anywhere from a week to a few years. Many of their guests went on to become *shomer Shabbos* and still express their gratitude to Yisroel and Leah every time they cross paths — even today, so many decades later.

Caroline Gabay, who was hosted by the Neubergers decades ago, wrote the following in a letter, an example of the feelings of many whom the Neubergers influenced and helped:

My fiancé, David, invited me to his friends' house out in Long Island for a holiday. What holiday could it be? Rosh Hashanah and Yom Kippur had just passed! Leah and Yisroel were warm, welcoming, and nonjudgmental. The house smelled delicious, and the children were all happy, brimming with excitement.

My father, a Holocaust survivor who had me very late in life, asked how it went. My response: "It's so strange.

They live in a beautiful home, but we ate outside in a hut decorated with X-mas lights."

My father responded, "It's Succos!"

"What is Succos?"

Why had my father never before spoken that word? I knew he grew up in a very religious home back in the Ukraine, but it was astonishing to me that he apparently had a clear knowledge of the holidays that we never celebrated. He lost his entire family during the war. Maybe it was just too painful for him.

After that life-altering Succos experience (now I could actually name the holiday!), I spent many Shabbosos and holidays with the Neubergers in their warm, loving home along with many other guests. Needless to say, it inspired me to have an observant home of my own. I am very grateful for the Neubergers' hospitality and love.

◆ ◆ ◆

Over the next four decades, thousands of guests spent time in the Neuberger home. Besides those who came just for a meal, there could be up to six people sleeping over on a Shabbos.

One Shabbos they hosted a young man who had been raised by Jewish parents who had chosen not to reveal their Jewishness to their son. They were so good at hiding their Jewishness that Scott* never even dreamed that he and his parents were not the gentiles they pretended to be. They had even changed their very Jewish last name to one that gave the exact opposite impression.

One day, when Scott was in his twenties, he went up to the attic. In one dusty box, he found a sheaf of astounding documents that showed that his entire life had been a lie. He was a Jew and not a "regular" American as he'd always thought.

As you can imagine, Scott was profoundly shocked by this discovery. He decided that he wanted to know more about this hidden world. A question here, a question there, and like so many others, Scott found his way to Hineni.

By this time Yisroel and Leah were the official Hineni Shabbos hosts. Leah would stand up at every class announcing that anyone who wanted to come for Shabbos should speak to her after the class. Leah made the same announcement when the Rebbetzin was giving her class to ten people or, later — at KJ on the Upper East Side — when fifteen hundred were attending each week.

People couldn't believe their ears.

"But you don't even know us!"

"That's easily remedied," she would reply.

So they came, enjoyed, and stayed in touch for years.

On the Erev Shabbos when Scott was to be their guest, Mrs. Perie Hirshaut, one of the Neubergers' neighbors, was preparing for Shabbos. It so happens to be that Mrs. Hirshaut has a large window overlooking the entrance to the neighborhood. As she was working, she heard a roar, which proved to be the sound of a motorcycle entering the quiet streets of Lawrence. Scott had arrived.

Scott loved every moment that he experienced that Shabbos: the Kiddush, the *zemiros*, the *seudah*, the *divrei Torah*, the shul. He loved it so much that, by the time Shabbos arrived the next week, he was already learning in Yeshivas Chaim Berlin complete with black hat and a suit, with tzitzis hanging over his belt.

Scott was the polar opposite of the minister who took twenty-six years to change his lifestyle. Leah was concerned that he had moved too quickly, but he remained *frum*, and the Rebbetzin eventually set him up with a Bais Yaakov girl whom he married.

Shortly after Scott's first Shabbos, Mrs. Hirshaut met Leah, who happened to mention the enthusiastic guest who had arrived on a motorcycle. "He's learning in Chaim Berlin!" Leah said.

Mrs. Hirshaut retorted, "I should have known that the motorcycle was saying, "*Fruuummmmm, fruuummmmm, fruuummmmmm!*"

At the end of the day, it depends on the person. Some make the decision to change the moment they hear the truth. For others, it takes decades. But no matter in which category they belonged, Yisroel and Leah opened their home and welcomed them in, determined to give them a Shabbos they would never forget.

♦ ♦ ♦

Just as every person is different and relates to life in his or her unique way, it's the same thing when it comes to guests. The Rebbetzin had a conversation about this with Yisroel and Leah way back in the beginning.

"Some people are extremely grateful for everything you have done for them," she told them. "They go out of their way to keep in touch for years to come. But there are others who spend time with you, and after they leave, you never hear from them again."

At first, Leah and Yisroel were perturbed by this. After all, they went out of their way for these people. They opened their home and hearts to them. In some cases, a guest might literally live in their home and become part of the family. How could they disappear after sharing such a relationship? How could a person just leave without ever calling or writing to let them know how he or she was doing?

The Rebbetzin explained that people sometimes don't want to remember where they were in life before they were observant. "They prefer to forget about that part of their lives," she said. "Since maintaining contact with people who know their past reminds them of that time, they cut off all contact."

Then she added another line that resonated:

"But Hashem knows what you did and that's the main thing."

More difficult was when a guest whom they welcomed into their home turned out to be seriously problematic. It was a rare occurrence; the guests whom they hosted in their home were generally a delight, but there were a few times when this wasn't exactly the case.

There was one young man whom Rebbetzin Jungreis helped to extract from a Florida-based cult. Somehow she convinced him to do *teshuvah* and to leave Florida, explaining that he would never be able to change while still in close proximity to the cult's headquarters.

The Rebbetzin called the boy's mother, who had asked her to save him in the first place. "I have great news for you," she told the mother. "With the help of Hashem, I managed to convince your son to leave the cult."

"That's wonderful!"

"Yes, and I want to send him home to you so that he can start a new life."

There was a sudden pause and a sharp intake of breath from the other end.

"No," the mother burst out.

"No?"

"No. Thank you for getting him out, but you can't send him to me."

It seemed that the boy wasn't an easy person to deal with, to the extent that he had a hard time getting along with his own mother.

Rebbetzin Jungreis sent him to Roy and Leah instead. Among other things, Leah explained to him some of the basic rules of kashrus, showing him that there was a sink for meat and a separate sink for milk.

She had to go out for a short while, and when she returned, she found him cooking chicken with yogurt in one of her pots!

Leah tried explaining the rules again, but it didn't take long to realize that he just wasn't going to listen. In the end, they were forced to ask him to leave.

◆ ◆ ◆

Of course, this wasn't the rule, and most of those they had hosted over the years were very welcome and would remain forever grateful for the Neubergers' impact on their lives.

Sheila* arrived after attending one of the Rebbetzin's classes, where she was advised to spend a Shabbos with the Neubergers. That she had even met the Rebbetzin in the first place was a beautiful thing. Sheila worked at a candy store on Wall Street that was owned by a Sephardic Jew. The longer she worked at the store, the more her boss came to realize that the people in her life weren't a good influence on her. She was hanging out with a non-Jewish crowd, many of whom were tough people from the streets.

"Why don't you go to hear Rebbetzin Jungreis at Hineni?" he suggested. "You will hear some interesting ideas and meet some nice Jewish people."

May G-d bless
you and give you
strength and answer
all your prayers.

Leah & Yisroel

Sheila's siddur, used every day for over thirty years, with Yisroel's inscription on the inside cover

For whatever reason — maybe even she was a little scared of her "friends" — Sheila took her boss's advice. That small step led to Shabbos after Shabbos at the Neubergers'. Sheila came to love Shabbos, to love spending time at their home. It wasn't long before she had become a regular at their table.

Sheila eventually moved in with the Neubergers, and everyone was happy that she had managed to escape from her old life without mishap. Then Sheila moved away, and the Neuberger family didn't hear from her anymore.

Eighteen years later, a letter arrived:

> Dear Yisroel and Leah,
>
> Do you remember me? I was a very confused young girl when I lived in your home. I want to thank you and Rebbetzin Jungreis for everything that you did for me. I still have the siddur that you gave me. I daven from it every day. I live in Israel, and I am married to a man named David.* We have two sons and two daughters. Our son's bar mitzvah is coming up in a few months, and we are planning on holding it in Jerusalem.
>
> Please, please come to the bar mitzvah! It would mean so much to us!
>
> Sheila

"We were overjoyed to hear that Sheila was doing well," Leah says, "and we were extremely touched at having been invited to share in her *simchah*. At the same time, it wasn't easy to just pick ourselves up and arrange a spur-of-the-moment trip to Israel."

But in the end, it worked out beautifully: Yisroel and Leah's daughter Sarah had married a boy from Yerushalayim and was living in Israel, where she had given birth to a baby whose bris was taking place right around the time of the bar mitzvah. This meant that they were going to be in Jerusalem at that time, so they were able to accept Sheila's gracious invitation and attend her special celebration.

"Seeing Sheila with her family, I was reminded that you can never give up on anyone. You never know what Hashem has in store for them. Ever since then, we've kept in touch with Sheila and her family. We always attend each other's *simchahs*. We have visited their home. The more we know them, the more we realize how blessed we were to have been granted the opportunity of hosting such a special girl when she needed us most."

Chapter Seventeen
Growing With Hineni

The seventies was a dangerous time for the Jewish people. Cults operated by charismatic people, many of whom had spent years in India studying under the swamis, were rampant, and young Jewish men and women were drawn to them like bees to honey.

When any part of *Klal Yisrael* was suffering, Rebbetzin Esther Jungreis tried her best to help. In many cases, this meant driving the Hineni van[10] wherever it was needed to take part in demonstrations. And whenever there was a demonstration that she decided to attend, Yisroel and Leah were there.

Reverend Sun Myung Moon was a major cult leader in the 1970s and '80s. A Korean preacher, he founded what was called the Unification Church, proclaimed himself the Messiah, and

---

10. The Hineni van was a vehicle completely equipped to be set up as a movable stage with a powerful sound system. The Rebbetzin and Barbara Janov would drive in this van to events such as demonstrations on behalf of Soviet Jewry. In the case of Reverend Moon's massive convocation at Yankee Stadium, the Rebbetzin spoke outside the stadium and attracted a large number of Jewish kids who otherwise would have entered and listened to the cult leader addressing the crowd. Some of these kids went on to attend the Hineni School and came to Yisroel and Leah's home for Shabbos. Sometimes the Rebbetzin would take a group to Midtown Manhattan and randomly speak to Jews on the street.

became famous for holding mass wedding ceremonies. Many Jews were attracted to his movement, whose followers became known as "Moonies." In his heyday, the reverend was so popular that he filled Yankee Stadium with his followers.

On the day of one of his events, the Hineni van was driven to Yankee Stadium, and the Rebbetzin spoke to whoever would listen, trying to dissuade them from attending the event. She herself was no stranger to gigantic venues. She had already given one of her famous speeches at Madison Square Garden by then and would give another famous speech years later when she was invited to give the invocation at the Republican National Convention. But it was never about the size of the crowd. If there was a possibility of saving even one Jew, the effort would have been worthwhile. So she didn't think twice about standing in the shadow of Yankee Stadium, even with the amplified voice of Reverend Moon ringing out for all of New York to hear. It was challenging, but thousands of Jewish lives were at stake.

What was challenging?

For Yisroel and Leah it was not natural to approach passersby and ask whether they were Jewish. If they answered at all and the answer was "yes," they would attempt to engage them in conversation and invite them to Hineni. This was not easy, but… the Rebbetzin had asked them and they were part of the team! In fact, many people's lives were changed through these encounters.

Yisroel and Leah had done this with the Rebbetzin many times, whether it meant rescuing Jews from the Hari Krishna people — the ones in the orange robes and strange hairstyles — or to protest the Russian government's suppression of Torah and Torah-observant Jews.

One of the people they met at the Moon rally that day was a very sweet Israeli guy named Avi,* who ended up spending many Shabbosos with the Neubergers, where he became known as *Bli Gezer* — "without carrots" — on account of his liking for all of Leah's salads except for the carrots.

"I'll never forget teaching Avi how to make a *berachah*," Leah says. "He was Israeli; he knew Hebrew, but a *berachah* was new to him. It was difficult for us to grasp the concept of Jews being raised in a Jewish country and not knowing anything about their heritage."

"Bli Gezer" ultimately became religious and a happy man.

But he still doesn't like carrots.

◆ ◆ ◆

Not long after their move to North Woodmere, Yisroel began frequenting a neighborhood bakery on Friday afternoons to purchase their Shabbos challos and cakes. He'd been going there for a while when he noticed that many trays of beautifully decorated cakes and fresh bread, rolls, magnificent challos, and cookies were being thrown into the dumpster every Friday afternoon because they would become stale by the coming Sunday.

Yisroel approached the owner and asked, "How can you throw out all these wonderful baked goods?"

"We can't sell it," he explained, "and I need all fresh stuff for the customers on Sunday."

"Let me take it."

"You're not serious."

"I'm perfectly serious. I'll take all the leftover baked goods and distribute them to shuls and yeshivos who will be very happy to receive them. Your baked goods will find their way to good homes, and you will have a tremendous merit."

That's how Hineni, and the shul where Rabbi Meshulem Jungreis was rabbi, Congregation Ohr Torah, became the recipients of free challahs and baked goods every Erev Shabbos, courtesy of Yisroel Neuberger.

Yisroel drove a station wagon in those days, and there were times when there was so much cake and challos stuffed into his car that he couldn't see out the rear window. Sometimes there was barely enough room for him to get into the car himself. After Yisroel made his rounds, Rabbi Jungreis made a point of visiting every widow in the congregation before Shabbos, giving each a challah. Some of the cakes and cookies were used for the *kiddush* in shul.

On Motza'ei Shabbos, whatever was left went to Brooklyn to

the home of the Rebbetzin's parents, where Mama would work her magic and make everything disappear, either distributing to any one of the *chesed* projects she was running (Mama fed more people than it's possible to imagine...) or to the kids at the elementary school Mama and Zeide had opened in Canarsie, Ateres Yisroel. Mama would stand at the doorway of the school when the buses arrived and welcome every child by handing them a pastry and telling them to make a *berachah*. The welcome at Yeshiva Ateres Yisroel was like coming home. And, of course, there were always Jews from the Soviet Union coming and going at Mama's home, and all of them knew that whenever they arrived, Mama would find something delicious for them to eat.

◆ ◆ ◆

In the 1980s the Rebbetzin's class moved from Canarsie in Brooklyn (her father's shul) to the new Hineni Building in Manhattan and then to Kehilath Jeshurun, a huge shul on the Upper East Side. Yisroel and Leah were there week in and week out, to welcome everyone who walked through the doors.

In those days, it seemed almost unbelievable that twenty- and thirty-year-old nonobservant, professional Jews would flock to a Torah lecture every week at a synagogue in New York City. But Rebbetzin Esther Jungreis's Torah lecture on Tuesday night at Kehilath Jeshurun was the place to be if you were single and interested in meeting a fellow Jew. At its peak, fifteen hundred people attended every week, and the main sanctuary as well as the women's balcony were packed. The Rebbetzin was warm and welcoming, as well as a brilliant orator.

After every lecture, the participants would mingle and line up to speak to the Rebbetzin, with Leah and Yisroel Neuberger at her side. They welcomed everyone they could speak to and formed friendships that have endured to this day. Lives were changed every week. Immediately after the Rebbetzin finished speaking, Leah would take the microphone and invite anyone who was interested to come for Shabbos.

One young woman, Stacy, attended every week for two years,

and she couldn't help but be impressed by the Neubergers and their story. With a combination of Leah's calm demeanor and Yisroel's exuberance, they shared their compelling journey from well-educated, secular Jews to *baalei teshuvah* who decided to become fully observant. Those sitting there, unaffiliated, unlearned in Torah, were blown away.

At one point, Stacy took up Leah on her offer to learn one-on-one, anything she wanted, and Leah became her first *chavrusa*. Right there, in the sanctuary at KJ following the lecture, Leah taught Stacy how to pray from a siddur. Leah was patient and non-judgmental. Stacy asked her to show her the parts of the weekday Shacharis that were most essential because her mornings were usually rushed getting to work, and she didn't have time to say it all. Unflinchingly, Leah happily obliged.

"Leah and Yisroel treated me like family," Stacy recounts. "They introduced me to their children and grandchildren, took me along to shul, took me to Shabbos *shiurim*, and graciously let me bring the cheesecake on Shavuos! I remember one time walking through their front door and seeing Leah under the dining room table fixing something. She worked hard to prepare a beautiful Shabbos meal and table, smiling all the while.

"Yisroel and Leah had so much compassion for my frustrating single status. They encouraged me and even set me up. I danced at their daughter Miriam's wedding, and they both danced at my wedding. I was honored that they attended, as I realized that they probably got so many wedding invitations from the hundreds of singles they knew. And they didn't just attend my *chasunah* — Yisroel and Leah danced and celebrated! They are always fully present.

"Thinking back on that time in my life, I'm so grateful for the opportunity to have met Leah and Yisroel, and for all they've done for me. Today, I proudly consider myself to be a *baalas teshuvah*, and I'm deeply grateful to be the wife of the most wonderful man, a *ben Torah*, the mother of precious *frum* children, and even a *shadchan*, in large part due to Leah and Yisroel's influence. I treasure their friendship and many beautiful memories."

♦ ♦ ♦

Helping the Rebbetzin with her *avodas hakodesh* was Yisroel and Leah's way of saying thank you to Hashem for saving them and to Rebbetzin Jungreis for reaching out to them. When every class was over, Leah would stand up in front of the room and invite everyone in the crowd to their home for Shabbos. There were also gatherings for singles events, and Yisroel ran those as well. The truth is that both of them became involved in pretty much every aspect of the Hineni operation, attending every single Torah class, hosting guests for Shabbos, and running singles events.

Among other things, Rabbi Meshulem Jungreis gave a *Chumash shiur* to the women of the shul every Wednesday afternoon. During the summer months, when he took a break, he asked Leah if she would be willing to take over. She agreed and the classes were held in her home every week,[11] accompanied by delicious refreshments. In retrospect, that was the beginning of what would be a lifetime of public speaking and teaching.

The Rebbetzin also asked Leah to take on the responsibility of preparing *kallahs* for their weddings and teaching them what they needed to know so that they could build kosher Jewish homes. Leah put a lot of thought into how to teach the women in the most effective way possible.

Before she would teach the *kallah*, she would meet with the couple. She would talk about Jewish marriage, with a lot of focus on the importance of Shabbos to married life. "The more you bring Shabbos into your home," she'd explain, "the more the serenity of Shabbos will fill your home even during the week." When Leah spoke about *shalom bayis*, she focused on teaching her students how to handle anger, which is such a destructive force in a marriage.

Later Leah would speak to audiences on "Successful Dating and Marriage," contrasting the Torah's idea of love and marriage

---

11. This was in addition to the Shabbos afternoon classes led by Chaya Sora Jungreis.

with the Hollywood version and explaining why the Torah's path offers the optimum road toward genuine marital happiness. Of course, it included much of what she had been taught by the Rebbetzin.

"More important than looking into one another's eyes," Rebbetzin Jungreis used to say, "is that you're both looking in the same direction, that you share common aims and goals."

Leah would talk about how people have to think about the consequences of their actions and words. When someone lashes out in anger, it's possible to inflict emotional wounds that may never heal. Words are powerful.

"Rebbetzin Jungreis would talk about what to do if you get angry. She would say, 'Go to the sink and wash your face. Walk around the block. Get some fresh air. Cool down. Don't speak when you're angry. If you're angry, zip your mouth closed.'"

For his part, Yisroel also took on myriad responsibilities to help Congregation Ohr Torah, the Jungreises' shul, run as smoothly as possible. He became extremely active in the shul and after only a few years in North Woodmere became the shul president, with Leah serving as president of the Sisterhood.

Rabbi Jungreis had revolutionized North Woodmere by creating an Orthodox shul, but there was still much to accomplish. Ensuring that they had minyanim for all the *tefillos* was an ongoing challenge at Ohr Torah, one that the rabbi and Yisroel (even before he was president) dealt with constantly.

There was a man who lived in a neighboring community. He used to rise early and walk every morning before commuting to the city. His walking route took him past Ohr Torah at the same time every day. One morning, Rabbi Jungreis went outside before Shacharis to see if he could lasso a passing Jew for the minyan, and he stopped this man, introduced himself, and asked if he was a fellow Yid.

He was.

"Could you perhaps spare a few minutes and join our minyan as the tenth man?" Rabbi Meshulem asked.

From that early-morning meeting, a life-changing story emerged.

Yisroel, of course, went out of his way to welcome "the walker" (as he was lovingly dubbed) to their minyan, and it wasn't long before he invited his entire family to the Neuberger home for Shabbos. The parents and one daughter soon became regulars at the shul every Shabbos and joined the Neubergers afterward for the daytime meal.

The walker (let's call him Walter Bergman*) did have a job other than walking: he was a legendary suit salesman at the iconic Saks Fifth Avenue in Manhattan. He had some high-profile clients, including Moshe Arens, who at that time was defense minister of Israel. Mr. Arens bought all his suits from Mr. Bergman, usually purchasing more than a dozen at a time and devoting half a day for this purpose on his regular diplomatic trips to the United States. Whenever he came to Saks, the entire store would be closed as a security measure.

Ruthie, the Bergmans' daughter, wanted to become a doctor, and her parents watched with pride as she became first a PA, then a physician, and then a highly trained specialist. When her parents passed away years later, Ruthie became like a daughter to the Neubergers.

By that time, Yaffa — remember the little girl with the broken arm? — was all grown up and married to the Jungreis's son Rabbi Osher. She was also a successful shadchan. Yaffa decided it was time for Ruthie to get married, so she started telling everyone she knew about Ruthie.

One Shabbos, a couple named Robert and Bianca Gordon, who had met each other at Hineni, were hosting a wonderful young man at their seudah. In the middle of the meal, Bianca heard a voice, as if someone were whispering in her ear, "Bianca, don't forget, you need to find a shidduch for Ruthie! She's a great girl!"

It took her no time to identify the voice as that of Yaffa Neuberger, who had spoken those words to her so many times. Somehow, Bianca was hearing Yaffa speaking, even though Yaffa wasn't there!

And there he was, right in front of Bianca.

In short, Bianca made the *shidduch* and everything turned out beautifully. It was a story that really began early one morning outside Congregation Ohr Torah, when Rabbi Meshulem Jungreis "lassoed" Walter Bergman into joining his minyan, convincing yet another Jew to join the shul and changing lives in the process.

◆ ◆ ◆

One evening a man showed up at Hineni where the Rebbetzin gave her talks. Tuvia* was dating a non-Jewish woman, and to his shock, he happened to walk in just as the Rebbetzin was delivering a speech against intermarriage. That speech led directly to his breaking up with his girlfriend. Soon he was a regular at Hineni. There was a nice girl there who expressed interest in him, but Tuvia wasn't ready to start dating again.

Yisrael devoted a lot of time speaking with Tuvia to convince him to give it a try, until finally he agreed to go on a date. One date led to another and another. Eventually they got engaged. But it was never simple, and there were times when Tuvia wanted to break it off. Every time Tuvia was on the brink of calling the whole thing off, Yisroel would sit down with him and convince him that it was just a bad case of nerves, that it was going to be different this time.

Eventually, they married (not before Yisroel felt like he'd used up most of his allotted words for the year on getting the *chassan* to the finish line) and went on to build a *bayis ne'eman b'Yisrael*. Not long ago, they sent Yisroel and Leah a picture of them marrying off one of their children. And every time the Neubergers have the opportunity to attend one of their family *simchahs*, Tuvia and his wife thank them again for everything they've done for them. Tuvia would point to the large group of kids running around and say, "These are your children just as much as ours..."

Years later, Tuvia's wife wrote a very beautiful and forthright account of what happened:

> I came to Hineni to learn from Rebbetzin Jungreis but mostly to find a husband. While I was learning, Yisroel Neuberger and his beautiful wife Leah came up to me and

invited me for Shabbos. I had heard of Shabbos before, but didn't think of it as anything special. *At the very least, I thought to myself, I'll eat well.* So I accepted their invitation. Needing a ride from Brooklyn to Long Island, Yisroel found me one with my future husband.

Because of Yisroel Neuberger, my life would change forever. I arrived at his house wearing pants. His daughter Yaffa, who was then eight years old, answered the doorbell and said, "Why are you wearing pants?" I was so taken by surprise, all I could say was "I don't know."

Without missing a beat, she said she would get me a skirt for Shabbos. I had one in my suitcase anyway, but that was my entrance into their world. Soon Leah lit the Shabbos candles and the feeling of being in another world began. She not only lit the candles, but she sat down with us (there were many others there for Shabbos, too) and explained their significance.

Before I knew it, Yisroel and whoever was with him came home from shul, and we all sat down at their dining room table. Yisroel stood up and I thought he was going to make Kiddush. Instead, he sang *Eishes Chayil*, and I was dumbfounded. I had never seen anyone do that before.

Everyone at the table was quiet. I was really flabbergasted. You had to be there. He was singing so beautifully, and I felt again that I was in another world. I thought to myself, *If I come here next week, I'll see this again.*

The look on Yisroel's face told us that there is a G-d in this world. Without a doubt. His Kiddush was almost mystical to me. If you saw his face during those moments, you would understand what I'm saying. *Here is a man who really believes in Hashem. Here is a man who learned what Hashem wants of him and he goes and does it.* I was convinced I wanted to be like him. I wanted to believe, too, and to have a home just like his, to have children just like his, who are so foreign to wearing pants they had to ask me why.

To make a long story short, I started to date the man who gave me the ride to their house and back. After some time, Yisroel came to us and said that when Jewish people date, they date for the purpose of marriage. Either we decide to get married, or we decide not to see each other anymore.

I was shocked. What happened to the nice guy who headed the kind of family I wanted to have? Even though I was devastated, Yisroel stood firm where the Torah was concerned. As kind as he was, he wouldn't budge on this point one way or the other. Hashem's word is the law, and Yisroel would not stand by and see two people doing anything to violate it.

We did stop dating, and much to my everlasting joy we got married instead!

And who was our *shadchan*? We are always proud to say it was Yisroel Neuberger!

♦ ♦ ♦

Among their contributions, Leah and Yisroel started hosting classes given by Chaya Sora, the Rebbetzin's eldest child, to members of the shul every Shabbos afternoon. Chaya Sora wasn't enamored with the idea of teaching her own classes, but the Rebbetzin knew that she was a natural and insisted. Chaya Sora began giving a Shabbos afternoon *Pirkei Avos* class in the Neuberger living room, and afterward Leah served *shalosh seudos*. There was plenty of homemade challah (whole wheat, of course) and other delicacies.

The *shiur* and communal meal that followed became something the shul members came to look forward to. Eventually Chaya Sora's class became so popular that it had to be moved to the shul itself.

I remember how excited we all were when we heard the big news. The Neubergers, who were regular attendees of my mother's *parashah* classes, were moving to North Woodmere. And not just to any block. They were moving just two blocks down from our home on Hungry Harbor Road. My mother sent me over to help them settle in, and that was the beginning of a most special relationship.

The Neubergers embraced their new life with incredible *simchah*. Shabbos became the highlight of their week. They wanted to share the beauty of Shabbos with those who had not yet experienced it. My mother appointed Yisroel and Leah as the "Shabbos Hospitality Chairmen," and their home soon became a "Shabbos House," always open to anyone who wanted to experience a genuine Shabbos.

The Neubergers never said no. There was always room at their table for one more. So many people who never had experienced a Shabbos tasted not only the flavors of Shabbos, but they found their souls rising to great spiritual heights because of the Neubergers' open and warm home.

Yisroel and Leah also became active in my parents' shul, Ohr Torah, and hosted a weekly *shalosh seudos* for the shul members in their home, which was just a few steps away from the shul. My mother asked me to give a *shiur* in their home prior to *shalosh seudos*. The Rebbetzin was a big believer in "leaping in and taking the plunge." I was just a high school student, but my mother believed in me.

My father joined the shul members for *shalosh seudos* at the Neubergers, always with an insightful and timely *devar Torah* that spoke to everyone. He had the kindest and most beautiful way of touching everyone's soul with his soft-spoken words. Of course, he made a point to always thank the Neubergers for their hospitality.

Yisroel would sit right beside my father and make sure that the singing at *shalosh seudos* was lively and spirited. The highlight was when my father would sing *Mizmor L'David*, closing his eyes in deep concentration and swaying ever so gently to the beautiful melody. When he finished, my father would rise and we would all follow as Abba led us in accepting upon ourselves the kingship of Heaven, calling out, "*Hashem melech Hashem malach Hashem yimloch l'olam va'ed* — Hashem is King, Hashem was King, Hashem will be King," and "*Shema Yisrael Hashem Elokeinu Hashem echad!*"

The first Shabbos that my then husband-to-be, Rabbi Shlomo Gertzulin, joined our family, we of course made our way to the Neubergers for *shalosh seudos*. He told me soon after how touched he was by the entire experience, particularly at seeing the incredible hospitality and warmth shown by the Neubergers not just to the members of the shul but to all those whom they had invited to their home to a "real live" Shabbos.

We will always remember it.

♦ ♦ ♦

Not long after Yisroel and Leah made their journey back to *Yiddishkeit*, the Rebbetzin encouraged Yisroel and Leah to tell their story to as many people as they could reach. And so the Neubergers wrote their story, which Rebbetzin Jungreis published in her weekly column, "The Rebbetzin's Viewpoint," in *The Jewish Press*. In addition, the Rebbetzin encouraged them to speak at Hineni events, telling them that they needed to share their story with the world. "To declare the miracle" was the way she put it. "Declaring the miracle is the way to thank Hashem for taking you out of your personal Egyptian exile."

This was one of the ways the Rebbetzin made it clear to them that just as she had inspired them and changed their lives, now it was their turn to do the same for other Jews and pass the torch along.

At a speech they gave in Monsey, they met Dimitri.* He was very moved by their story. After the speech, he introduced himself, explaining that he and his mother had arrived from China not long before and that they were trying to learn as much as they could about *Yiddishkeit*.

"Why don't you come to Hineni?" they suggested.

And so Dimitri began attending classes at Hineni, and he was captivated by everything he learned. He also began coming to the Neuberger home for Shabbos on a regular basis. A short while later the Rebbetzin announced another trip to Israel, and Dimitri decided to sign up. That trip was particularly memorable because Dimitri celebrated his bar mitzvah at the Kosel at the age of thirty-one. The Rebbetzin's line — "Thirty-one is thirteen backward" — was widely reported by every journalist who covered the emotional event.

Dimitri's mother was a Russian Jew who had had a relatively good job working at the Chinese embassy in Moscow. There she met a Chinese diplomat who asked to marry her. That's how a Jewish girl from Moscow ended up moving to China. There they had a son, Dimitri.

As the years passed, Dimitri's mother felt more and more trapped by life in China. Though she never served pork, a staple in every Chinese home, she also never told her husband that she was Jewish. But now, overwhelmed with feelings of discontent and unhappiness, her *Yiddishkeit*, latent for so long, began to surface. After all, when someone feels alone in the vast world, it's quite possible that he will remember the one thing that is most valuable in his life, and that's what happened with Dimitri's mother. She couldn't stop thinking about the life she had left behind in Russia, Even though her family had not been religious in Russia, she still felt guilty about giving up all connection to Judaism and she felt isolated in a completely alien environment; yet she kept the truth from her husband and son.

No doubt life would have continued on its path with Dimitri remaining unaware of his true roots — except for one thing: he loved building shortwave radios. One night he was tinkering with his radio when he suddenly picked up a broadcast from the *Voice of Israel* live from Jerusalem. When he heard Jewish music blaring from the radio and the Hebrew language being spoken, it touched him deeply. The discussion on the radio concerned the Jewish people's victory in the Six-Day War. Dimitri felt his skin tingle.

When he told his mother about what he had heard and his reaction, she broke down and admitted that she had a secret to share. She told him the story of a young girl whose parents had died. The young girl had been raised by a non-Jewish family. She hated her life and eventually ran away to Moscow, where she married a young Chinese diplomat.

"Did you ever tell my father that you're Jewish?" he asked her.

"No," she admitted, "I was afraid to tell him."

She told her son everything she remembered from her childhood. She told him about the city of Jerusalem, and she shared with him a prayer that she recalled.

"It is called the *Shema*," she said.

"What does it mean?"

"I don't know exactly, but my grandmother told me that by saying it a person can connect with G-d."

Time passed and life became increasingly challenging for both Dimitri and his mother. They realized that they had to leave Communist China, but the question was how to achieve that goal. Dimitri's mother applied for exit visas for herself and her son. Since she was a foreigner, she eventually received them. So it came to pass that a Russian Jewish woman who had spent a large portion of her life in China and her Jewish (but Chinese-looking) son were able to leave Red China for the United States of America.

There Dimitri eventually met the Neubergers, who connected him with the Rebbetzin and Hineni. But the story wasn't over yet.

During the Hineni trip to Eretz Yisrael, Dimitri became friendly with a young woman from Brooklyn who had also joined the trip. It didn't take long for the two of them to realize that they had much in common, though she had been born and raised in the States and he in Red China. The Rebbetzin was concerned that her parents would be uncomfortable with the *shidduch*, but after they got to know Dimitri, they saw that it was a good match. The children got engaged, and Zeide and Rabbi Meshulem Jungreis presided over the wedding.

Whenever the story of Dimitri's wedding would come up in later years, the Rebbetzin would say that it epitomized the story of the Jewish people itself: no matter where *galus* takes us, our *pintele Yid* will come to the fore in the end. That is what happened with Dimitri and his mother, and that is what happened countless times throughout the generations. Even though a person may drift so far away, there is always something inside that can draw us back.

To think that a young Chinese boy found his way back home and ended up building a beautiful Jewish family due to a short-wave radio that he built all by himself in the vast emptiness of China.

◆ ◆ ◆

Like so many others, a medical student named Debra heard Yisroel and Leah speak at a Hineni singles event, and she decided to call and tell them how inspired she was by their story. She added that she had never experienced Shabbos and would like to join them sometime. Of course, Yisroel and Leah extended a warm invitation.

Debra became a regular Shabbos guest and fit in beautifully with the family. Her own family lived far away and was distant from *Yiddishkeit*. The entire Neuberger clan became very fond of Debra, and each one of them kept her in mind to try to find a *shidduch* for her.

One night, at a *simchah*, the Neubergers met a fine young man — refined, intelligent, and sincere — whom they felt was just right for Debra.

"Thank you so much for thinking of me," Debra replied after they told her a little about his background. "But I don't want to meet him. There's no way someone who grew up religious will understand me."

"Why don't you go out just once?" Leah suggested. "You never know."

So they went out on a date.

And guess what. They got married! Today Debra is a *bubby* many times over.

"Sometimes a person thinks that they know exactly what they

need," Leah says, "and they are unwilling to consider anything else because it's inconceivable to them that Hashem may have other plans for them. One needs to be willing to consider other options, just as Debra did."

It's not that a person has to be overly open-minded and go out with every person suggested to them. As Rebbetzin Jungreis used to say, "Some people are so open-minded that their brains fall out." But it pays to keep a range of options on the table and be willing to think outside the box even when you're certain you know what you need.

Because you never know.

Chapter Eighteen
Miniature Ambassadors of Torah

Many times over the years people have asked Yisroel and Leah if they hadn't been worried about opening their home and inviting the world to enter. In their minds, there was never a question. Whereas some people hide their past, trying to present a façade that's unlike the reality of their lives, Yisroel and Leah never tried to hide anything. In fact, they went out of their way to share their story with their children and guests. The children heard their parents' story hundreds of times and were familiar with every detail.

Along with everything else, the children became accustomed to meeting new people. They learned to teach them how to make a *berachah*, how to say *Shema*, how to wash *mayim acharonim*, or how to *bentch*. They even sat with them in shul and taught them how to daven. They became miniature ambassadors of Torah.

But even though they had a relatively open house, there were always standards at their Shabbos table. The guests caught on to the way they spoke to one another and to the types of things they talked about. Rare was the moment that they needed to correct someone because they weren't being respectful. The opposite was true: the guests were captivated by the sight of a six-year-old showing them how to wash their hands and gesturing to them not to talk afterward, with a finger on his little lips…

The atmosphere brought out the best in virtually everyone who crossed the threshold. The children often slept in one room if their rooms were needed. They did it happily and were so proud of what went on every single Shabbos, because they appreciated that they had the merit to grow up *frum,* unlike so many others who had found their way to Torah only when they were already in their twenties or thirties.

As their daughter Sarah attests:

> Our house was always full of guests, especially on Shabbos. There were many people who couldn't experience a Torah way of life in their own homes, and my parents, warmly and lovingly, invited these people to live with us and be a part of our family. My siblings and I never felt left out or jealous, because we played an integral part in making them feel at home. We genuinely enjoyed having them with us. Besides, we were constantly showered with love and knew how special we were — and are — to them.
>
> I remember doing a special dance with my sister Yaffa when we were little (we loved doing this dance) while my father sang a song at the Shabbos table. I remember the delicious and plentiful food my mother made for large groups of people: garlic bread, chicken with onions and gravy, raspberry syrup mixed with seltzer, roast beef, apple pie with whipped cream.
>
> I watched my father speak to people, Jew or non-Jew, and saw him personify what a Jew is supposed to be: a light unto the nations. I watched my mother greet countless guests with her noble and completely unruffled manner no matter what was going on around her.
>
> We went regularly with my parents to a nursing home to visit people and teach them Torah. And we would prepare hundreds of *mishlo'ach manos* before Purim and drive

all over New York delivering them on Purim, not only to friends and neighbors, but also to lonely widows, people in nursing homes, and Jews who didn't know what *mishlo'ach manos* was until we explained it to them. Although they were grateful for the delicious food that came with the *mishlo'ach manos*, they were even more moved by the obvious love and care my parents put into these packages. Purim was and still is my favorite holiday, and I will never forget the special Purim experiences of my childhood.

Many times people are admired, respected, and loved for the public persona they present to the world, but those who know them well think of them differently. As my parents' eldest daughter, I can say that people's perception of my parents as warm, loving, noble people who care about the Jewish people and for each Jew individually as if they were their brother, sister, son, or daughter is the absolute truth of who my parents are, heart and soul.

♦ ♦ ♦

Among those whom the Neubergers welcomed with open arms, even where others may have been reluctant to do so, was Anchi.

Anchi's* story was long and complicated. He was from a *chassidishe* family who had gone to speak to the Rebbetzin about their son. They were seeking her advice concerning a child who had been difficult from the time he was very young, and they had no idea how to handle him. When they realized that there was no chance that he would be able to succeed in an American yeshivah, his parents sent him to a yeshivah in Europe. He was there for only a short while before he was sent to Eretz Yisrael. But he left yeshivah and somehow found his way back to the States. He was a very tough, rebellious young man, bordering on dangerous. Eventually, he found his way to Las Vegas. By this time he was eighteen and he went by the name Andy, having given up on yeshivah.

Stupid he was not. It wasn't long before he'd become adept at playing poker. He would sit at the same tables where nonreligious Jews were playing. Since most people assumed that Andy was Italian, they had no compunctions about speaking Yiddish in front of him. But Yiddish was Andy's first language, and he understood everything they were saying. Frequently he was able to predict their moves and walk away the winner.

Andy became a little too successful and ended up branching out into a number of additional unsavory ventures. He committed several crimes before crossing paths with an undercover police officer and was arrested and sent to prison. From his new domicile, Anchi called his parents, contacting them for the first time in eight years since he'd left home at the age of thirteen.

The conversation didn't go incredibly well.

"Mommy, it's Anchi."

"Anchi! Where are you?"

"I'm in jail," at which point the phone dropped out of his mother's hand.

Nevertheless, a lawyer was dispatched to Vegas from New York. He drove to the jail, reviewed the case with Anchi, and managed to get his client released on a technicality. Anchi was escorted to the airport by an officer of the Las Vegas Police Department, who made sure that he boarded the plane and left the state.

Just before boarding, the officer looked him in the eye and said, "Listen, you had a good lawyer, and he managed to get you off. But if you show your face here again, I will personally see to it that you stay behind bars for a long time. Am I clear?"

Andy didn't have to answer. Both of them knew it wasn't an empty threat.

◆ ◆ ◆

Now Anchi was back in the old neighborhood, and his parents, still in shock, decided to try their best to rehabilitate him. They brought him to Rebbe after Rebbe. All spoke to him, but nothing worked. Anchi wasn't impressed.

His parents were at their wits' end when someone told them about Rebbetzin Jungreis, suggesting that she might be the one to achieve the miracle no one else could.

Anchi's parents brought him to a class and they met. The Rebbetzin took one look and got his measure, cutting through his bravado with a few well-chosen words.

"Take off your sunglasses."

It took him some time, but he obeyed.

"What's your name?"

"Andy."

"No, your real name."

He told her his Hebrew name — his real name. When she heard it, she was overcome. He had been named

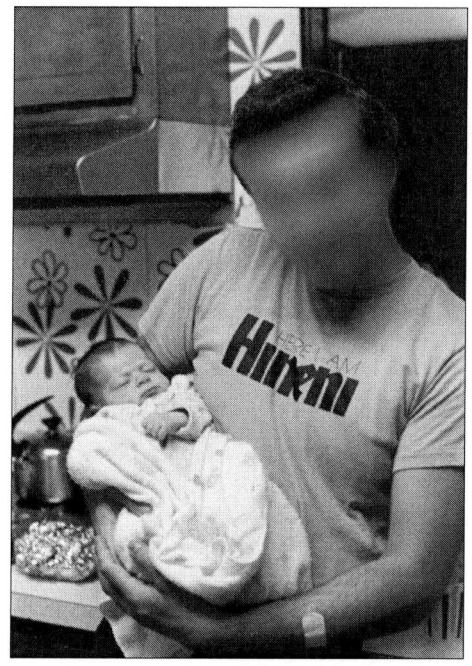

Anchi holding baby Ari Neuberger

after one of her ancestors as a *berachah* for healing him when he was a very sick baby.[12] Suddenly the room was filled with a new surge of electricity. It was the beginning of a new life for Anchi. After that, the Rebbetzin sent him to the Neubergers' — where he stayed for the next two years.

♦ ♦ ♦

He arrived on a Friday, his eyes covered by those ever-present shades, his face covered by a thick black beard. He wore a leather jacket, looking every inch a gangster. He accompanied his host to shul when Shabbos began like all the other guests, but at the Shabbos table Andy didn't utter a word. The most he was willing to do was mumble a response here and there. This behavior, understandably, was a bit disconcerting for everyone present.

---

12. As a baby, he had been very sick. His family was told by a Rebbe to name the child after the Czengerer Tzaddik as a *segulah* for good health.

After the first few Shabbosos, he began opening up. He even taught a *zemer* that he had grown up singing at his parents' Shabbos table in Williamsburg. Yisroel and Leah liked the song and began singing it every Shabbos.

Soon Anchi, as he was now calling himself, started to warm up. He spoke more often and took off his sunglasses at the table. He even began to smile. Clear progress was being made, even if it sometimes seemed they were taking one step forward and four steps back.

Still, what doesn't one do for another Yid?

◆ ◆ ◆

While living at the Neubergers, Anchi spent his time studying for his GED and managing security for Hineni events. The Neubergers were like family to Anchi, but they maintained contact with his parents, who were extremely grateful.

Much of Anchi's turnaround came about through the hours and hours of conversation that Yisroel devoted to him, helping him deal with his past so that he could focus on the future.

After he'd been in their home for about a year, they found out that Anchi had some legal business to clean up in Las Vegas. During his rebellious years, he had married a non-Jewish woman in casino land, and he needed to divorce her so that he could move on with his life and hope to build a Jewish family. (No "*get*" was needed, as she was not Jewish.) Knowing that he had to return to Vegas to deal with the situation and fearful that he wasn't ready to face the temptations he would find there, the Rebbetzin instructed Yisroel to go along and make sure Anchi stayed out of trouble.

"Go to Las Vegas and get Anchi divorced," she said.

The Rebbetzin booked them a flight that would leave late at night and land at around dawn. The plan was to go directly from the plane to the lawyer's office and straight back to the airport afterward, with little room for the Satan to cause trouble.

"You will land at six in the morning," she began. "Make sure you arrive at the lawyer's office by eight. I want the divorce to be finalized by ten and both of you back at the airport and on a plane by twelve."

That was the plan. But the best-laid plans…

As the plane flew over Chicago, a storm struck. It was a monster, and the plane had to travel hundreds of miles out of the way to avoid it. The flight took much longer than expected, and Yisroel and Anchi ended up with a sleepless night on the plane. All their well-intentioned plans were delayed.

By the time they arrived at the lawyer's office, they were exhausted and falling asleep on their feet. To make matters worse, the lawyer realized that Anchi was missing an important document and wouldn't be able to finalize the divorce that day.

"You're going to have to make a return trip to Vegas," he told them.

Terrible news.

"I knew I had to get Anchi onto a plane and out of Vegas as soon as possible," Yisroel says. "It was obvious to me the instant we landed in Vegas that he wasn't the Anchi I knew back in New York. He was Andy again. One glance into his eyes, and I could see that he was reverting to his previous persona. His eyes were hooded and dark, as if all the light of the previous year had been sucked out of them and replaced with the poison of his earlier life."

Yisroel looked at the young man he'd all but adopted with trepidation, afraid that he was going to lose him in the moral quicksand of Las Vegas.

"Let's go back to the airport," he told Anchi.

"No, you go back without me," Anchi told him. "There are a few things I have to do here."

Exactly as Yisroel had feared, the *yetzer hara* had grabbed hold and wasn't going to let go easily. Yisroel had no leverage, but he did his best.

"You can't stay here."

"I'm staying."

The look in Anchi's eyes was dangerous.

What to do? What to do? A Yid's life was at stake. Yisroel had a strong feeling that if Anchi stayed in Vegas, he would never see him again.

Suddenly, Yisroel had an idea.

"You do whatever you have to do," he told his companion. "I have to make a phone call."

Something in Yisroel's words caught Anchi's attention.

"Who are you calling?"

"Sergeant Peterson at the Las Vegas Police Department. Your old friend, remember? You told me he escorted you to your flight. I'm sure he'd like to know you're here."

For a moment, Yisroel thought Anchi was going to attack him. He could see the battle raging in Anchi's eyes. It was as if the angels who had sat with them around the Shabbos table week after week had shown up to protect them both — Anchi from ruining his own life and Yisroel from losing his friend.

Yisroel felt he used up a lot of his angelic protection that day.

Although Anchi was angry, the threat did break through his trance. Yisroel got him to the airport and onto a New York–bound plane. By the time they were nearing JFK, Anchi was more or less back to normal and his eyes had lost that dangerous glaze.

When they returned to Vegas, they came prepared. Anchi himself was mentally ready to deal with any challenges that might arise. Everything went smoothly, and they were in and out within a few hours. But Yisroel would never forget the look in Anchi's eyes when he threatened to pick up the phone and call the police. At the same time, he knows that he would have done the same thing all over again, because it was a matter of saving another Yid's life.

Chapter Nineteen
The Lives That Were Changed

Over the years, Yisroel and Leah had close relationships with so many people in their capacity as the official welcoming committee of Hineni. They had seen that what people really needed was someone to listen to them. They provided them with that listening ear, and the results were life-changing. It often doesn't even matter if you actually have advice for the other person. The fact that you care enough to give of your time and listen is enough.

More, that Yisroel and Leah were willing to share their own struggles meant that people felt they weren't talking down to anyone but treating them totally as equals. This made them more open and accepting of the Neubergers' help and caring.

The Neubergers met Dr. Jonathan Berenstein at Hineni. He was fifty years old and still not married. He was dating someone, but it wasn't working out. He started coming to Yisroel and Leah for Shabbos. Yisroel would tell him, "You have to have *emunah*. How do you know why this is happening?"

"You don't understand," Jonathan would say. "This is never, ever going to work out."

Yisroel went on to tell him stories of other people his age and how everything had worked out for them.

"But that was different," Jonathan insisted. "How am I ever going to get married and have children? This was my last chance!"

"No matter what," Yisroel said, "Hashem has His ways of doing things. All you need to do is have *emunah*. We will be at your wedding and we will see your children."

Jonathan had never met people with such *emunah*. In the meantime, he was still distraught about breaking a relationship that everyone knew was no good for him. He felt it was his last chance to get married.

Yisroel just kept saying, "We will be at your wedding and we will see your children."

Who could ever imagine it would come true!

"As a doctor," Jonathan says, "I see a lot of patients who are very sick, and I say to them, 'The doctor is not the one who decides what will happen. We'll do our best for you, but don't let the doctors tell you that you're not going to make it. Because trust me, if you have faith, it's an unbelievable gift.

"It's the same unbelievable gift that the Neubergers transmit to people. What's amazing is that they transmit it to total strangers. What, after all, was our relationship? I was just another participant in Rebbetzin Jungreis's class, yet they treated me like a nephew. They helped me through some of the toughest days of my life. I kept saying, 'You don't understand…' and Yisroel kept saying, 'Just have *emunah*.'

"Only last week I was thinking, *How lucky I am! How did this ever happen? I'm sitting at the Shabbos table and I have a wife! I have children! At fifty-three years old I had children! Who has ever heard of such a thing!*"

◆ ◆ ◆

Reuven Rosenthal first got to know Yisroel Neuberger at Rabbi Osher Jungreis's Monday night Gemara *shiur*. From the start he discovered that Yisroel understood his struggle working in the financial market, an occupation that completely contradicted his nature. Yisroel's empathy and warmth were a wonderful pick-me-up to help him face the coming week's battles in the trenches of Wall Street.

Usually, when two people meet, it's their commonality that connects them. But when they meet in *shiur*, it's more than that. It's the Torah that creates their true commonality, and because the Torah is eternal, their friendship becomes eternal as well.

But even eternal friendships have a beginning. And sometimes, those beginnings don't go as smoothly as one might wish.

Reuven also attended the Rebbetzin's weekly class at Kehilas Jeshurun, where she would always end her class with an open invitation to join Yisroel and Leah for Shabbos. Although Reuven heard this weekly invitation, his brain didn't register it. He hadn't yet experienced Shabbos and didn't know what it really meant. Spending Shabbos with another family? In the secular world, people generally stop having sleepovers sometime in their teens. So, like a person listening to a foreign language, he simply didn't pay attention.

But he wasn't going to get off so easily. After a month or two, Yisroel approached him with a personal invitation for Shabbos. Since Shabbos was a foreign concept at that point, Reuven wasn't sure how to react. Nevertheless, as his friendship with Yisroel steadily grew, he knew that he had no need to doubt his sincerity. He also came to realize that if the Rebbetzin suggested something, then G-d probably thought it was a good idea, too, so he should at least give it a try.

Shabbos was like nothing he had ever experienced before. Ritual hand washing, drinking from silver goblets, communal eating from large loaves of braided bread, singing songs in the middle of a meal — it was all alien to him. And Yisroel spoke about the weekly Torah portion with passion and enthusiasm the likes of which Reuven hadn't heard from any of his university professors.

For Reuven, an unmarried professional living in Manhattan, dinner usually meant a bottle of Coke, maybe a can of tuna in the cupboard, and a lot of takeout. Leah's lemon chicken and mashed potatoes were like a taste of Heaven on earth. But it wasn't only a five-star banquet of delicious food that she served. It was a five-star banquet of delicious food that she served with love. It expressed a giving and caring heart that served a guest not only to satisfy the body, but also as a means to satisfy the soul.

Reuven was also taken aback at the participation of all the children. That the children were even sitting at the table with the adults for a formal dinner was a foreign concept to him. No table for the grownups here and for the children over there. Not only that, each of the Neuberger children contributed their ideas on the *parashah* and joined in the conversation. Ari, the Neubergers' son, helped Reuven find the right place in the *bentcher* and graciously let him sleep in his room.

Years later, when Reuven went to Eretz Yisrael to learn, he discovered that the unique brand of Neuberger hospitality extended well beyond the shores of Long Island. That first week after he arrived in Jerusalem wasn't easy. He had come on his own, leaving a group of close friends behind. He had no family or friends in Israel, and although the rebbeim and students in the yeshivah were very friendly and inviting, he felt lonely. (Those were also the days before everyone had a laptop and cell phone.)

A few days after Reuven's arrival, he received a call from Ari Neuberger, who was then learning in a Jerusalem yeshivah, inviting him to join him for Shabbos with his older sister Sarah's family in Beit El. There he found another home away from home.

When Reuven married, the *chasunah* was held in Long Island, and it was the Neubergers who hosted him and two close friends, while their daughter and son-in-law, Rabbi Osher and Yaffa, hosted his wife's family. After the *chasunah*, when all the guests had gone home, Yisroel personally drove the newlyweds around town to deliver the leftover food to a local *gemach*.

Their relationship continues to grow even today, and the Neubergers continue to be a source of inspiration and support for Reuven and his family.

◆ ◆ ◆

One day Yisroel heard that a missionary group was actively trying to convert Jewish patients in a nearby home for people with physical disabilities. The person who told him asked him if he would be willing to give the patients a *shiur*, and Yisroel agreed.

He began delivering a *parashah* class there every Sunday morning. After a few weeks, there was quite a number of people in attendance. One day, Yisroel asked the group if anyone had an idea for a more permanent place for the class. A woman named Jane,* who suffered from cerebral palsy and for whom the class was the highlight of her week, graciously offered the use of her room. After Yisroel had gotten to know her better, he asked if she would like him to place a mezuzah on her doorpost. She loved the idea.

One day Yisroel discussed the concept of *techiyas hameisim*. Jane, whose beloved mother had recently passed away, could not control her excitement. "I'm going to see Mum again!" she said over and over. "I'm going to see Mum again!"

As in many parts of their lives, Yisroel and Leah involved their children in this latest undertaking. So it was that Sarah and Yaffa were introduced to Jane, and they became very close. It was their job to say *Shema* with her whenever Yisroel was ready to end a session. Jane would cover her eyes and recite the *Shema* with tremendous devotion. Seeing this woman with severe disabilities reciting the *Shema* was sufficient to move anyone to tears.

The success of the *shiurim* and the residents' love for the Torah they were learning helped convince the missionaries that this wasn't the right place for them, and they moved on. Of course, even after they left, Yisroel continued giving his *shiurim*, with Sarah and Yaffa in attendance.

Jane passed away at a relatively young age. Her father and stepmother asked Yisroel to speak at her funeral.

Yisroel described the unique relationship he and his family had shared with Jane. He spoke about how focused on spirituality she had been, and he told the assembled that after so many years Jane was finally reunited with her mum and how happy this surely made both of them in *Shamayim*, where Jane is now in perfect health.

◆ ◆ ◆

One of the most amazing Jews Yisroel has met is a young man from Ethiopia. Raised in a Jewish family that was religious back in Ethiopia, Menashe* was drafted into the Ethiopian army — are you ready for this? — at the age of thirteen. Of course, he didn't want to be in the army. He was too young and petrified about what he would be facing.

He was small, wiry, and incredibly fast. One day he fled, running into the wilderness that surrounded the base. Soldiers fired their machine guns at him, and the bullets whistled past on both sides, but angels were clearly protecting him because, against all odds, the bullets missed.

When he was finally out of range, Menashe was able to slow down and catch his breath. He ended up walking across much of Africa, close to two thousand miles (at times taking refuge from wild animals by climbing trees), until, after many months, he finally reached the South African border fence, which was electrified and impossible to scale. He found a nearby tree, scaled it, inched his way across a branch, and then dropped down onto the other side, into South Africa and relative safety.

Menashe made his way to Johannesburg, where he met members of the Jewish community and eventually ended up in Yerushalayim. He met Yisroel at a speaking program. Yisroel introduced his new friend to a *shadchan*, who introduced him to his future wife, and they are living a beautiful Jewish life today.

From the veldt to the Holy Land!

◆ ◆ ◆

While Yisroel was still working at *The Long Island Press* and needed legal advice, he asked a fellow editor to recommend a good lawyer. "I have a great lawyer," he said. "Bernie Landau."*

Yisroel and Bernie, who as a super-liberal Democrat was active in Long Island politics, hit it off. Their relationship developed beyond that of lawyer and client — and it was all because of Bernie's daughter and Yisroel's listening ear.

She had never connected with her Jewish roots and had begun investigating other religions as a result of her lack of spiritual satisfaction. When he saw that his daughter was becoming more serious about Messianic Judaism, a Christian movement, Bernie was alarmed. Sure, he was a liberal who believed in free choice, but for some reason, what had been so clear to him in theory was no longer clear when his own daughter wanted to live the life of a Christian.

Clueless as to how to handle the situation, Bernie turned to his friend Yisroel for advice. When he heard Yisroel's voice on the phone, he burst into tears. Real tears.

"Yisroel, my daughter was searching for G-d and I failed her. My Jewishness isn't enough for her. And now…now she believes in Yoshka! She thinks she can be both Jewish and Christian."

The pain behind Bernie's words was evident. He could hardly speak. Though an intellectual, he was also highly emotional, and he couldn't bear the pain of seeing his daughter reject her Jewishness.

"She'll intermarry and raise her kids to be Christians," Bernie choked out. "This is the end! I knew from all those questions she was asking us about what we believe and who we think was the Messiah that she was either thinking about becoming a rabbi or…this."

Yisroel listened with compassion. "Would your daughter come to us for Shabbos?" he offered. "She's welcome to be with us and see what Shabbos is like."

That same week, Anna* called from college. She wanted to discuss the situation with her parents, whom she dearly loved. She wanted to know that they would accept the path she wanted to take in her life.

It was Anna's mother who answered the phone. Bernie couldn't bring himself to speak to his daughter. The ache in his heart was too intense. When her mother extended the Neubergers' invitation to Anna, she responded, to her mother's great relief, "Wow! That would be great! I would love a chance to meet real Orthodox Jews who actually keep Shabbos!"

With Rebbetzin Jungreis's advice as their guide, the Neubergers knew that they should avoid addressing Anna's questions about the differences between Judaism and Christianity at the Shabbos table.

"Let her taste Shabbos without the focus on Christianity," the Rebbetzin advised. "Let her just experience what Shabbos is really like."

So it was that Anna experienced Shabbos for the first time in her life at the Neubergers' home. One of the most powerful turning points for her was when it was time to wash her hands before *hamotzi* on Friday night.

"Ari, can you help Anna say the *berachah*?" Leah called to her six-year-old son.

The two stood together in the kitchen, Anna the college student and Ari, the Neubergers' little boy. She gazed at little Ari, who was looking up at her with a big smile on his face as he told her how to pour the water over her hands and then guided her in what to say: "*Baruch Atah Hashem Elokeinu melech ha'olam asher kideshanu b'mitzvosav v'tzivanu al netilas yadayim!*"

Ari chanted the *berachah* in his sweet six-year-old voice.

And Anna's heart melted.

Wow, this six-year-old knows more about Judaism than I do at age twenty-three, she thought. *I need to know more.*

Within a short time, Shabbos began working its magic and Bernie's daughter lost her interest in Messianic Judaism. She went on to become a religious Jew in every sense of the word — and she spent many more Shabbosos with the Neubergers.

Three years later, the Neubergers hosted Anna's Shabbos *kallah* before her *chasunah* in the White Shul in Far Rockaway, where they celebrated with Anna, her *chassan*, her very relieved and tremendously happy parents, and all of their extended family at an authentic, joyous religious Jewish wedding.

Decades later Anna, who was by then living in Eretz Yisrael with her husband and many children, invited Yisroel and Leah to speak at a neighborhood N'shei event. When she introduced them to the crowd, she credited them for saving her life and for everything she had become.

At the N'shei gathering, the Neubergers understood for the

first time the depth of what they had done for Bernie's daughter. Needless to say, they were very emotional by the time they started giving their own speech. They couldn't help but feel a special connection to Anna's children and grandchildren. In a sense, they were their grandchildren, too.

After all, it all started back at their Shabbos table.

♦ ♦ ♦

Although Bernie Landau had been extremely worried about his daughter converting to Christianity, he hadn't been very happy (to put it mildly) with Yisroel for turning his little girl into a Jewish "fanatic" either. But Shabbos had worked its magic, and there was no turning back.

Bernie used to complain to Yisroel about how religious his daughter had become.

"How could you do this to me? Look what she turned into!"

"I don't understand you," Yisroel would respond. "Would you rather that she lived like a non-Jew?"

So it went on for years.

"We were at the wedding of one of Bernie's grandchildren," Yisroel says. "It was a few decades after his daughter had become religious. Bernie was older and not in the greatest physical shape, but he managed to fly to Eretz Yisrael for the wedding. At the wedding, Bernie and I had a conversation. He told me how happy he was at the way things had turned out and how much *nachas* he had from his daughter and her family."

And Yisroel remembered how it all began.

With a Shabbos.

(Author's note: "Anna" was a very special woman whom I happen to have known fairly well from many interactions through the years. Unfortunately, Anna herself passed away a few years ago at a young age. She was a woman who truly embodied Torah life in everything that she did. She will be forever remembered by the incredible family that she raised and by her many, many friends.)

Chapter Twenty
Serve Food and They Will Come

It was at Ohr Torah, the shul established by the Jungreises in North Woodmere, that Yisroel and Leah learned that if you want people to come, serve food. There was a *kiddush* in the shul every Shabbos, which Leah was in charge of, and when Yom Tov came around, the *kiddush* only grew more elaborate, which in turn drew more people to the davening.

Rabbi Jungreis, being Rabbi Jungreis, would make sure to go down to the kitchen and compliment the Sisterhood members who were making the food, emphasizing that it was their efforts that were pulling together the entire community. He was a master at making everyone feel appreciated. When he told them that they were doing the loftiest mitzvah possible, his words struck their mark because he really meant them.

In keeping with this principle, Leah would prepare a *mishlo'ach manos* for every person who came to hear the Megillah at the shul, as well as many members of the community, especially if that person lived alone. Many of those people didn't receive *mishlo'ach manos* from anyone else. The Neubergers' visit was often their sole connection to Purim.

They ended up preparing over three hundred and fifty *mishlo'ach manos* every Purim, which led to another tradition.

Every year, when the children were young, Yisroel would take them to Williamsburg in Brooklyn to Flaum's, which among other famous goodies also contained vast bins of every color and kind of candy you could imagine. They filled the station wagon and returned home, where the candy was accompanied by tangerines, nuts, and hamentaschen, and the assembly line was put into action, producing hundreds of *mishlo'ach manos* and turning the kitchen and dining room into a *mishlo'ach manos* factory.

The actual delivery on and even before Purim (otherwise, how could it all be done?) was another adventure. A detailed route and geographically organized list of names and addresses were prepared, so that all the stops would be made in the most efficient manner. The station wagon was loaded with cartons of *mishlo'ach manos*, and Yisroel and the children would set out to the accompaniment of joyous music.

The look of joy on the faces of the recipients was worth the entire trip. It was a day of happiness — the kind of happiness that comes from giving.

One of the widows they visited with a *mishlo'ach manos* lived alone in Washington Heights. She had emigrated from Russia long before and was an old friend of the Neuberger family. Until she became too old, she spent her days at the nearby Columbia Presbyterian Medical Center doing a unique *chesed*. Those were the days when Russian Jews were just beginning to trickle out of the Soviet Union. When they needed medical help, there was often a language barrier that prevented them from communicating with the doctors and nurses. She was there to translate, and this was a huge comfort to untold numbers of Russian Jews. In fact, she saved many lives.

Every year the entire family would drive to Washington Heights just before Purim to bring a special *mishlo'ach* manos to this wonderful lady. Just as she brought comfort to hundreds, if not thousands, of Russian Jews, so the Neubergers brought comfort and joy to her.

♦ ♦ ♦

No one knows better about the central role of food in outreach than Jamie Geller, the well-known cookbook author, who came to know the Neubergers — where else? — at their Shabbos table. (Her sister brought her!)

New to the culture of Shabbos meals, she thought, *This is great! What magnificent food! If I keep eating like this, I'll hit 250 pounds in no time!*

Enamored as she was of the spiritual riches at her hosts' Shabbos tables, the caloric impact of a chocolate mousse trifle at the end of the traditionally heavy meal didn't escape her either. It seemed to her that it is impossible to be confronted with all this fabulous food and not succumb to the temptations of overdoing it. Must celebrating Shabbos translate into chronic overeating?

"I didn't want my waistline to expand along with my Jewish knowledge," Jamie says. "But I love food, and Shabbos is like a weekly Thanksgiving banquet — or, actually, three of them in a row in the course of twenty-five hours. Now, that presented a real challenge.

"Then I was invited to the home of an incredible, prominent, and spiritually alive family. Yisroel and Leah Neuberger had been down the same road that I was now treading, and they had figured out how to balance the physical and spiritual aspects of Shabbos with exquisite intelligence and taste. My experience in their home was one of those life-changing events that turn on all the lights in a clueless mind."

Friday evening began with one of the most moving expressions *of Shalom Aleichem* she had ever heard. Yisroel sang as if from his soul, with all his heart, beckoning the Shabbos angels to enter their home and bless their lives. Jamie half expected to see some winged apparition come fluttering in at his call.

Leah stood by his side. Jamie took a long look at her.

She is an elegant woman, relaxed and smiling, trim and fit. She believes in exercise and taking good care of herself. Moreover, everyone in the family leads a healthful lifestyle. If I didn't love them so much, I'd be mad jealous.

It turned out that Leah was also an elegant cook. Every dish was delicious — not overdone, not overly heavy, not overly anything. That was Jamie's first introduction to the idea that the spiritual fulfillment of Shabbos can be linked to eating right. Until now, she had always stuffed herself without a care, savoring all the Shabbos delights abundantly available until she needed to sleep off the effects. (Cholent became the perfect antidote to insomnia.) Yet, some deep instinct kept badgering that genuine Judaism can't require such gastronomic excesses. Now she had finally met a hostess who cooked healthily, serving light dishes that kept you alert to all the wonderful things going on around you.

Jamie doesn't remember all the details of the daytime meal except that for dessert Leah served a pie she had decorated with fresh blueberries. What registered were the Torah insights that were shared and how impressed she was with the Neubergers' personal journey toward observant Judaism. Their family — children, grandchildren, not to mention numerous guests — lingered at the table, unhurried, just taking in the pleasure of being in each other's company and enjoying the Shabbos atmosphere. You could close your eyes, breathe it in, and be uplifted by its fragrance.

Then came a light, third meal — *shalosh seudos* — consisting of fresh salads and fish. At the conclusion of a delightful Shabbos of meals, singing, Torah study, prayer, relaxing, and napping, they reached the closing ceremony of Havdalah, and Jamie figured the food fest was over. But no! The family sat down once again to enjoy a mini-smorgasbord of cakes, as if they hadn't eaten in days.

It was then that she learned about the custom of a repast called *melaveh malkah* — literally, escorting the Shabbos Queen as she leaves — traditionally eaten when Shabbos is over. It's a very special mitzvah, one that starts off your week with uplifting songs and the lingering sweetness of Shabbos on your tongue.

"Looking back," Jamie goes on to say, "I realized that unlike me, the family had been eating sparingly for the entire Shabbos. They had enjoyed just enough of the delectable fare to propel them into a satisfied state of *oneg Shabbos*, but not a crumb more. So now they actually had room, literally, for the icing on the cake.

"I thought a lot about that Shabbos and learned a great deal from it. Leah fascinated me. I reflected on the fact that her warm home was always open to guests, yet she didn't seem pressured at all. If I were to live like that, I'd be a nervous wreck. How did she stay so relaxed?

"I think motivation has something to do with it. To Leah, making people comfortable in her home, explaining about Shabbos, sharing her experiences, is no chore; it's a mitzvah and one she relishes. She won't let something so potentially important and downright pleasurable become a burden. Burdens burn you out; mitzvos keep you fresh. Everyone at Leah's table felt relaxed because she had the time and energy to engage her guests.

"Thinking of her style, I looked for a few good rules I could incorporate into my life. For one thing, she wasn't out to impress. If preparing a lot of food takes up too much of your time, ultimately you'll resent doing it. You don't need myriad choices. The meaning of Shabbos can get lost in an elaborate menu, both for you and for your guests.

"You also don't need to get stuck on the same traditional heavy foods. You can expand your horizons and create your own Shabbos experience. With any luck, you might even entertain someone like me — a budding *baalas teshuvah* who was under the serious misimpression that 'eating Jewish' means downing vats of fatty, cholesterol- and calorie-rich dishes.

"'That's not it at all,' you will say nonchalantly, as you pass her a bowl of basil and garlic quinoa. 'Shabbos is a time to do what's best for both your body and your soul.'

"Don't be surprised if she looks stunned."

PART 5

"I read your manuscript,
and I couldn't put it down!"

Former Hollywood actor Steven Hill

Chapter Twenty-One
Yeshiva Ateres Yisroel

In 1978, Yisroel accepted the position of English principal and administrator of Yeshiva Ateres Yisroel, the elementary school that the Rebbetzin's parents had founded in Canarsie, where they lived. Yisroel dedicated himself to the school for more than a decade, from 1978 until 1990.

The Hebrew principal at that time was Rabbi Yanky Jungreis's wife, Rebbetzin Shifra (Teigman) Jungreis. Rebbetzin Shifra is a story all on her own.

In the year 1963 (the year Yisroel and Leah married), there was a television quiz show called *College Bowl*. Colleges from all over the United States would send teams of four students to compete against one another. The winning team earned a cash prize and generated positive headlines for their college. It was all very exciting and dramatic. Since the show was so popular, it was big news when Yeshiva University was invited to take part.

YU sent a team of four students, captained by none other than Rebbetzin Shifra Jungreis, who was then a student at Stern College. She made major headlines — especially in *The Jewish Press* — when she appeared on the show wearing a sheitel and led her team to victory for five consecutive weeks, which was a record for any university, let alone a Jewish one.

Rebbetzin Shifra Jungreis as captain of the YU team on College Bowl

Needless to say, Rebbetzin Shifra was a brilliant woman, the kind of person who could speed-read the Sunday *New York Times* and then repeat every word she had read. All this was combined with rare humility and selflessness. But the best part was that she used her prodigious talent to teach generations of Jewish children the greatness of Torah life. Through her work at Yeshiva Ateres Yisroel, she was able to get hundreds of young people into top-level yeshivah high schools. She remembered every graduate and took great pride in all their careers.

♦ ♦ ♦

Yeshiva Ateres Yisroel accepted children that no other school would admit. They took in children from the poorest families, families who had no way to pay tuition, and children fresh off the boat from foreign countries who couldn't read a word of English, let alone Hebrew. At that time there were many Jews with little Jewish education living in Canarsie. Yeshiva Ateres Yisroel welcomed them with open arms.

While the school had been established by Zeide and Mama, the Rebbetzin's parents, the one who actually ran the school was their son Reb Yanky. It wasn't in his character to press the impoverished families who sent their children to the school for money, which meant that it was left to Yisroel as administrator to raise money to keep the school running. There was never a time when the yeshivah wasn't under a huge deficit, and for years, Yisroel took no salary. The fact of its continued existence was an open miracle.

♦ ♦ ♦

"My days at the yeshivah began with a major dose of Zeide," Yisroel recalls.

Since his job as English principal began in the afternoon, when the students studied secular subjects, he had the mornings free. It was Yisroel's privilege to spend those mornings driving Zeide, Rebbetzin Jungreis's father and founder of Yeshiva Ateres Yisroel, anywhere he needed to go. Yisroel felt as if this was his yeshivah on wheels. He absorbed Torah just from being in Zeide's presence.

"If we went to Manhattan, we took the same route every time: Canarsie to Crown Heights (passing Chabad's iconic building at 770 Eastern Parkway) and continuing on to Bedford Stuyvesant and then Williamsburg. From there it was over the bridge until we reached the Lower East Side of Manhattan. The transition between Bedford Stuyvesant, where groups of tough-looking men hung out on the street corners, and (*l'havdil*) Williamsburg, where you'd see men in chassidic garb hurrying home from *shtieblach* and women pushing baby carriages, never failed to fascinate me. It was like going from Mitzrayim to Eretz Yisrael in one block!"

Yisroel used to think that he would be able to feel the difference in the very air even if his eyes had been closed. A step into Williamsburg and the waves of *kedushah* washed over you.

Many times, they would stop in Crown Heights on the way to Manhattan to visit an elderly shoemaker. He was a European Jew who had been repairing shoes for decades. When Zeide would walk into the store, the old man's face would light up as if Mashiach himself were visiting him.

On other days Zeide directed Yisroel to drive him to Brookdale Hospital, one of the main medical centers for the residents of Canarsie. This meant that members of his *kehillah* had been hospitalized, and Zeide would visit them to cheer them up and give them *chizuk*. He continued to visit the hospital even later in life when it was very difficult for him to walk. And whenever he walked through the doors of Brookdale, the head of the hospital (a parent at Yeshiva Ateres Yisroel) made a practice of walking at Zeide's side as he made his rounds.

In the weeks before Pesach, their route took them to Kedem Winery, whose headquarters were on the Lower East Side. Zeide had known the Herzog family, the owners of Kedem, back in Europe. Zeide and Rabbi Herzog would sit together in a cavernous room filled with barrels of wine as Zeide would purchase wine and grape juice for his congregation and for needy families for the forthcoming Yom Tov.

From there, they would often go to Rabbi Biegeleisen's famous *sefarim* store on Division Street. This was nothing short of a *sefarim* lover's paradise, high-ceilinged rooms filled with shelves of *sefarim* for which you needed tall ladders to reach the high shelves.

Before leaving Manhattan, Zeide would instruct Yisroel to stop at the iconic Ratner's Restaurant on Delancey Street. The coffee there was unforgettable, and Zeide — who remained in the car while Yisroel went inside — always made sure that Yisroel buy himself one of Ratner's delicious pastries to go with his coffee. Zeide was content with a coffee, but Yisroel had to have a fresh pastry. Zeide insisted! And Yisroel gave in. What else could he do? Zeide's orders!

Yisroel's association with Ratner's dated back to his own father, who had been a frequent visitor to the famous Manhattan culinary landmark during World War II.

Captain Neuberger's City Patrol Corps helmet

Roy Senior had wanted to fight for his country during the Second World War, but, since he was past draft age, he enlisted instead in the City Patrol Corps, a volunteer police force. With the rank of captain and about ten men assigned to him, he would spend three nights a week — after a full day's work on Wall Street — patrolling the Williamsburg Bridge, on the lookout for German submarines coming up the East River.

At midnight, when their tour of duty ended, the men would go down Delancey Street to Ratner's, which was open twenty-four hours a day and where the waiters all wore red Chinese-style yarmulkes with tassels. It was a classic Old New York Jewish scene. Roy Senior was particularly fond of the old-fashioned black pumpernickel bread.

As the days became longer, Yisroel would join Zeide for Minchah at the family shul, which was situated right behind the Jungreis home. In the winter months, he would daven Maariv there, too, after which Mama would serve them huge dinners with platters of food piled high.

This was Mama: always the giver. The yeshivah's annual dinner took place every year at the famous Aperion Manor in Flatbush and was catered by the Schick family. There was no question about the dinner being held anywhere else since Mama, Rebbetzin Jungreis's mother, was closely related to the Schicks. When the event was over, you would find Mama in the kitchen making sure that no food went to waste. Yisroel and Leah would stay for hours after the dinner, helping to load up as many cars as were needed to transport every drop of leftover food to Mama's basement, where there was a long line of freezers that Mama used for storage. Nothing ever went to waste, with the food going either to the yeshivah or to the needy immigrant families who lived in the neighborhood.

♦ ♦ ♦

One of Yisroel's responsibilities at Ateres Yisroel was to make sure that every child safely boarded the correct school bus at the end of the day. The bus company was owned by an ex-boxer who had two sons in the business.

One day eight-year-old Yaffa Neuberger spent the day with her Abba at the yeshivah. Yisroel was overseeing the boarding process when the owner of the bus company, an aggressive man with a quick temper, started arguing with him. Suddenly the man grabbed Yisroel by his jacket and pushed him up against the side of a bus.

Yaffa, who had been watching from the sidewalk, saw the man grab her father and shove him against the bus. Little Yaffa didn't hesitate. She flew into the street straight at the ex-boxer, who couldn't for the life of him understand where this little dervish had appeared from. One moment he had been peacefully beating up an English principal, and the next he was being pummeled by a flurry of little fists.

He released Yisroel on the spot and suddenly became almost deferential to the man he had been fighting with only moments earlier.

◆ ◆ ◆

Speaking of school buses, Yisroel was once raising money to purchase a new school bus. Among those he called was a woman named Maya whose parents had been part of the Neuberger parents' circle of friends and whose brother had been in Yisroel's brother's class at Fieldston, so the connection bridged two generations.

While Maya's father moved to America, her uncle settled in Israel. His son grew up to become a celebrated IDF general and then prime minister of Israel. His name was Ariel Sharon.

"The one time I met Ariel Sharon," Yisroel says, "was at the *levayah* of Maya's mother. He had flown in for the funeral."

Maya, a poetic and spiritual person, appreciated how Yisroel and Leah had adopted a Torah lifestyle and was excited about being able to help the yeshivah. She gave a large check toward the purchase of a new bus, but the check ended up going instead to a different project — namely, the school payroll.

Yisroel later admitted to himself that he could have tried to prevent the check from veering off course, but there was terrible financial pressure, as there can be in a yeshivah. He feels that he should have fought harder to make sure the money went where it was originally supposed to go.

One day, Maya visited the yeshivah. She saw the school buses, but none had the lettering on the side that would have indicated her significant contribution. That's when Yisroel became embarrassed, because he was usually straight as an arrow. In this case, the arrow went off course. Maya found out what had happened and was upset that her donation had been used for something other than what was intended.

"Neither she nor I ever forgot this incident," Yisroel says. "And because I knew that I'd let her down, the relationship between our families became awkward."

The guilt ran too deep. There were no excuses, and Yisroel had nothing to say. From that moment on, he couldn't bring himself to face Maya.

Many years passed. Although they didn't stay in touch, he was still consumed by guilt. One day he mentioned the story and his resultant guilt feelings to his *chavrusa*, Rabbi Shaul Geller, who said, "Why not just call her? Tell her the truth. You'll feel better and so will she."

So twenty years after the incident, Yisroel picked up the phone.

Maya's daughter Corey answered. When she realized who was on the phone, she got very excited and said, "I have to tell you something."

"What's that?"

"We talk about you and Leah all the time! Where have you been?"

When Maya got on the phone, the conversation was unexpected.

"I haven't been able to live with myself," Yisroel said, and he told her the whole story. Maya was grateful. She understood and appreciated the fact that he had felt pain at this, just as she had felt pain.

Yisroel was extremely gratified that he had made the call, rectifying something that had been on his conscience for decades. And it just goes to show you how valuable is the advice of a good friend like Rabbi Shaul Geller.

Chapter Twenty-Two
Life in Canarsie

Much of Yisroel's everyday life during the decade that he served as administrator was spent making sure that the Jungreises' yeshivah had sufficient funds to stay open, since the majority of its student body came from homes that found it very difficult to pay tuition. The school never had enough money — and that was before the city made life even more challenging for the yeshivah.

In the 1980s, the city of New York passed a regulation that made it a criminal offense if a private school didn't have emergency lighting. The problem was that many of the schools in question didn't have the funds to install these expensive systems. The upshot was that the city's demand was being ignored.

Some of the bright lights working for the city came up with a brilliant idea. "Take legal action against the principals," they said. "That should do the trick!"

This held serious consequences for Yisroel because he could be held criminally accountable for the fact that Yeshiva Ateres Yisroel lacked emergency lighting. Soon threatening letters began arriving at the yeshivah, summoning him to appear in court.

Yisroel was, to put it mildly, a little concerned.

Seeing that the problem wasn't going away, Yisroel turned to the yeshivah's legal adviser, Shmuel Prager, who was at that time the Assistant General Counsel for Agudath Israel of America. On the appointed day, Reb Shmuel accompanied Yisroel to the courthouse in downtown Brooklyn. The case was heard in a gigantic courtroom, which was filled with what looked like a hundred private-school principals, all of whom were facing criminal charges. As the proceedings dragged on, Shmuel left the room for a few minutes. When he returned, there was an excited gleam in his eye.

"I just got an idea."

Yisroel watched hopefully as his lawyer approached the bench.

"Your Honor? May I have a word with you?"

The next thing he knew, the judge and the lawyer were deep in conversation.

Suddenly the judge stood up. Lifting his gavel high in the air, he banged it on the podium and bellowed, "Case dismissed!"

The city's lawyers protested, but the judge wouldn't budge.

"Case dismissed!"

The second they heard the judge's pronouncement, one hundred principals jumped out of their seats, grabbed their belongings, and were gone before the judge could change his mind. Within a matter of minutes, the huge room had emptied out.

Yisroel turned to Shmuel and asked, "What on earth did you say to him?"

"As you saw, I left the room for a few minutes. In the corridor, I happened to look around, and suddenly a thought occurred to me: *There is no emergency lighting in the courthouse!*"

Shmuel rushed back to the courtroom and approached the bench.

"Your Honor," he said, "the city has put dozens of school principals on trial for neglecting to install emergency lighting in their schools."

"That's correct," said the judge.

"But the thing is, Your Honor, I was just in the corridor, and there is no emergency lighting in the courthouse building. How can the city put so many upstanding educators on trial for something that it is guilty of not doing itself?"

The judge looked at Shmuel and said, "You are one hundred percent correct!" He banged his gavel on the podium and dismissed the case.

The next day the story was headlined on the front page of *The New York Law Journal*. In the years to come, Shmuel Prager would go on to enjoy a successful legal career in private practice. He and Yisroel remain close friends.

As for Yisroel himself, the next day found him (and the rest of the private-school principals) happily back at their desks doing their job.

◆ ◆ ◆

Aliza Schaeffer* got to know Yisroel Neuberger during the years that he served as administrator of the yeshivah. Their interaction changed her life.

This is her story:

◆ ◆ ◆

Alan* and I met in 1971; we were married in 1973. He was born in a DP camp in 1950 to Polish Holocaust survivors. He came to America by ship in 1951.

I was an American girl with American parents. At the time I didn't fully comprehend what his parents had gone through.

Alan grew up in a religious home. His first language was Yiddish. As a child, he attended shul with his father and brothers, but he struggled to assimilate into American culture. His only friends were nonreligious boys from the neighborhood, even though he attended Yeshivas Chaim Berlin, which was located in East New York at the time. Alan wasn't happy in the yeshivah and fought with his parents until they agreed to let him leave the yeshivah after the sixth grade and attend public school.

He struck a deal with his father: he would always wear his yarmulke, attend Talmud Torah after school, and keep going to shul. But the pressure of American culture in the late 1960s was too much to resist. Today, he mightily regrets the rift and wishes that his father had lived to see what became of his middle son.

He would have been so proud of his grandchildren and great-grandchildren.

I grew up in a nonreligious home, although my mother lit candles Friday night and kept kosher for the sake of her parents. I remember driving to Coney Island in the summer on Saturdays. In 1961, my father became friendly with a rabbi who convinced him to transfer me, along with my two younger brothers, from public school to yeshivah.

I wasn't happy to be plucked from my second-grade class, taken away from my friends, and put into this strange environment. The school, located in Boro Park at the time, didn't even want to accept me, not until the rabbi made a plea. The school put me in second-grade English but in a lower grade for the Hebrew classes.

It was torture. Everyone seemed more religious than I, and I felt alone. Eventually I made friends with other girls who were also leading "double lives." After graduating the eighth grade, I attended public school with these same girls.

I couldn't have known that one day I would be grateful for those few brief years of yeshivah education. Learning to read Hebrew and daven were invaluable to Alan and me on our later path back home to *Yiddishkeit*. It would have been so much more difficult, even daunting, if we hadn't had that knowledge.

So there we were in 1971, two yeshivah dropouts, not at all religious. Alan had just finished military service; thank G-d he wasn't sent to Vietnam. American culture at that time was nothing short of insane. Somehow, and we're not sure why, Alan and I didn't get caught up in the wild things we saw going on all around us. Maybe we were drawn to each other for that reason. And, it is now obvious to us, G-d was watching over us.

♦ ♦ ♦

Our eldest daughter was born in 1979. Three other daughters were born in 1981, 1985, and 1988. Life was good. We lived in Canarsie. Down the street on the corner was a modern-looking yeshivah. It was coed and had a three-year-old nursery program.

The boys and girls exiting the school didn't look particularly religious. In those days, public schools didn't have pre-K classes; public school started at age five. So everyone in the neighborhood sent their young children to this yeshivah, which was run by Rabbi Jacob Jungreis.[13] I had no clue how famous the family was or what their mission was. Our plan was to send our firstborn there until she was old enough to enter public school. At no time was there ever a thought in our minds that this would turn into a long-term commitment.

When our eldest daughter was about to turn five, we had her tested for the gifted program at the local public school, and she was accepted. Our plan was in place. In September, she would start public school, and our second daughter would start the toddler program at the yeshivah.

All that spring I had a gnawing feeling in my heart. Our daughter was happy at school. She came home every day full of excitement, asking questions, singing Shabbos or holiday songs. She talked incessantly about what her *morah* said and did. The questions were hard for me to answer. "Mommy," she would ask, "how come we don't have a white tablecloth Friday?" Or "Mommy, how come you never buy challah?" By the end of August, I had made up my mind: we could do this for one more year. Just one year. Alan said we could probably manage it, and we were confident that the gifted program would still take her the following year.

But G-d had other plans.

◆ ◆ ◆

That year, pre-1a was magic for her. She hung on to every word the *morah* said. Like a sponge, she seemed to absorb everything she learned. She would come home and say things like "Morah Libby said I have to say a *berachah* when I wake up" or "Morah Libby says we have to have two challahs on Friday night."

Needless to say, Morah Libby became a main player in our family structure. Somehow, I didn't mind. In fact, I happily started taking orders from our five-year-old. I was already lighting candles

---

13. The same person as Yisroel's friend and mentor, Rabbi "Yanky" Jungreis.

every Friday night because my mother did, and I had to make dinner anyway, so I guessed I could make dinner a little fancier. Maybe Alan would even come home early for dinner, I thought. Now that would be really nice!

Actually, not only did that happen, but he started to recite Kiddush!

As the year played out, I started worrying about the following year. Months in advance, I was already fretting. We had both had our yeshivah education cut short. How could we do less than give a complete yeshivah education to our children? I thought back to when we got married. I had thought then that the crazy culture of the times couldn't possibly get worse. How wrong I was. It was so much worse! TV was getting worse; there was less and less that the girls could watch. The nice little Jewish girls on the block that our daughters played with were dressing like their mothers — let's say, not exactly *tznius*. My girlfriends started to poke fun at me when we didn't follow suit. "C'mon, you're being silly. What's wrong with it? It's cute. It's the latest style."

My worries about sending our daughter to public school kept me up at night. How would I tell Alan? What should I do? I kept thinking that maybe we could manage another year of tuition at the yeshivah, though the gifted program would no longer be available to our daughter. It was just the two girls; maybe this could work.

I waited until the summer to discuss it with Alan. We didn't need to send the girls to summer camp, I told him; I would keep them occupied. The money we saved could go for tuition. Alan never tried to change my mind or talk me out of it. He said, "Don't worry, we'll manage."

My friends were shocked that we decided on one more year of yeshivah. "That's your Disney money," they reminded me.

"So be it," I said, actually shocking myself.

This continued for the next two years. Somehow we made it work.

By the time our eldest was in the fourth grade, we had another entering second grade, another entering pre-1a, and our baby was ready to enter the three-year-old toddler program. Unfortunately, that year our financial situation changed. Alan was unemployed for a little while and decided to start driving for a private car company. It was supposed to be temporary until he could transition to something else.

But, of course, G-d had other plans.

With a mortgage to pay and four children in private school, Alan found himself working twelve, fifteen, and sometimes eighteen hours a day. I couldn't let him kill himself. I wasn't ready to go to work. The solution was clear: I didn't register the children that spring. It was over. I'd find a way to explain it to them. The kids would understand.

◆ ◆ ◆

In late August, about a week before school was to start, the phone rang. It was Mr. Neuberger, the English principal.

"Mrs. Schaeffer, why haven't you registered the children for next year?"

I started to stutter. After composing myself, I told him about our situation and the decision to transfer to public school. He said I must come to the school the next morning to speak with him. "We can work this out," he said.

I didn't see any way we could work it out. I didn't mind groveling for my children, but the yeshivah had been more than generous with us until this point. I knew there would be nothing more they could do.

The next morning, Mr. Neuberger reminded me that I had volunteered to help the school in the past by working on obtaining an important grant from the electric company. We talked about what I had done before we had children. When I told him that I had worked as a medical secretary at a hospital and had done medical billing, he smiled and offered me a job.

"It's done," he said. "There's nothing else to discuss."

I was dumbfounded. He said, "You need your kids in school here, and the school needs a bookkeeper. See you next week!"

◆ ◆ ◆

The monumental decision to keep the girls in yeshivah changed everything. There was no turning back. We would be safe until they were in the eighth grade. By then, things would be different.

Our friends thought we were crazy. "Why are you encouraging your kids to live a different lifestyle from your own?"

In fact, I had noticed that our friends' kids were calling all the shots at home: where to go on vacation, what new tech toys they wanted, what they wanted for dinner, where to go out to eat, and what time to go to bed. Disrespect had become the norm. We had none of those issues with our girls. We were respected, and we were in charge.

It must be the school's education, I thought, *or maybe not allowing them to watch TV shows depicting disrespectful kids who claim to know more than their parents.*

I couldn't care less what my friends thought, and thankfully Alan agreed. Peer pressure at any age can be huge. Sometimes I felt as if my friends were acting like they were in junior high school. But these were college-educated women. Maybe misery likes company, and they just wanted me to go along with their lifestyle.

Things went smoothly for the next few years. The girls were happy as they learned more and more about their faith. On their own, the two older girls had stopped eating foods that were not marked "kosher." *Okay*, I thought, *I'll start shopping at Kosher City. No big deal.* Another big decision because the prices there were so much higher.

One day, one of the girls came running into the house breathlessly asking, "Mommy, what time did we finish dinner?"

"Why?" I asked.

Her friend up the block was having ice cream cake for her birthday.

At that moment, something powerful dawned on me. If a nine-year-old could have such self-control and wait to have ice cream while watching her friends enjoy it, then how important that self-control would be when she was older.

♦ ♦ ♦

The next life-changing decision came in the early 1990s.

Our Brooklyn neighborhood started to change. A new government regulation known as the Fair Housing Act allowed low-income buyers to purchase houses with almost no down payment. Almost immediately, our beautiful two- and three-family homes started looking like boarding houses. Our neighbors started moving out. Anyone with children in public school moved to the suburbs, and I couldn't blame them. Crime soared. The yeshivah started to lose students. But we couldn't think of moving. We put bars on our windows. We were safe for now. Then it became too much. Even Kosher City closed.

But where would we go? We were being urged by friends and relatives to move to the new communities of Marlboro, New Jersey, or Staten Island. We were told that we could have a bigger house and no tuition. The schools were great there. We could lead a different life.

A big decision, but we decided that we couldn't do that to the kids. There were no Orthodox shuls within walking distance in these new subdivisions. Funny how things change: when we bought our house in Canarsie, we hadn't given a thought to where the nearest shul was. Now it was the first question we asked ourselves.

The vibrant Jewish communities we were interested in were very expensive. Our two older daughters were already in yeshivah high school. Tuition was high even with the generous scholarships we were granted. What could we do?

Mr. Neuberger came to the rescue. Again. "I know a wonderful real estate broker. She'll find you something you can afford in North Woodmere."

"I don't think it's possible," I told him. "We don't want to waste her time."

"Just meet her and give her a chance."

Well, of course, Mr. Neuberger was right. The agent was patient and wonderful. We were sure that she made very little commission on us. We were able to buy a house in a beautiful community, a fixer-upper within our budget and only a short walk to an Orthodox shul.

The kids were elated. A house we could afford in a neighborhood that we couldn't afford! For us, this was a new beginning. We started going to shul every Shabbos. No one knew our past religious indiscretions.

I think the biggest decision we made over the years was allowing ourselves to let our children influence us. I made fun of friends for letting their children call the shots, but this seemed different somehow. The world was spinning out of control, but our girls were home reading on Friday night while our friends' children were out dancing in bars and drinking.

We discuss this all the time with our girls, and even with our older grandchildren. We always remind them that things would have been so different if we had been weak and influenced by family, silly friends, the latest fad, or the latest "in" neighborhood.

Now, years later, with the girls all married to wonderful husbands and with wonderful grandchildren who are all attending yeshivos and leading Torah-filled lives, we can see it all so clearly. So many of our family and friends' children, who played with our children way back when, have married non-Jews, gotten involved with drugs, didn't marry at all, or are divorced multiple times. So sad! Their lives could have been so different if their parents hadn't been so concerned with the cultural norms of the day.

This is how I like to explain a yeshivah education to our family and friends whose grandchildren go to public school: We have insurance on everything we own. Our house, our car. We have flood insurance, life insurance, and health insurance. We pay premiums every month, hoping that we never have to use the insurance or put in a claim. Yeshivah tuition is the same: you pay every month for each of your precious children. But it's also different, because at the end of the day, you will get dividends back, dividends beyond what money can buy.

We think that's a pretty good deal!

We are so thankful to Yisroel Neuberger for going out of his way to help us save our children from the fate suffered by so many people around us. And just as he did this for us, no doubt he did the same thing for so many others. Who knows how many fine, upstanding members of *Klal Yisrael* are living Torah-filled lives today because of the actions he took during his time as principal of Ateres Yisroel?

Chapter Twenty-Three
A Stop on Wall Street

It was the year 1990. For the past decade, Yisroel had served as English principal at Ateres Yisroel, and he had done good work there, but he was ready to move on.

He sat down with his father and said, "I feel it's time for me to take responsibility to support my growing family."

Yisroel's salary at the yeshivah was minimal, and at times he even declined to take a salary at all because of the school's financial problems. He needed a job that would bring in a higher income.

"What do you want to do?" Roy Senior asked.

"I was thinking of a career on Wall Street."

"If you're ready to start swimming in the deep," his father said, "I'll speak to some friends and see if anyone has a decent position for you."

♦ ♦ ♦

There were plenty of people Yisroel's father could reach out to. Roy Senior spoke with Harry Gordon,* a major player in New York real estate, and he agreed to hire his son.

Yeshiva Ateres Yisroel made Yisroel a farewell party. He felt a little guilty about leaving, but the die was cast and it was time to move on.

Harry Gordon's firm had a division that invested in the stock market. This fund was managed by a young Wall Street professional named Phil Stern,* who was about ten years younger than Yisroel. A nice Jewish boy from Westchester, Phil taught Yisroel the tricks of Wall Street and served as his mentor. The two of them got along on a certain level, but Phil was totally focused on business, while Yisroel had other things on his mind.

Yisroel's first day at the office was the day after Pesach. The previous night, Motza'ei Yom Tov, Leah had been up on a ladder putting away the Pesach dishes when the phone rang and they'd heard that their daughter Sarah, who was living in Israel, had given birth to their first grandchild.

But there were health issues, which, at the time, were extremely frightening. The next day, his first at the office, Yisroel did his best to put on a professional face, but all he could think of was his granddaughter in the NICU.

♦ ♦ ♦

That first morning, a secretary showed him around and introduced him. Before anything else, she took him to the patriarch, Harry Gordon, who was ensconced in his palatial office. Harry stood up and they shook hands. He was about a head taller than Yisroel.

Looking down, he said, "What's that thing on your head?"

"It's a yarmulke, Mr. Gordon."

"We don't allow that here."

When he walked out of Harry's office, Yisroel's initial inclination was to bid farewell to Gordon Brothers. But he knew it would be a mistake to make a hasty decision. Knowing that he needed advice, he headed over to the Jungreises' at the end of the workday.

"I feel like quitting," he told the Rebbetzin.

"You're not going to quit," she said calmly. "You think it's so easy to find a job?"

"But the boss told me I can't wear a yarmulke!"

"This is what you need to do," said the Rebbetzin. "Go to

Claire Accuhair on Avenue M —
the *sheitel macher* — and order
a professionally made toupee
that you will feel comfortable
wearing during work hours."

Rebbetzin Jungreis was rec-
ommending a hairpiece that
would be completely indistin-
guishable from Yisroel's natural
hair. In fact, Claire, the propri-
etor, turned out to be an expert
at this. This wasn't the first time
she had been given such an
assignment.

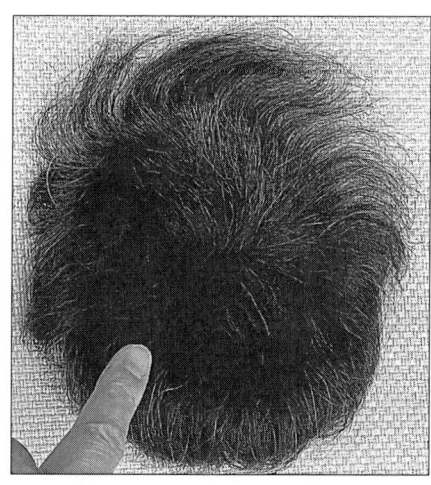

Yisroel's hairpiece (having been
stored in a box for years, it lost
some of its original color).

Claire produced something
special. It was the size of a normal yarmulka and was meant to
be worn on the center of Yisroel's head. And it blended perfectly
with his hair. It took two weeks until the hairpiece was ready,
which was fine, since Yisroel and Leah had been planning a trip to
Israel to visit their new grandchild. He had informed his employer
that he might be leaving immediately after first starting work, so
in effect he would really be starting the job upon his return.

♦ ♦ ♦

When they arrived in Israel, Yisroel and Leah went straight to
the hospital to visit Sarah and the baby and then straight to the
Kosel, where they davened their hearts out.

This was their first grandchild. Instead of the unadulterated
joy that should come with such a milestone, they found themselves in the throes of excruciating worry.

The Ribbono shel Olam answered their *tefillos*, and everything
turned out fine. The relief was indescribable. Yisroel and Leah
remained at their children's side until it became clear that the
baby would be okay. (Today that baby has children of her own.)

While they would have wanted to stay with their daughter and
granddaughter for another month, Yisroel had a new job waiting

for him in New York. So it was back to the airport and a new life in corporate America.

♦ ♦ ♦

The first day back from Israel, Yisroel walked straight into Harry Gordon's office sporting his new hairpiece.

"Good morning, Mr. Gordon."

"Good morning, Roy."

"I wanted to tell you that I understand what you said about the rules you have in place for your employees. Nonetheless, I have to follow Jewish law, so I've purchased a head covering to wear at work. You can't see it, but I want you to know that I'm wearing it right now and I'm covering my head in accordance with Jewish law."

Harry Gordon stared at his new employee, trying to figure out what the man was talking about.

"Mr. Gordon," Yisroel went on, "do you know why Jews cover their heads?"

"Yes," the other man replied. "My rabbi said that it all goes back to Israel thousands of years ago. There was a great rabbi who one day caught a cold. Because he wasn't feeling well, he covered his head. That's how it all started."

Yisroel realized there was no point in continuing the discussion. It was sufficient that Harry Gordon knew that he was covering his head. And every afternoon at 2:15, Yisroel left his office and walked to a neighboring building to catch the Minchah minyan at Bear Stearns. It was quite a large minyan, in the stairwell of all places, but there were probably about seventy people there. Then he covered his head with the yarmulke that he kept in his pocket.

This was his introduction to Gordon Brothers. Not auspicious, but certainly interesting.

♦ ♦ ♦

Big companies on Wall Street generate annual reports that are discussed at serious meetings. Investment firms make a point of hosting these meetings, at which analysts grill representatives from a wide assortment of American and foreign companies, asking for details of their earnings, projections, competition, new product lines, and so on. They're expected to know how much they will make (or lose) per share in the next quarter, next half, and even a year or years into the future. The analysts are frequently brilliant and keep endless lists of numbers in their heads.

Phil Stern attended these meetings, and since Yisroel was supposed to be learning the ropes, he attended as well. Every day, many thick (and slick) annual reports would pour into the office from different companies: Johnson and Johnson, Coke, Pepsi, General Motors, Apple.

It didn't take Yisroel long to figure out that he had no head for the numbers. The analysts could gobble up the reports and remember every detail, while Yisroel would fight to keep his eyes open.

Sometimes Phil would say to him, "I don't really understand why you're in this business. All you want to talk about is Torah!"

◆ ◆ ◆

One day a prominent entrepreneur walked into Yisroel's office. The owner of an innovative telecom company, he had developed a new type of telephone switch that he claimed was going to revolutionize the industry.

"How much does it cost to manufacture a switch?" Yisroel asked.

"Sixty-four thousand dollars."

"And how many switches do we need to invest in?"

"As many as you want. Ten, twenty, a hundred. It's up to you."

Yisroel didn't grasp the significance of the switch and turned him down. Within a year the $64,000 switch had a million-dollar price tag.

"During the two years that Yisroel worked for Gordon Brothers," Leah says, "he was very stressed. His stomach would hurt. It's a miracle that he didn't develop ulcers."

Yisroel remained there for two years. Finally, thanking

everyone at Gordon Brothers, he realized it was time for him to move on.

But now what?

◆ ◆ ◆

Since he felt his strength was visual and not numerical, Yisroel became interested in charts and graphs showing stock movement. This was akin to the technique that his father had mastered. This wasn't so surprising, since both Yisroel and his father were visually oriented. Yisroel hoped that this method would allow him to find success on the Street, and he broached to his father the idea of opening his own hedge fund.

At that time there were three young men who operated a fund in midtown Manhattan whom Yisroel had befriended over the past couple of years: Orin Hirschman, Richie Grossman, and Paul Packer. He asked them if he could rent space from them for his own fund. They cordially agreed.

They were exemplary Jews and smart businessmen, and they hosted a daily Minchah minyan in their office every day. And there was never a word of *lashon hara* spoken, all of which created an atmosphere that Yisroel sought in a workplace. It was a beautiful place to work (and no one objected to Yisroel's yarmulke!).

There was a certain trading technique that Yisroel had read about that he began using on a regular basis with a certain degree of success. He was trading S&P futures and beginning to make some money. He had started his fund with one client, his father. The plan was that when he had proved himself, other clients would come knocking. In the meantime, his father invested enough money to get him started.

It was 1998. For the first time in his life Yisroel was finally making money and the fund was beginning to grow.

With every day, Yisroel's confidence level rose, and he contemplated life as a successful businessman. There was one problem: the technique stopped working.

One year it worked.

The next year it didn't.

Yisroel would never be able to explain why the technique that had been so effective in 1998 suddenly fell apart in 1999. At first he thought that maybe he hadn't been patient enough and he tried again. S&P futures are extremely volatile; you can gain or lose money rapidly. When he had a losing trade, he would think, *Maybe it's going to work next time, the way it did last year!*

Life suddenly became very tense. His 1998 profits were a thing of the past. And then his father started to worry. The stress had returned, only worse. Yisroel would wake up in the morning and wonder if today would be the day he'd throw in the towel — or perhaps today things would turn around.

He had so wanted to make his father proud, so wanted to show his father that he'd inherited his genes. But in the end, he was forced to concede that, unlike Roy Senior, he wasn't cut out for the world of business.

Sadly, he had no choice but to say goodbye to Orin, Richie, and Paul. Carrying a cardboard box filled with his belongings, he headed home.

The fool will never acknowledge the truth.

The wise man recognizes defeat.

And Yisroel was no fool.

Chapter Twenty-Four
From Central Park to Sinai

The year was 1999. Yisroel Neuberger was no kid anymore.

What was he going to do for the rest of his life? He had worked in city government, and it wasn't for him. He'd worked in the newspaper industry, and he'd had enough of that. He'd been a school principal until he felt it was time to move on. He'd worked on Wall Street, and it hadn't worked out.

What now? What could he do with his life in order to feel like a productive human being who is accomplishing *ratzon Hashem*? He was feeling down. All the questions and self-doubt resurfaced in a torrent of emotion.

He was well past fifty and what had he accomplished? Sure, he and Leah had hosted thousands of Shabbos guests and been instrumental in inspiring them to live a Torah life. But inside his heart, he knew he had to chart his own course, to respond to his own unique set of abilities. He felt he had a destiny that had not yet been explored. The time had come for Yisroel Neuberger to forge his own path.

But where did that path begin and where did it lead?

Yisroel sat on the train on the Long Island Rail Road on his way home, with the cardboard box at his feet. He looked out the window at the passing scenery, the homes and trees and cars, all the details of thousands of lives flashing by.

And then, suddenly, a thought.

Maybe it was time for him to write his book.

Yisroel has always loved to write. It was the most natural way for him to express himself, and it was where his natural abilities truly lay. But when he had tried writing a book in the past, it hadn't been a success (and that was putting it mildly). The problem was, he knew, that at the time he had a gigantic void in his soul, a gulf so deep it threatened to swallow him whole. And because he didn't know what he was lacking, it was manifest in his writing.

Things were different now. He was different.

Maybe Hashem was sending him a message: "Yisroel, stop busying yourself with things that aren't right for your soul's mission on this earth! It's time for you to satisfy the cravings of your *neshamah*! It's time for you to write..."

Almost in a trance, he got off the train, found his car, and drove home. He deposited the cardboard box on the dining room table and went into his study. He sat down in front of the computer.

He was going to do this. He was going to write.

But would he find the words to tell the story? Would Hashem help him?

There was only one way to find out.

He placed his fingers on the keyboard and began to type.

♦ ♦ ♦

The words appearing on the screen were clear and beautiful, flowing like a brook filled with winter rains.

It was his story.

He wrote every detail, every nuance, and somehow he was never dry. He barely had to think twice before finding the right word or phrase. Writing the book was a time of *siyatta diShmaya* — an *eis ratzon*, if you will — especially coming as it did on the heels of such pain.

Most of the book was about his and Leah's story, but he included a significant section on the Jungreis family and their ancestors, and for that he spent much time interviewing his friend Rabbi Yanky Jungreis, who was intimately familiar with his family history.

He wrote about his journey from a Central Park childhood to the night of January 10, 1966, when he'd begun to turn his life around. He described what it had been like for Linda and him before that day, how they had spent so much time searching for the truth, how it had always been just a little beyond their reach, like the pot of gold at the end of a rainbow. And then how everything had changed when they met Rebbetzin Jungreis and all the guests who had walked through their doors.

Writing the book turned out to be the easy part.

The difficult part was getting it published.

Yisroel walked around nervous and worried that his "baby" was never going to find a home. He felt like he had when he was dating Leah. It just had to work out, but he wasn't quite sure how it would work out! Both seemed *bashert* to him — his *shidduch* and his book — necessary ingredients to the fulfillment of his mission in this world.

Sometimes lightning strikes suddenly and illuminates the darkest night. After a year of frustration, Yisroel discussed his problem with Rabbi Yechiel Perr, the beloved rosh yeshivah of the Yeshiva of Far Rockaway, who directed him to Jonathan David Publishers, who enthusiastically agreed to publish his book.

The book came to be called *From Central Park to Sinai: How I Found My Jewish Soul.*

Yisroel had found his calling, and he never looked back.

◆ ◆ ◆

Though Roy had been calling himself Yisroel for a long time now, he signed his books and articles as Roy Neuberger. People asked why he used the name Roy in particular for the byline of a book that tells the story of his life. Why shouldn't a book about his new life feature his new name?

The answer tells a lot about how Yisroel and Leah work.

They discussed this question with rabbanim and the conclusion was that Yisroel should use a name that would connect with potential readers who weren't familiar with the world of Torah. If all those Jews out there who were in the same place where Roy had been saw a book by someone named Yisroel, would they buy it?

Probably not. The name Yisroel would sound too alien. Yisroel wanted to connect to those who had never met a Yisroel but for whom the name Roy wouldn't sound strange. He wanted to speak to his readers in a way that they'd feel comfortable. That is how he writes and that's how he and Leah speak: heart to heart.

From Central Park to Sinai turned out to be extremely popular in the religious world as well. Observant Jews gained a new appreciation for the life of Torah and mitzvos they had grown up with, seeing how Yisroel and Leah struggled and searched until they found it. They also became inspired to reach out to their assimilated brethren. They gained respect for those who had rejected the popular culture and had come home to Torah. And they gained respect for themselves!

♦ ♦ ♦

After Yisroel finished writing *Central Park*, he gave it to several people to read, among them Dr. and Mrs. Leonard Feiner (whose son, Rabbi Eytan Feiner, is the well-known rav of the White Shul in Far Rockaway). Mrs. Feiner is the daughter of long-time family friends, the Russaks.

Yisroel first met the Russaks in 1982, the same year that Roy Senior and Marie Neuberger celebrated their fiftieth wedding anniversary. Two weeks after the anniversary celebration, Yisroel's brother Jimmy started complaining about a mouth sore that wouldn't go away. The doctors ran a series of tests, and he was diagnosed with cancer. It was a major shock.

Their sister Ann told Jimmy about a doctor in England who had developed a treatment called fast neutron therapy for exactly the type of tumor that Jimmy was suffering from. Yisroel called her.

"Your brother doesn't have to travel to London," the doctor said. "It so happens that I am going to be lecturing at the Hutchinson Institute in Seattle, next week. Your brother can consult me there at one thirty next Friday afternoon."

Yisroel would be accompanying Jimmy to the appointment. He called Rabbi Meshulem Jungreis and asked what he was supposed to do about Shabbos. Rabbi Jungreis contacted Rabbi Moshe Londinski in Seattle and asked him to find a place for Yisroel and his brother for Shabbos.

"The premiere address for *hachnasas orchim* in Seattle is the home of Joe and Adina Russak," Rabbi Londinski informed him.

Yisroel called the Russaks. He had barely finished speaking when Joe Russak graciously extended an invitation for the two brothers to stay for as long as they needed.

Yisroel and Jimmy flew into Seattle on a Thursday night and took a taxi to the Russaks' home. Yisroel still remembers the delicious fragrance emanating from Adina's kitchen, where she was preparing tongue in raisin sauce, as he and Jimmy walked in. The aroma of Shabbos made Yisroel feel very much at home, and he sensed that Joe and Adina were special people from the moment they were introduced.

Joe Russak was a successful real estate developer. He was also

Yisroel with Joe Russak

a successful ambassador for Torah and delivered a *daf yomi shiur*. For Yisroel, who was still new to *Yiddishkeit*, meeting a man like Joe Russak showed him what he could aspire to.

Although Jimmy opted for surgery instead of fast neutron therapy, he recovered completely and is healthy today.

After that Shabbos, the Russaks and the Neubergers became very close.

♦ ♦ ♦

Now, after Yisroel had written his book, Mrs. Feiner read the manuscript and told Yisroel, "You need to get Steven Hill to write a blurb for the cover."

"Who's Steven Hill?"

"You don't know Steven Hill?"

"I've never heard of him."

Steven Hill as he appears in Yisroel's PR video

"He was a famous actor before he became religious. Steven Hill grew up in Seattle, and my father knows him well. You should talk to my father about contacting him."

Joe Russak was happy to make the call and wasted no time doing so.

"Steve, I want you to read a manuscript."

"Joe, I have no time."

"Do me a favor and read one chapter. Even just a few pages."

"Okay, Joe. Just for you!"

Joe gave Yisroel the go-ahead, and he overnighted a copy of the manuscript to Mr. Hill in Monsey, New York.

A few days later, Yisroel's phone rang.

"Hello."

"My name is Steven Hill. I read your manuscript and I couldn't put it down. I love it! I want to meet you!"

Thus began a beautiful relationship.

"I drove up to visit Steven Hill," Yisroel says, "and we became close friends. Later, when we filmed a PR video about the book, I asked him to be in it, of course. (Who else if not the master of the medium?) In the video, he's reading *Central Park to Sinai*. Then he looks up at the camera and says, 'Words from the heart enter the heart...' It's beautiful and moving."

That was Yisroel's connection with Steven Hill, a great Jewish soul himself.

Shortly after the book was printed, Yisroel and Leah also sent a copy to a certain rebbetzin, who was in the hospital recovering from a serious operation. She was in such pain that even strong narcotics weren't able to relieve it.

Then she read *From Central Park to Sinai*. She later told Leah that reading that book was her only respite from the suffering. While reading the book, she forgot about her pain. For her, Yisroel's book was literally a life-saver.

◆ ◆ ◆

From Central Park to Sinai: How I Found My Jewish Soul was released shortly after Succos in the year 2000. Tsemach Glenn, a friend of the Neubergers starting from the days when he was a yeshivah classmate of their son Ari, as well as a well-known photographer of *gedolim*, pointed out that *sefarim* stores probably wouldn't stock the book because they were unfamiliar with Jonathan David Publishers.

"What do you suggest?" Yisroel asked.

"Let's make the rounds of the major booksellers and personally introduce them to the book. We'll go to Zundel Berman. We'll go to Moznaim. We need to get the guys who sell the books interested in your book. Let's meet after Minchah at Torah Vodaath" (where Tsemach was then learning).

On the appointed day, Yisroel and Leah drove to Brooklyn and met Tsemach. They had the books and were ready to make the rounds.

But Tsemach also had another idea.

"Before we go around to the stores and distributors, there's someone I'd like you to meet."

Yisroel with Rav Avraham Pam, October 2000

Yisroel and Leah followed Tsemach around the corner, where he knocked on the door of a private home belonging to none other than Rav Avraham HaKohen Pam, the legendary rosh yeshivah of Torah Vodaath. The rosh yeshivah was very welcoming, and soon Yisroel was telling him his life story, in essence the story of the new book. The meeting lasted a long time. "Rav Pam insisted that we keep on talking," Yisroel says. "And so we did."

At the end of their conversation, Yisroel made a comment and Rav Pam started to laugh. Tsemach utilized that moment to snap a picture of the scene, an iconic picture that was incidentally featured on the cover of *Mishpacha* when Yisroel's second book, *Worldstorm*, was published in 2003.

♦ ♦ ♦

They left Rav Pam with the rosh yeshivah's warm and gracious *berachah* ringing in their ears. From there they drove to Zundel Berman, a major bookseller, who accepted the book with no questions asked. The same thing happened with Moznaim. After Moznaim, they decided to stop at Eichler's superstore in Boro Park and asked whom they could speak to about the new book.

"See that guy at the back?" they were told. "That's Shuey. He's very busy, so I don't know if he'll have time to speak with you, but he's the one in charge of the English books here."

Shuey was only twenty years old but sharp as a tack. He was the kind of salesman who could sell you anything if he put his mind to it.

Normally, Yisroel might have been worried that he wouldn't find the right words to explain what his book was about. But not that day. Not after the one-in-a-million *berachah* that Rav Pam had just given them. Yisroel would never quite know how it happened, but they instantly became best friends with Shuey, who ended up reading the book and loved it with the kind of unconditional love that's normally reserved for the best book you've ever read in your life. Before you could turn around, there were gigantic piles of *From Central Park to Sinai* sitting beside the front door of Eichler's, and Shuey was telling everyone who walked through the doors, "You *must* buy this book!"

"But I don't know if I want it," the customer would inevitably say.

"You want it. Believe me, you want this book!"

Inexplicably, the best salesman at Eichler's had decided to turn their book into his personal favorite and sell it in a way that went above and beyond anything they could have imagined. Shuey didn't just sell the book for a few weeks. He pushed it from after Succos until Shavuos, and within about six months, Shuey had personally sold 915 copies at that store alone. This was unprecedented (except for cookbooks!).

"I really believed in it," Shuey says. "I wouldn't sell something I didn't believe in, so it's not like I sold it because I liked Yisroel (which I did), but I really loved the book. There was something special about it, and it got to me."

Back then Country Yossi would call Shuey every week to get a list of the ten top bestsellers so he could feature them in the weekly bestseller list in *Country Yossi Magazine*. And every week, *From Central Park to Sinai* was at the top of the list.

One week Shuey went to Lakewood to spend Shabbos at his sister's house. There he happened to meet Yisroel's son, Ari, who said to him, "You're Shuey Rhine? My father can't stop talking about you!"

Then Ari said, "My father wants to have you for Shabbos."

Shuey was hesitant — what did he, a young single guy, have in common with this older couple — but Ari promised he would be there as well.

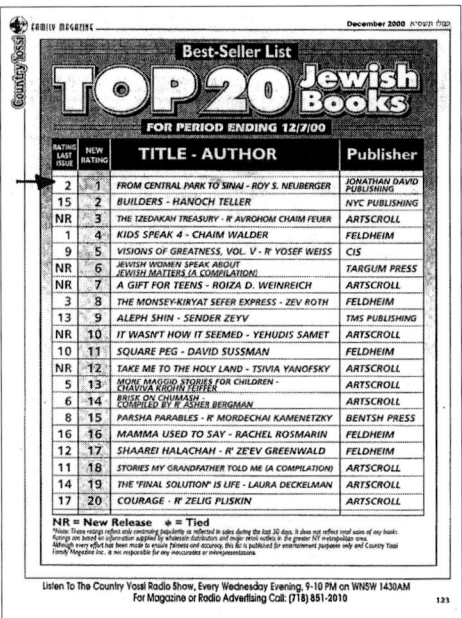

Country Yossi bestseller list, spring 2001

Shuey with Roy Senior

Shuey ended up becoming a regular at the Neuberger home. More than that, Yisroel became a surrogate father to Shuey after he lost his own father.

But when Ari got married, Shuey was reluctant to go. He was still single and didn't want to feel like a *nebbach*. Yisroel said, "If the family makes a wedding, you have to be there!"

It was a *potch* — but one given with love. "You're part of our family," Yisroel insisted. "You don't get to play hooky."

When Shuey himself got married, Yisroel made a *berachah* under the *chuppah*. After all, what was the question? He was family.

They are still as close as family today, over twenty years later. And it all began a few hours after they left Rav Pam's house with a *berachah* and hearts full of hope.

♦ ♦ ♦

The book didn't make waves only among Eichler's readership. When it was released just after Succos in 2000, *From Central Park to Sinai* was officially launched in Roy Senior's apartment in the Pierre Hotel (right across the street from Central Park). Many guests were invited, along with select members of the press. This was followed by a slew of interviews and book reviews.

The book launch at Roy Senior's apartment in the Pierre Hotel

Yisroel and Leah were interviewed on WOR Radio, a popular station that had talk shows around the clock. They were featured on news shows on cable TV and numerous Jewish radio and television shows. One late-night radio interview was with Joey Reynolds. The studio was located in midtown Manhattan. When they arrived at around 1:30 a.m.,

Yisroel on *The Barry Farber Show*

they found the host, the producer, and a bunch of other people sitting around drinking coffee.

The producer pulled Yisroel and Leah aside and said, "Here's the way it works. Joey is a tough host. He takes people apart."

Now Yisroel and Leah were getting a little nervous.

"If Joey likes you," he went on, "he'll keep you on the air for twenty minutes. If he doesn't like you, you'll be out of here in thirty seconds."

Nothing like a little pressure. In the end, they were on the air for ninety minutes.

At the end of the night, Joey said to them — on the air — "I'm a Catholic, but I can tell you one thing: you're the roots and I'm just a grafted branch."

"I never saw anything like it," the producer said to them as they were leaving. "I don't remember anyone being on as long as the two of you."

For months they were busy with all sorts of PR and speaking engagements around the country. It was a whirlwind. The Ribbono shel Olam had given them a way to make a *kiddush Hashem* and reach out to many people with their personal message.

So it was that the book didn't just create an international[14]

---

14. *From Central Park to Sinai* was translated into Hebrew, Russian, and Georgian. Yisroel and Leah have told their story in fifteen countries, including a massive *kiruv* rally in Manchester, England, and all across the former Soviet Union.

storm, but it was incredibly successful on a personal level as well, creating a bond between the author and countless readers who recognized themselves in the powerful prose that they just couldn't put down.

Chapter Twenty-Five
A New Chapter

In the wake of *Central Park to Sinai's* astounding success, Torah Umesorah decided to sponsor a book tour for Yisroel and Leah Neuberger that would bring them to speak at kiruv *kollels* all over the United States. Rabbis Nate Segal[15] and Tzvi Bloom[16] were especially excited about this idea. Rabbi Segal made many calls to kollelim and kiruv centers on the Neubergers' behalf, which led to programs all across the United States.

The next thing they knew they were flying to Boston, Chicago, Denver, Seattle, Miami, and Phoenix. Boston was the first stop and the organizers asked Leah to speak at the local Bais Yaakov. This came as a surprise.

Rabbi Nate Segal

---

15. Director of Community Outreach and Development at Torah Umesorah.
16. Executive Director of Torah Umesorah.

The Neubergers had imagined that since Yisroel wrote the book, he would be delivering the speeches. But they quickly realized that audiences wanted to hear both of them.

Before long, Yisroel and Leah cultivated a joint way of speaking in which Yisroel related their story up until a certain point and then Leah took over. Having been married for a very long time, they quickly developed a rhythm and a way of speaking that went over equally well on college campuses and at kiruv events.

The students loved the way they bantered with one another. Yisroel would say, "I was the middle child, which is why I'm kind of crazy…" whereupon Leah would interrupt and say, "You aren't crazy… just intense!"

The students loved watching a married couple who really seemed to like one another. Many wrote to them that they hoped their marriages would be like theirs.

The feedback was powerful. Yisroel and Leah struck a chord with their audiences no matter their age, affiliation, or background. Suddenly their days were action-packed, and they were traveling all over the country, going from one speaking engagement to another.

Part two of their life had begun.

A life of speaking and traveling, of sharing their story with others, of providing inspiration to *Klal Yisrael*.

A life worth writing about.

◆ ◆ ◆

Although Yisroel had imagined himself doing many things in life, public speaking was not one of them. But often Hashem has other plans for a person that he doesn't expect. Although his and Leah's speaking careers were launched into the stratosphere after the book release, it wasn't the first time Yisroel spoke in front of an audience.

The first time was on Chanukah in the early 1980s, when Rebbetzin Jungreis was scheduled to speak in front of the Jewish inmates at Rikers Island Prison in New York, and wasn't able to make it. She asked Yisroel if he would be willing to step in. He was willing, but he had no idea what to do.

"I'll never forget that day," Yisroel says. "It was Chanukah. Rikers Island is situated on an island in the East River and is one of the most famous jails in America. It's the main intake for all of New York City's prison facilities. You can see it on your right when coming in for a landing at La Guardia Airport. It's a tough place. Anyone trying to swim off the island will find that the currents are deadly."

One reaches Rikers Island by driving there on a causeway from Queens. No ferry to Rikers. The causeway is long, with several checkpoints. The guards ask a lot of questions and request papers and documents.

There are many prison buildings on the island, and it took Yisroel a while to find the right one. To enter, he had to pass through an electric door that slid open, admitting him into a long corridor with glass walls on both sides. As he walked down the corridor, security personnel on the other side of the glass stared at him... intensely. He felt as if he were under a microscope. At the end of the corridor was another electric door. Both doors were never open at the same time.

"I remember thinking, *I am never getting out of here!*" Yisroel says, "even though I was just a visitor. It is frightening to be behind bars."

A warden led him into a room filled with Jewish inmates. Yisroel began by telling them about Yosef HaTzaddik, who didn't allow himself to get depressed even though he was incarcerated in an Egyptian dungeon.[17] He told them that despite his dire situation, Yosef kept up his spirits and looked for ways to help his fellow inmates. He had every reason to be bitter, since he had been falsely accused and imprisoned for no reason, but he didn't let that deter him.

"When you smile at someone," Yisroel said, "just because you want him to feel better, you also feel better. That's the way it works."

---

17. Amazingly, this took place during the week of *Parashas Vayeishev*, which tells of Yosef's imprisonment in Mitzrayim.

It's always a challenge to tailor a speech to the audience. You want the people to connect to your message. Otherwise, what have you accomplished? The prisoners connected to Yisroel's message. It was simple and straightforward.

Especially since Yosef eventually was released.

Yosef emerged from a prison that was much worse than Rikers, and it happened in the blink of an eye. More than that, he became the ruler of Egypt. He rose to the top.

Yisroel also shared some of his own story. He told the prisoners what it felt like not knowing who he was or where he was. He had also been a prisoner, a prisoner of his rejection of G-d. He wasn't trying to push an agenda; he was just honestly sharing his own experiences.

Yisroel would always remember Rikers Island as something that started off as frightening but ended as a beautiful experience. The prisoners' gratitude was immense. Many thanked him for coming out on a cold night just to speak to them. Being a prisoner is challenging, and they were appreciative of his honesty about his own life struggles.

This is something that stands out about Reb Yisroel Neuberger: he wears his heart on his sleeve and says things as they are. That is why so many people connect with his message.

◆ ◆ ◆

Though Yisroel and Leah had spoken several times to Hineni audiences since the Rikers Island speech, Yisroel and Leah suddenly found themselves in demand as speakers after the book's release. Sometimes they would rent a car and go on a road trip, driving to speaking engagements all over the States. It could be in Boston, Chicago, Florida, Denver, Ohio, or Indiana, where they visited a host of *kiruv* centers and Jewish communities.

One of their favorite destinations was the Pacific Northwest, where Rabbi Avrohom David of Seattle runs a network of *kiruv* centers from British Columbia all the way to Oregon. Yisroel and Leah would land in Seattle, drive north to Vancouver, and then work their way south to Oregon, speaking along the way at many locations. Some of the towns where they spoke were small, and sometimes the crowds they addressed were comprised of just a few people. It didn't matter. The main thing was to inspire people, wherever their mission took them. Rabbi David would arrange the logistics. All the Neubergers had to do was show up and give a speech. The trips were so successful that they reprised them often over the years.

Yisroel with Rabbis Avrohom David (left) and Elinatan Bitton, both major *kiruv* personalities

One memorable experience was a Shabbaton in Eugene, a college town in Oregon. Driving there from Seattle takes a good five hours. On Erev Shabbos, during Minchah, a young man walked into the shul with his mother. Juan Ortega* had a very distinctive look, with masses of curls on his head.

While Juan's father was Mexican, his mother was Jewish. Yisroel and Leah became close with him and kept in contact with him after that Shabbos. Juan was a pilot but later moved to Michigan to attend medical school, and the Neubergers introduced him to their close friend Rabbi Avraham Jacobovitz, who had established a successful *kiruv* program at the University of Michigan, where the Neubergers spoke on many occasions. Rabbi Jacobovitz eventually officiated as *mesader kiddushin* at Juan's wedding.

It all began in Eugene, where Juan had first tasted the delicious flavor of Shabbos.

On one trip, which also began in Seattle, Yisroel and Leah spoke in Victoria, the capital of British Columbia. The rabbi in BC was a *chashuve Yid* named Rabbi Shaya Greineman, who had grown up in Bnei Brak and ended up doing *kiruv*. One has to take an hour's ferry ride just to reach Victoria, making the decision to establish a *kehillah* there a true act of *mesirus nefesh*. It's gorgeous but utterly remote.

One time someone came over to Rabbi Greineman in the supermarket and asked him, "Why do you have spaghetti hanging off your belt?" That gives you some idea.

◆ ◆ ◆

Yisroel and Leah met Neese Azose in Seattle.

For his day job, Neese worked as an engineer for Boeing, but he was also very involved with the Seattle Community Kollel. Yisroel and Leah sometimes stayed at the Azoses' home when they visited Seattle for a speaking tour, and it didn't take them long to realize that this man was an angel of *chesed*.

One night, driving from British Columbia, Yisroel and Leah reached Seattle at two in the morning. They had asked their host not to wait up for them, but as they pulled into his block, who was waiting in the street for them, fully dressed and welcoming them with outstretched arms as if it were the middle of the day?

This was typical Neese Azose *hachnasas orchim*.

During that trip, Yisroel was suffering from sciatica. He could barely walk, let alone shlep cartons of books (people always want to purchase his books after the Neubergers speak), so Neese graciously took the next day off and placed himself at their disposal, shlepping books all over midtown Seattle.

That day featured a lunch-and-learn program at a local lawyer's office. After the speech, Yisroel starting talking to a man named David Cassius.

"What do you do?" Yisroel asked.

"I'm a doctor."

"What's your specialty?"

"I'm an orthopedist. I specialize in sciatica."

Yisroel did a double take. "Wow! You are just the man I need! May I come to your office later?"

Shortly thereafter, Dr. Cassius gave Yisroel an emergency shot, and suddenly he was able to walk again. It brought new meaning to the *berachah* of *zokeif kefufim*.

Thus began a long and continuing friendship, both with David Cassius and Neese Azose. It was Neese who first suggested that

Yisroel with Neese Azose (left) and Dr. David Cassius

Yisroel write weekly essays on the *parashah*. Yisroel thought he couldn't do it, but with Neese's encouragement, he did. Those weekly essays became a regular column, which ran for thirteen years in the *Yated Ne'eman*. It also led to regular articles appearing in *The Jewish Press* and the *Jewish Connection*.[18]

◆ ◆ ◆

Another western city where Yisroel and Leah have spoken several times is Phoenix, Arizona. Once they travel out of town, they usually spend at least a week there, giving several speeches in the surrounding area. They spoke for Rabbi Jordan Brumer's JAC (Jewish Arizonans on Campus), Rabbi Tzvi Holland's *kollel*, Rabbi Ariel Shoshan's shul in Scottsdale, and at the University of Arizona in Tucson.

One memorable speech took place at the home of Dr. Steve and Lynn Kanner, to which the Kanners invited many friends. Rabbi Holland told the Neubergers that they were able to reach

---

18. Roy continues to send out these weekly essays in written and video form via email.

people the rabbis couldn't reach because listeners identified with them. As a direct result of that program, two couples decided to make a commitment to keep Shabbos.

One Friday morning in Phoenix, they had free time. They asked their host for suggestions.

"What do you like doing?"

"We like hiking."

"I have something perfect," he told them. "Climb Squaw Peak."

Squaw Peak is the second highest point in the Phoenix Mountains. At 2,610 feet above sea level, it rises dramatically over the city. Had it been summertime, they would never have considered such a climb, because temperatures in Arizona can reach 120 degrees. But it was just after Pesach, and the weather was pleasant, so they said, "Why not?"

They climbed and climbed. The entire way Yisroel and Leah kept saying, "If he can do it, we can do it..."

But after a while, they began to say, "How are we going to get to the top?"

Along the way, they met a man who climbed the mountain every day carrying a backpack filled with bottles of water for

Squaw Peak with Phoenix in the foreground

those who didn't realize how much water they were going to need. There were also people jogging past them. It reminded them of their days running up and down Mount Scott. It had been so much easier then. Even though they were still in good shape, Squaw Peak was tough. With effort they reached the top.

Later that afternoon, just before Shabbos, they couldn't help but ask their host how he could have sent them on such a difficult hike. More than that, they wanted to know how he himself had been able to accomplish such a feat.

"I've never climbed it," he admitted cheerily. "But you said you like to hike, so I thought you would enjoy it."

◆ ◆ ◆

For events in Chicago and the surrounding area, it was Rabbi Zev Kahn who would arrange Yisroel and Leah's speaking tours.

Rabbi Kahn, who is known as the Rugby Rabbi, has his own fascinating story. He was raised in a traditional home in South Africa, where he developed a prodigious talent for rugby. He was so good that he was chosen to represent South Africa at the Maccabiah games in Israel, and that's how he "happened" to visit Yeshivas Ohr Somayach and learned that there is something called Torah.

Back in South Africa, he connected with Rabbi Akiva Tatz. Then his new life began, continuing at Ohr Somayach, where he fell in love with Torah learning.

Fast forward and Zev — now Rabbi Kahn — is in charge of the *kiruv* programs for the Chicago Community Kollel. Yisroel and Leah had met him at a convention of the Association for Jewish Outreach Professionals (AJOP). In November 2000,

The Neubergers in Chicago
with Rabbi Zev Kahn, 2006

Ironic moment: Roy in front of the Chicago Society for Ethical Culture.

Rabbi Kahn was running an innovative program called Buffet of Jewish Thought. An elegant monthly luncheon would be served at a downtown hotel where businesspeople could hear exciting Jewish speakers. Rabbi Kahn invited Yisroel and Leah to speak at one of the gatherings, and the program was a great success.

Over the ensuing years, the Neubergers returned to Chicago many times. By then, Rabbi Kahn had opened his own *kiruv* organization called JET (Jewish Education Team), to reach out to college students and young professionals.

Yisroel and Leah spoke for JET in and around Chicago and on several college campuses. Rabbi Kahn didn't care if there were five people at a speech or a hundred fifty; every Jew was precious. Since this was Yisroel and Leah's *hashkafah* as well, they understood one another.

♦ ♦ ♦

In July 2004, after one of their speaking tours in Chicago, Yisroel and Leah drove to South Bend, Indiana. They timed their journey so they would arrive well before their eight o'clock speech. They were making good time on Interstate 90 when they caught sight of a sign that shocked them.

"You are now entering the Eastern Time Zone."

Oh no! One hour lost!

Suddenly they weren't early anymore.

They made it with three minutes to spare.

"It was a hot summer's night," Yisroel recalls. "I was filled with emotion as usual. I was starting to perspire. Then I reached the dramatic moment

Entering the Eastern Time Zone

in our story when Walter Grunfeld shouted at me, 'What kind of a Jew are you? Are you made of stone?!'"

At that instant, the moment Yisroel uttered the words "Are you made of stone?!" they heard a loud thunderclap from outside the room.

BOOM!

Everyone jumped.

A moment orchestrated by the One above, adding an unforgettable touch to a memorable night.

After everyone had left the shul, it was just them and the president of the community, Mr. Mike Lerman. They watched (and helped) as he cleaned up and returned *sefarim* to their places. It is his family that has, over the years, supported all the community institutions, yeshivos, and shuls and makes South Bend a presence on the Torah map.

Mr. Lerman was the last man out, shutting the lights as they left. This made a major impression. He was humble and self-effacing, while at the same time he was the well-respected benefactor of the entire Jewish community.

Soon afterward, they left South Bend, moving on to the next program. Another evening on the road, inspiring Yidden and being inspired themselves.

◆　◆　◆

About forty-five minutes south of Chicago is the town of Munster, Indiana, just a few miles from the shores of Lake Michigan. Rabbi Kahn put Yisroel and Leah in touch with a very special couple there by the name of Howie and Barbara Pielet, forever to be remembered by the Neubergers with admiration for the incredible *kiruv* work they did all by themselves for so many years.

Munster has many Jews, but very few are observant. The Pielets decided, on their own, to become a two-person *kiruv* organization, organizing speakers, events, and classes for the growing number of Munster Jews over years and years. Howie is not a rabbi but an engineer, a graduate of MIT. Yisroel and Leah were astounded by the Pielets' success in bringing their Jewish brethren back under the wings of Torah. Visiting Munster was an eye-opening experience, demonstrating what it means to stand on the front lines of *kiruv*.

It was a hot summer day when they arrived in Munster. Barbara served them cold gazpacho soup — the perfect welcome. The plan was to speak that evening at a program the Pielets had organized and then stay overnight at their home. There were a hundred people at the program, and the crowd loved it. The Neubergers' story is one that resonates with everyone, especially since they have no problem being honest with their audience and honesty always talks to people.

A number of years after their memorable visit to Munster, Yisroel and Leah were walking in a park off their street in Yerushalayim, where they now live. As they strolled down one of the tree-lined paths, they happened to notice a young rebbi sitting on a bench, deep in conversation with a *talmid*.

"*Shalom aleichem*," Yisroel said.

The rebbi responded, "*Aleichem shalom*."

"What's your name?" Yisroel asked.

"Yaakov Pielet."

Yisroel looked at him and said two words: "Munster, Indiana."

The rebbi almost fell off the bench.

"How do you know where I'm from? How do you even know there's a place called Munster, Indiana?"

With Howard and Barbara Pielet in Munster, Indiana, 2004

"How do I know? We spoke in your hometown, and we stayed at your parents' house, that's how I know. And your mother served us amazing gazpacho soup."

A conversation ensued. Yisroel and Leah learned that the Pielet children had moved to Israel and were teaching Torah with warmth and enthusiasm. With all their children living in Israel, the parents had followed them across the ocean and were now also living in the Holy Land.

Yisroel and Leah couldn't help but appreciate the outcome of this story. Howie and Barbara Pielet had chosen to spend their lives spreading Torah in the middle of a spiritual desert and were rewarded with children who became *talmidei chachamim, roshei yeshivah,* and *roshei kollel.* And then the entire family merited making aliyah and living together in the Holy Land of Israel.

Chapter Twenty-Six
Ice Cream in the Snow

While it was Rebbetzin Esther Jungreis who initially sent Yisroel and Leah to deliver many speeches over the years, their speaking career really took off in the wake of the success of *Central Park to Sinai*. Suddenly everyone wanted to hear them tell their story. They first embarked on the speaking circuit around North America, but with time they were contacted by people in other countries as well.

In January 2012, Rabbi Zvi Bloom of Torah Umesorah connected them with someone named Abdo Chacalo from the Syrian Sephardic community in Mexico City. "I'd like to invite you to spend eight days with us in Mexico," he told them. "We'll take care of everything, from plane

With Abdo Chacalo in Mexico City

tickets to hotel arrangements. All you need to do is fly down and speak."

There are two Syrian communities in Mexico City, one with Jews from Aleppo, the other with Jews from Damascus. All the material and spiritual needs of the members of these *kehillos* are well taken care of, with committees to provide for every aspect of their lives. Yisroel had never seen such a beautiful *mikveh* as the Syrian *mikveh* in Mexico City. The water was so clear he felt he could drink it. All those who come receive a warm bathrobe, sandals, and a wrapped toothbrush, as well as soap, shampoo, and other supplies. It was like a spa.

There were also two very large Bais Yaakov high schools. During Yisroel and Leah's speeches, the girls wore headphones through which they received a real-time translation into their native Spanish. Leah loved the girls, who were friendly and respectful, wonderful representatives of the community their parents had built. In both schools, after Yisroel and Leah finished speaking, a crowd of girls ran up onto the stage for a *berachah*.

Leah surrounded by Bais Yaakov girls after a speech in Mexico City

Xochimilko

Yisroel and Leah spoke two or three times a day during those eight days, including Shabbos. At every speech, someone was on hand to translate for anyone who didn't speak English.

The Neubergers spent one afternoon in Xochimilko, a resort area near Mexico City, known for beautiful gardens and waterways and surrounded by mountains, some of which are active volcanoes.

The Pacific coast of Mexico is prone to severe earthquakes. Shock waves take a matter of minutes to reach Mexico City. After a horrific earthquake that killed thousands of people in 1985, the government installed warning systems to alert people the moment an earthquake strikes the coast, but still there are only a few minutes in which to act. Every public building is equipped with an alarm system complete with sirens and an evacuation plan that everyone has to study.

"There was actually an earthquake while we were there," Yisroel says. "It wasn't so big, but we felt it. I was reminded of the time when I stood in the eye of the storm and helped the hotel

Giant Mexican volcano

owner put away his deck chairs before the storm hit us again, and I recalled the summer Leah and I spent living at the top of a mountain and lightning struck our cabin and fiery sparks buzzed off the metal shutters so that we were forced to take shelter on top of the insulated beds. When I was young, I thought that nature was a power in itself. When we were introduced to Torah, we learned that nature is a creation of Hashem, Who rules over every atom and molecule."

It certainly changes one's perspective on "natural" occurrences.

An email arrived shortly after their return from Mexico: "I am emailing you from the Bais Yaakov Ohr Hajayim. You were there on Wednesday. Sorry on my English. I just wanted to thank you because you changed my way of life. May Hashem bless you with the best *berachot*. Thank also your husband please. Thank you very mucho! Happy Purim!"

♦   ♦   ♦

Yisroel with Shlomo Axelrod in Riga

In 2013, soon after returning from Mexico, Yisroel and Leah flew to Riga, in Latvia, and to Vilna, Lithuania.

There is no kosher food to be purchased in Riga. On the day they arrived, the rabbi brought them bread, smoked salmon, cucumbers, and tomatoes, and that's what they lived on while they were there.

They spoke to a small group of Jews (there aren't many Jews there these days). One of them, a man named Shlomo Axelrod, gave them the impression that he was sleeping while Yisroel was speaking. The truth was the opposite. He was so overwhelmed by their speech that he could barely stop himself from breaking down. His *neshamah*, which had been sleeping for decades, suddenly woke up, and a spark was ignited by the words he heard that day.

Later, they received a letter from his sister, who wrote, "You have revived my brother. He's come back to life..."

Yisroel and Leah remained in touch with Shlomo long after their initial meeting. Needless to say, it had been worthwhile to travel all the way to Riga for the *zechus* of lighting a spark even for one *neshamah*, especially a *neshamah* like the one possessed by Shlomo Axelrod.

♦ ♦ ♦

Speaking in Vilna held great meaning for Leah since the Rabinowitz family, on her father's side, hailed from that city. They were introduced to the chazzan of the city's main shul, Shmuel Yatom, and his wife. Shmuel Yatom wasn't raised in Vilna, but his grandfather, who had been murdered by the Nazis, had been the

Yisroel with Reb Shmuel Yatom
in Vilna

Rabbi Chaim Burshtein slicing his
homemade bread in Vilna

chazzan there. Growing up, Reb Shmuel had a dream to take his grandfather's place at the *amud* where his *zeide* had stood for so many years. His dream was to carry on his *zeide*'s legacy.

And his dream came true.

Rabbi Chaim Burshtein was the chief rabbi of Lithuania at the time. While in Vilna, Yisroel and Leah ate all their meals at his apartment, since there's no kosher food available. One of the many rabbinical figures who live in Israel and commute to the former Soviet Union for about half of each month, Rabbi Burshtein had become proficient at making his own bread.

Every few weeks, Rabbi Burshtein would take a circuit tour, leaving his home at four in the morning and driving for hours all over Lithuania. He visited every community, from bigger cities to tiny hamlets, making sure every Jew received the attention he or she needed.

◆ ◆ ◆

Yisroel and Leah also traveled to Vienna, where they spoke before a large group in the magnificent shul and were put up in a quaint but comfortable hotel. In the morning, Yisroel walked

Old World sugar cubes

over to the local Satmar shul for Shacharis. When davening was over and he was putting away his tallis and tefillin, an older Yid approached him and greeted him with a warm "*shalom aleichem.*" He was holding a steaming mug of coffee in his hand along with a bowl of sugar cubes made the old-fashioned way, meaning that they weren't perfectly square, but each came in a different shape.

"Have a nice hot coffee, please," he said to Yisroel, with heartfelt Yiddish *varemkeit.*

The gesture warmed Yisroel's heart more than the coffee (although the coffee was more than welcome!). At that moment, Yisroel felt as if Mashiach couldn't be far away. A seemingly small act can mean so much to a person. The love and brotherhood

Yisroel with Rabbis Yaakov Kugel and Sender Garber (right) in Vienna

emanating from those words sank into the depths of Yisroel's soul and filled him with immense joy at having the merit of being a member of *Klal Yisrael.*

♦ ♦ ♦

One day Yisroel and Leah got a call from Shvut Ami, the first Russian-speaking yeshivah in Yerushalayim, which was established by Rabbi Eliezer Kugel. Not only did the yeshivah teach Russian immigrants how to learn, it also trained many of the *talmidim* to become rabbis in their own right and then encouraged them to return to the lands they had come from to teach Torah and lead communities in the former Soviet Union. The rabbis would continue to live and raise their families in Israel (the children needed to attend Jewish schools, which don't exist in those countries) and travel to Eastern Europe for two weeks out of every month.

In 2013, Rabbi Yaakov Kugel, grandson of the founder, was running Shvut Ami. He had *From Central Park to Sinai* translated into Russian, and then invited the Neubergers to fly with him to the former Soviet Union and speak with his people there, many of whom had already read the book in Russian and were thirsty to meet Yisroel and Leah in person. Rabbi Kugel would eventually translate another of Yisroel's books, *2020 Vision*, into Russian as well, a work that also went over well with their Russian fans.

Leah and Yisroel had grown up hearing about the mystique of the Russian winter, and here they would be walking right through the snowy door. Ironically, although temperatures had been well below zero before the Neubergers arrived, that winter turned out to be mild by Russian standards. During their trip, temperatures never dropped lower than seventeen degrees Fahrenheit. To put things in perspective, when they flew to Edmonton, Canada, the temperatures were way below zero. "Someone in Edmonton had moved there from Texas years earlier," Yisroel recounts. "He told me that the first time he got there, it was fifty below zero. He was warned that if he went outside with exposed skin for more than thirty seconds, he would definitely get frostbite."

Compared to that, Russia was a piece of cake.

◆ ◆ ◆

So it was that in January 2013, Yisroel and Leah flew to Moscow from Israel with Rabbi and Rebbetzin Kugel and Richie Levine, Shvut Ami's public relations director. The flight itself was four and a half hours — no big deal — and it was afternoon when they landed.

When they reached passport control, the official faces staring at them were grim and unsmiling. This led to a little bit of a comic scene where Yisroel misunderstood directions and tried to make his way through a gate that was locked. He then stepped backward and bumped into Leah. Yisroel was sent through one turnstile, Leah through the next, and no matter how they tried, they just kept on getting things wrong, all this under the blank stare of the Russian border control agent whose stoic face never changed expression throughout the show. The scene, had it been

Leah with the Kugels and Richie Levine at the Moscow airport

In front of the Moscow hotel with the Kugels

filmed, could have been titled, "Slapstick Comedy at the Moscow airport." Eventually they got through passport control and met up with the Kugels and Richie Levine.

They took a cab into the center of Moscow. Traffic was intense, and the drive took a while. They passed through a long stretch of countryside before entering the city itself, and when they finally reached Moscow, they drove past mile after mile of drab Soviet-style tenement buildings, each giving off prison fortress vibes. Only when they had reached the center of the city, where some of the neighborhoods had been built before the Russian Revolution, were they able to see any architecture with heart and soul.

Finally, the taxi dropped them off at their hotel, a nice little place, complete with all the necessary amenities and a bowl of fruit on the coffee table. They were given a few hours to rest, and that night they went out to give their first two speeches of the trip at the Moscow *kollel* and at a *kiruv* center.

♦ ♦ ♦

The excitement that greeted them when they walked through

the doors of the *kollel* was palpable. This wasn't a place that boasted many visitors. That the Neubergers had chosen to make the trip was enormously appreciated by the local religious community, many of whom had read Yisroel's book and were anxiously waiting to hear what he and Leah had to say.

Minutes after their arrival, Yisroel was telling their story, and they found that their message was received just as clearly as it had in the States, and maybe even better, since the Russian Jews were able to relate completely to their tale of an endless search for meaning.

Rabbi Yaakov Baum, Shvut Ami's *rosh kollel*, was the man on the scene, which was interesting, since he himself didn't speak any Russian, communicating instead in Hebrew and his special brand of warmth. Yisroel and Leah spoke English themselves throughout the trip. Some of the local Yidden inevitably spoke their language, but there was also a translator on hand at the speeches for those who spoke only Russian.

From the *kollel*, they drove to the *kiruv* center, which was run

Speaking at the Moscow *kollel*

by Mrs. Sarah Katz, and once again, they found a room filled with young Jews who were ready and eager to listen to every word they had to say.

It was an auspicious way to start a trip.

◆ ◆ ◆

They ate supper that night at a restaurant located in the magnificent Moscow Choral Synagogue, which was probably more than a hundred years old. The restaurant featured soft, colored lighting with elegant drapes, tables, and chairs that brought to mind the era of the czars. The setting also brought back memories of the traveling Yisroel and Leah had done in Europe when they were students at Oxford University. Tea was served along with those old-fashioned sugar cubes. The food was surprisingly good, with a wide array of salads and delicious main courses. All in all, it was hard to reconcile the idea of a Russia that boasted abundant kosher food with the days of the Soviet Union, which were not so far in the past.

The Moscow Choral Synagogue

Leah at the restaurant in the Moscow shul

♦ ♦ ♦

They were picked up from their hotel the next day at noon. It was Erev Shabbos and the day was extremely short. (During the winter, the sun sets in Moscow as early as 3:56 p.m.) The van would be taking them on a forty-mile drive to the village of Popovka, which was home to the biggest yeshivah in Russia, Toras Chaim, run by an Israeli rosh yeshivah, Rabbi Moshe Lebel.

It was a fairly isolated area, situated in the middle of a forest. This was where they were scheduled to spend Shabbos. A major program was planned, with people traveling to the yeshivah from all over the country to hear them speak.

The van driver spoke only Russian, of which Richie Levine spoke a mere smattering (not enough to really understand or be understood), while the rest of them couldn't communicate with the driver at all.

It took time to get out of Moscow, and after an hour on the road, it was already beginning to get noticeably darker, even though it was still early afternoon.

Welcome to winter in Russia.

On a regular day the onset of night would have made no difference, but with Shabbos coming, there was a sense of urgency about reaching their destination, especially in a country where they were unable to communicate.

They had been assured that "everyone" in Popovka would be able to give them directions in case they got lost. When they reached there, however, the driver asked the few people whom they saw on the streets how to get to the yeshivah. No one knew what he was talking about. The general response ranged from "What yeshivah?" to "What's a yeshivah?"

Not encouraging.

The sky was getting darker. No matter whom they asked, it seemed no one in the village had ever heard of a yeshivah situated in the nearby forest.

They called Mrs. Katz in Moscow, who is Russian. Although she was able to give the driver directions, he was having trouble figuring out what she meant since there were no street signs. The sky was growing ever darker, and the passengers in the van were getting nervous, not knowing whether they were going to make it to the yeshivah, or even whether there was a yeshivah at all. Then the driver found a grocery store (in a log cabin) and went inside to see if anyone perhaps knew where the yeshivah was.

He emerged a few minutes later with a man in his early twenties who was eating an ice cream cone. (Remember, the ground was covered with snow.) The man got in the van and announced (in Russian) that he was going to help them. He kept on licking his ice cream cone even as he gave them directions. And then the newcomer gave the moment another surrealistic twist when he tried handing out ice cream to everyone in the van.

"Ice cream for everyone! For you and for you... What about you?"

Everyone, of course, turned him down. Unfazed by their polite refusals, he continued licking his cone with enjoyment.

He began telling the driver where to go: right, left, then right again. Soon they had arrived at the edge of the village.

"Stay on this road," he told the driver.

"And go where?"

"Straight. That's all. Just keep on going. That will take you where you need to go. I'm getting out here. Good luck!"

With that, Mr. Ice Cream waved goodbye and left the van.

The sky was even darker now, the sun a ball of orange light hovering ever closer to the horizon, which they glimpsed through the thick trees of the endless Russian forest.

Following the directions, they continued driving down the road, which led them deeper into the forest. Soon the road grew narrow, and then narrower. The trees on either side brushed the windows with their leaves and branches. The snow was much thicker here, and the wheels were having trouble gaining traction. Just as they thought the situation couldn't get worse, they realized that, well, things had gotten a lot worse, because the road suddenly ended in a snowbank.

The friendly, smiling, ice-cream-licking Russian had played a trick on them, sending them on a road to nowhere. He had known

Arriving at Yeshivas Toras Chaim just before Shabbos

they would get lost and that it would be extremely challenging for them to turn around in the middle of the forest. Yet he had been very happy to send a vanload of Jewish visitors exactly where they didn't want to be at a time that could hardly have been worse.

The driver backed down the road, through the snow, until it widened enough for him to make a U-turn. Of course, by that time the sun had descended ominously, and the eastern sky was turning dark.

As they sat on the road with no place to go, they started to worry in earnest that they would find themselves stranded in a van in the middle of a Russian forest for Shabbos, without a shul, minyan, kosher food, or shelter. At that moment, it seemed as if they were starring in a very dark Russian drama.

And then, just when things were looking totally bleak, they noticed a taxi heading in their direction. The van driver began honking for the taxi to stop. He got out and asked the cab driver if he knew about the yeshivah.

"Yes," the taxi driver said, "I know where the yeshivah is."

True to his word, he directed them to the yeshivah (Yisroel had started to wonder if it really existed), and suddenly, they were there.

Chapter Twenty-Seven

A Bachur
Named Benyamin

You had to see it to believe it.

They had left the village on yet another road through the forest, equally rutted, narrow, and snow-covered, but this time, after driving through the trees for a couple of minutes, they suddenly reached a clearing, and there they found Yeshiva Toras Chaim. Finally.

It was a large complex, ironically consisting of buildings that had previously been used as a vacation spot by none other than the KGB. Now they were home to *yeshivah bachurim* who sat and learned Torah day and night.

The "KGB hotel," where agents had been sent for vacation (or training for secret missions) by the Communist regime had been transformed. The apartments where agents used to stay had been turned into a dorm or living quarters for *kollel* families. The spacious entertainment hall was being used as a *beis midrash*.

The Toras Chaim *beis midrash* was packed that Friday night, and Yisroel opened his siddur with a heart full of gratitude, still not quite able to believe that they had made it. Leah, standing in the women's section of a shul that had served as an entertainment

The Toras Chaim *beis midrash*, a former KGB entertainment hall

hall for KGB officers, couldn't get over the fact that they were davening in such a place. Just listening to the sound of the Russian *yeshivah bachurim* davening Minchah, Kabbalas Shabbos, and Maariv was enough to bring her to tears.

Yisroel was sitting next to the *bachur* who was serving as the chazzan and couldn't help but be moved by his pleasant voice, demeanor, and *nusach*. After davening, Yisroel was introduced to him. His name was Benyamin, and he was soft-spoken and kind. After Shabbos, Yisroel found out that Benyamin was suffering from a serious medical condition that was very difficult to treat.

◆ ◆ ◆

After davening and the *seudah*, there was a delightful *oneg Shabbos*, and both Yisroel and Leah spoke.

The translator that night was a young handsome *bachur* who, they later learned, had been a Russian movie star before discovering Torah and doing *teshuvah*. Somewhat akin to Steven Hill, who gave up a life in Hollywood for Torah and Chassidus, this young man had given up the screen and stage and didn't seem to have any regrets. He was articulate and spoke beautifully, and after just a few minutes, it was clear why he had been a movie star before leaving that world.

"The more I spoke and told my story," Yisroel says, "the more this *bachur* got into it. At one point, he broke down and started to cry, recognizing himself in the story I was telling. Soon he wasn't able to speak, he was crying so hard. It was around the moment when I had my big breakthrough (*Are you there, G-d?*) back in Ann Arbor during the winter of 1966."

The *bachur* was so choked up from sheer emotion he couldn't speak. In the end, he just sat down, and someone else had to take over. The only words they were able to make out from him before he sat down were "This is my story... This is my story..."

So it went on a Friday night in the middle of the Russian forest, with snowdrifts on every side, as they sat and talked about what it means to be Jewish.

Yisroel and Leah had initially wondered what they had in common with a group of Russian Jews who came from a different culture and a different world. By the time they had finished giving their speech, everyone there felt like family and the atmosphere was charged. As they stood in the middle of that crowded room, they felt as if they were all one big, loving family. The boys came over to give Yisroel a hug and told him, "You have to come back to Russia. We'll get hundreds of people together to hear your speech next time you're here," while the women surrounded Leah as if they never wanted to let go.

It was as if Yisroel and Leah were the grandparents they never had, and they wanted to adopt them and make them theirs.

Many would do just that.

♦ ♦ ♦

Shabbos had been over for about two hours when the sound of singing wafted into the building from outside. It took Yisroel and Leah a few seconds to grasp that the yeshivah's *melaveh malkah* was taking place outside, in the snow. The *bachurim* had built a huge bonfire, and the aroma of roasting chicken spread to every corner. There were no side dishes that night, just the freshest, most delicious roast chicken you could imagine and as much vodka as you could desire.

Since the event was happening outside in the middle of the

Melaveh malkah in the snow…with vodka

Russian winter, a few shots of vodka were actually quite necessary to keep the heart pumping and the blood circulating.

Everyone was so friendly, wanting a turn to talk to them, smiling from ear to ear (a far cry from the Russians at the airport!). Then the *bachurim* started to dance, right there in the snow. Everyone joined hands, and the sound of music filled the air. Yisroel and Leah felt like they were dreaming.

"*Shir HaMa'alos…*" The words of the song soared to the heavens. "When Hashem will return the captivity of Tzion, we will be like dreamers. Then our mouths will be filled with laughter and our tongues with glad song…"

A *melaveh malkah* Russian style in a former KGB retreat.

In the snow.

With chicken and vodka.

◆ ◆ ◆

Later that night, when silence had finally settled on the yeshivah, Yisroel asked the rosh yeshivah about Benyamin. The rosh

Yisroel's group with the rosh yeshivah of Toras Chaim,
Rabbi Moshe Lebel, on Motza'ei Shabbos

yeshivah told him that Benyamin had already undergone surgery in Russia, but the condition from which he had suffered
had returned.

"What's going to be?" Yisroel asked the rosh yeshivah.

Then, suddenly, Yisroel had an idea.

There was a young woman named Ellen Silber who had been
a frequent Shabbos guest at the Neuberger home. Ellen was a
top-ranked nurse in charge of the operating room at a prominent
Manhattan hospital. She had reached a point in her career where
she was able to work with one doctor exclusively. It happened
that this doctor was the world's top expert in the exact condition
from which Benyamin suffered.

Yisroel had even met the doctor. It all began when a family
started attending Congregation Ohr Torah, the Jungreises' shul,
years earlier. One of the boys in the shul had a condition very
similar to Benyamin's, and no other doctor was willing to operate
because of the danger involved. In the end, the surgery was successful.

Benyamin under the *chuppah* in Moscow

Since the Neubergers knew the surgeon and the OR nurse, they were perfectly placed to help Benyamin. (And some people say that they don't see Hashem in the world...) Now the question became how to accomplish this, because another operation in Russia was out of the question.

As soon as they returned home, Yisroel and others began collecting money so that they could bring Benyamin to America for the complex and expensive operation. When they succeeded in putting together the funds, Benyamin and his mother flew to New York. They stayed for about six weeks until the doctor declared Benyamin fit to return. A year later, he returned for another operation. Both operations were successful.

A year later Yisroel and Leah Neuberger were invited to attend Benyamin's wedding in Moscow.

◆ ◆ ◆

Yisroel and Leah would return to Moscow a few years later, in 2018.

Rabbi Aryeh Katzin is the founder of the Russian American Jewish Experience (RAJE), where Yisroel and Leah have spoken

The midnight sun touches the horizon on the flight to Moscow

on many occasions. He also publishes two Russian-language newspapers and runs a popular radio show on which Yisroel and Leah were interviewed. A *talmid* of the Shvut Ami yeshivah, Rabbi Katzin was originally brought to the United States by Rav Elya Svei, the late rosh yeshivah of the Talmudical Yeshiva of Philadelphia, to establish Sinai Academy, a highly successful *kiruv* yeshivah high school for students from the former Soviet Union.

Rabbi Katzin invited Yisroel and Leah to join RAJE on a trip to Moscow and St. Petersburg in 2018. (Those were the "peaceful" days, before the Ukrainian invasion.) The Moscow-bound flight took them over the Arctic Circle, and since it was June, they had the unusual experience of watching the midnight sun rising without having set, a sight which they found disconcerting.

Yisroel wasn't sure whether the next day ever began because there had been no night, which meant he didn't know if he could daven Maariv or even Shacharis.

Once in Moscow, Yisroel was walking along the street when a religious Jewish man, who turned out to be a law professor, approached and told him excitedly that he recognized him from having read *Central Park* in Russian. He had borrowed the book and was very happy when Yisroel gave him a signed copy of his own on the spot. They shared a beautiful conversation in English

The law professor who recognized Yisroel on the street in Moscow

— which the man spoke fluently — then shook hands warmly and parted.

"We visited an opulent Chabad Center outside Moscow," Yisroel recalls. Rabbi Berel Lazar, the chief rabbi of Russia, was away, but we met the rabbi of the center, Rabbi Alexander Boroda. At the time, we were impressed with how good life seemed to be for the Jews living in the former Soviet Union."

Yisroel with Rabbis Boroda and Katzin at the Chabad Center near Moscow

Alas, things changed in the wake of the conflict between Russia and Ukraine. The midnight sun has been covered with dark clouds.

Chapter Twenty-Eight
From Tbilisi to Baku

After that incredible Shabbos and the grand *melaveh malkah* in the snow, Yisroel and Leah left the next morning, retracing their route through the thick Russian forest where they were almost forced to spend Shabbos. Soon they were back on the highway and speeding toward the airport to catch a flight to Tbilisi, Georgia.

Tbilisi is situated in a gigantic geological bowl ringed by the Caucasus Mountains, whose highest peaks stand at a lofty eighteen thousand feet and are clearly visible as you fly into the city. According to legend, one of those formidable mountains is none other than Mount Ararat, where Noach's ark came to rest when the flood subsided.

They landed at a modern airport with floor tiles spelling the words "Welcome to Tbilisi" in English. As they entered the arrivals area, a *frum* Yid approached them, calling out, "Hello, Linda Leah!"

It was the chief rabbi of Georgia, Rabbi Ariel Levine.

A native of Georgia, Rabbi Levine had been a refusenik under the Communist regime. He eventually left the country and became a *talmid* at Yeshivas Shvut Ami in Yerushalayim, then went back to serve as chief rabbi of Georgia. Rabbi Levine had read *From*

Chief Rabbi Ariel Levine wheeling the Neubergers' luggage
at the Tbilisi airport

Central Park to Sinai in Russian and loved it (which is how he knew both of Leah's names). After a beautiful greeting by a delegation of Georgian Jews where "Linda Leah" was presented with a royal bouquet of flowers, the chief rabbi insisted on personally wheeling their luggage out of the airport.

◆ ◆ ◆

It took forty-five minutes to reach the center of Tbilisi. The main road is called President George W. Bush Street and features a gigantic mural of none other than President Bush.

When you think about it, it's a strange sight. What's a street named after an American president doing in the middle of Georgia?

The Republic of Georgia actively fought against Russia's attempt to extend its rule into their country. President Bush was considered a hero for the assistance he gave to Georgia in their war against Russia. As a show of gratitude, the major road from the airport to the city center was officially named after him.

 პრეზიდენტ ჯორჯ ბუშის ქუჩა
PRESIDENT GEORGE W. BUSH STREET
N1-80

President Bush Street in Tbilisi

The city itself is a combination of the ancient and the contemporary. There are architecturally creative modern buildings and bridges strung with colored lights that light up the city at night and give it a magical ambiance. Jews have actually lived in Georgia since the time of Churban Bayis Rishon.[19] Close to the modern center of the city there are narrow streets where the Jewish Quarter is located.

The Shvut Ami group was dropped off outside their hotel in Freedom Square, named for the tank battle against Russia that had taken place in that very spot. At their hotel, they met a *National*

Illuminated bridge in the city center

---

19. Wikipedia

Geographic photographer on assignment to capture the magic of an ancient country that found itself in the midst of a modern world.

Tbilisi as seen from the ancient fortress above the city.

In general, Tbilisi and Baku, the capital of nearby Azerbaijan, are unfamiliar places to Americans. But aside from being major cities, both with populations exceeding one million, these places are enchanting, scenic, and even somewhat mysterious. Both cities were hubs of major importance on the spice routes of old. (And if you happen to visit Tbilisi, make sure to take the cable car up to the ancient fortress overlooking the city. The view is spectacular.)

The Old Shul in Tbilisi

Georgian Jews are proud of their heritage, particularly since they have been living there peacefully from the time they left Eretz Yisrael at the time of the destruction of the first Beis HaMikdash. The only time they suffered persecution was under the Russian Communist regime. After the Soviet Union collapsed, the community began rebuilding and regaining its former glory under the guidance of Rabbi Levine with the support of the Georgian government, which encouraged the Jewish renaissance.

In Tbilisi, Yisroel and Leah spoke at yeshivos, seminaries, boys' and girls' schools, even to young children who were just learning how to daven. The *mesirus nefesh* of those involved in outreach there is outstanding. Community members appreciated that Yisroel and Leah came to them from so far away, telling them over and over how grateful they were to them for making the trip.

◆ ◆ ◆

Chief Rabbi Levine loved Yisroel's books so much that he decided to have them translated into Georgian, a distinct language written in a script similar to Aramaic. He invited Yisroel and Leah to return to Georgia for the book launch, an invitation they gladly accepted. Their keynote address during that second trip was attended by hundreds of enthusiastic Georgian Jews who had been touched by their message.

Leah speaking in Tbilisi

Georgian edition of
From Central Park to Sinai

Georgian edition of
2020 Vision

During that speech, Yisroel spoke about how a Jew's natural gravitation toward Torah is a result of the learning he did with the angel for nine months in his mother's womb.

"Then," Yisroel concluded, "just before the baby is born, the angel gives it a '*zetz*' right between the nose and the upper lip, and he forgets the Torah he learned. The *zetz* he gets from the angel is the source of the indentation that everyone has above the upper lip (technical term: philtrum)."

After the speech, a line of people waited to speak with Yisroel and Leah. One woman explained that she was a psychologist who gave a lecture series on the relationship between different parts of the body and psychological phenomena.

"The only part of the body I've never been able to understand is the philtrum," she said. "Now I know!"

◆ ◆ ◆

From Georgia they flew to Ukraine, landing in the famous city of Odessa. (As we write this, the Russian army is invading

If it's Tuesday, we must be in Odessa

and attacking Ukraine. Our hearts go out to all our wonderful friends in Odessa and Kiev and other communities in this beleaguered country.) They stayed at a hotel that became famous in Neuberger lore because the elevator carpet was changed every day to reflect the day of the week. The day they arrived, the carpet said "Tuesday!" — an endearing touch.

On this trip (unlike Riga and Vilna), they were in cosmopolitan Odessa, and kosher food wasn't a problem. As in Moscow, the kosher restaurant was located in the main shul, a grand edifice. The restaurant was elegant, and the owner spent time at their table giving them a rundown of Jewish life in the city.

Once again, they spoke at a number of locations, including a kiruv center that resembled a nightclub, called the Platinum Club, in which all the young people looked like they had just come from spending hours dancing in discos.

"How will we reach them?" the Neubergers wondered.

But by the end of the program those young men and women were hugging Yisroel and Leah and begging them to return.

Yisroel gets a hug from a young man named Constantin at the Platinum Club in Odessa

A highlight in Odessa was Tikva, the Jewish orphanage, where some four hundred Jewish children from throughout the former Soviet Union, ranging in age from infants to twenty years old, resided. Some children were actual orphans and some were "social orphans," whose parents were either unable or unwilling to care for them. The director of the orphanage himself had been raised in the orphanage, evidence that this was an institution that succeeded in raising children to be ready for the outside world. The children

Igor Shveps playing the piano
at the orphanage

were taught Torah as well as music, art, and many other subjects in an environment that was clean and cheerful. The children were adorable, and many wanted nothing more than to be able to sit on Yisroel's and Leah's laps.

Needless to say, the Neubergers obliged.

They entered a room where, amid other activities, a young man was playing the piano. The music pulled at them; it penetrated the soul. The young pianist's name was Igor Shveps. He had a beautiful and sensitive face, and his music captured eons of Jewish struggle and the ability to prevail and overcome countless challenges. Yisroel gave him a hug. This young man and his music entered the Neubergers' hearts where they remain, even to this very day.

◆ ◆ ◆

From Odessa, they drove to Kiev with a short stop for davening and lunch in Uman. The pothole-filled, bone-jarring road

Yisroel with Rabbi Moti Neuwirth

never seemed to end. They were sure that the van would get a flat tire, but somehow they made it to Kiev without the need to resort to using the spare. It was hard for them to believe that they were on the main highway to the capital of Ukraine.

Kiev had its share of drab Communist-era apartment buildings, but the older part of the city was beautiful, with attractive modern buildings intermingled with elegant old-style structures. Here they met Rabbi Yaakov Bleich, the chief rabbi of Ukraine, and his colleague, Rabbi Moti Neuwirth, devoting their lives to *kiruv* and creating a strong Jewish infrastructure, including a modern matzah bakery, which was in full operation in preparation for Pesach.

"Growing up in Belgium," Rabbi Neuwirth says, "my mother used to tell me stories about the refuseniks who defied the Communist regime, gathering together to learn Torah secretly. As a child, they were my heroes, but I never imagined that one day I would be walking the very streets they walked. Yet here I am, doing *kiruv* in Kiev."

Leah speaking in Kiev

Rabbi Bleich told them that the Malbim is buried in Kiev. Yisroel feels a strong affinity with the Malbim, whose seemingly prophetic words pertaining to the War of Gog and Magog are quoted at the beginning of his book, *2020 Vision*.

"The Malbim was similar to Rav Shamshon Rafael Hirsch," Rabbi Bleich recounted, "in the sense that he was constantly standing up for Torah values while battling the *maskilim*, who tried their hardest to change the character of the European *kehillos*. One day the Malbim was on a train passing through Kiev when he fell ill and had to get off to find a doctor. He passed away in the city shortly thereafter. He was so hated by the *maskilim* that his family put up a tombstone in the local cemetery with his name on it but buried his body elsewhere. This way, if the *maskilim* would try to desecrate the grave, they would come away empty-handed. To this day, no one knows where the actual grave is located."

Rabbi Bleich also took them to Babi Yar, the forested ravine where the Jews of the city, thirty-seven thousand martyrs, were murdered by the Nazis and buried in a mass grave during the Holocaust.

There is a modern, miraculous sequel to that tragic story.

Many years after the war, the Russian government wanted to turn Babi Yar into a major commercial site. Not only were they not commemorating the atrocity, but now they wanted to turn the murder site into a huge building project.

They refused to heed the international outcry.

Just before work commenced on this project, Kiev was hit by one of the most torrential rainstorms in memory. The downpour

Rabbi Yaakov Bleich at Babi Yar

created a gigantic mudslide, dislodging tons of dirt. When every-thing settled, anyone passing by Babi Yar could plainly see thou-sands of bones sticking up from the mud and floating in the water, the bones of those who had been murdered by the Nazis and Ukrainians.

After that, all talk of a building project was shelved.

Today, Babi Yar is visited by those who come to daven at the burial site of the holy Yidden who died there *al kiddush Hashem*.

◆ ◆ ◆

The Neubergers became close with Rabbi Bleich and his right-hand man, a young man from Long Island named Jeff Cohen, who happened to be an amateur boxer. A few months after they returned from Georgia, the Neubergers were sitting at their Purim *seudah* in their Yerushalayim home when in walked Rabbi Bleich and Jeff. They were thrilled to see their distinguished friends.

Then they heard someone else knock at the front door. Leah went to the door, *tzedakah* and *mishlo'ach manos* in hand.

The man didn't introduce himself, but walked straight into the dining room. Clearly drunk, he was dressed as a *mekubal* with a tallis over his head. Sitting down at the table, he put his arm around Yisroel's shoulder, and soon his tallis was covering his host's head. Yisroel gave him *tzedakah* and wished him a "*Purim samei'ach.*"

Yisroel with Jeff Cohen

But the man didn't leave.

Yisroel was having trouble breathing under the tallis, and Jeff Cohen was seething at the obvious show of disrespect.

Yisroel tried again to tell the man that it was time to move on, but the man didn't respond. His arms and his tallis were still draped around Yisroel, who was seriously considering calling the police.

He didn't have to call the police.

Approaching the "*mekubal,*" Jeff literally lifted him off the floor and held him up in the air. Suddenly, the man's bloodshot eyes were taking in the scene from an unexpected viewpoint. Jeff carried him to the door and deposited him outside, making absolutely sure that he had left the property for good, which, by then, the other man was more than happy to do.

Yisroel and Leah were very thankful that Rabbi Bleich and Jeff had shown up at just the right moment.

◆　◆　◆

It was Rabbi Ariel Levine, the chief rabbi of Georgia, who suggested that Yisroel and Leah speak to the Jews of Baku, the capital of Azerbaijan, which sits on the shore of the Caspian Sea, the world's largest inland body of water. Rabbi Levine arranged their trip to this ancient city in the year 2015.

Baku is a modern city of two million people with gracious

Baku skyline on the Caspian Sea

and charming ancient buildings as well as modern skyscrapers. It's also a famous and ancient hub of the fuel-oil industry, sitting as it does on vast oil deposits, which have been the source of great wealth for centuries, especially since the technological revolution. Ninety minutes from Baku, there is an active volcano that's constantly shooting fire up into the sky, which the entourage wanted to visit until they learned that it is a place of idol worship.

Besides being a beautiful country, Azerbaijan is also of great strategic importance to the State of Israel, which uses it as a location from which to spy on Iran. Some believe that after the Mossad team abducted all the Iranian nuclear records in 2018, they escaped with them across the Azerbaijan border.

Though officially a Muslim country, the people are generally secular, modern,

Baku street sweeper

Davening in a Baku school

and friendly. The city is very clean, and older citizens can often be seen cleaning the streets with old-fashioned straw brooms. At one point, Yisroel and Leah were crossing the street and a police officer stopped them, informing them that one is not allowed to cross the intersection aboveground. Instead, they were directed to steps leading into an inviting underground arcade filled with stores, specially designed to make even crossing the street a memorable experience.

Yisroel and Leah remained in Baku for several days, speaking a number of times. Although the Jews of Baku at first seemed foreign to Yisroel and Leah, so different from the people and culture

Yisroel speaking in a school in Baku

familiar to them, as soon as they started speaking, they felt as if they were surrounded by family. This happened over and over. They also davened with schoolchildren, and Leah gave the girls a special speech about the role of women, with a lively discussion session at the end.

When the time came to leave, they said goodbye to this beautiful community, which expressed appreciation for their coming with heartfelt warmth. It turned out that the Baku airport was one of the most beautiful and modern airports they had ever seen, but there they learned that their Azerbaijan Air flight to Tel Aviv had been canceled. They had to reschedule on Turkish Air, with a stopover in Istanbul.

◆ ◆ ◆

When they landed in Istanbul, they found a very different airport. The Istanbul Airport is enormous, a major hub through which they had to walk for about a half hour to reach the gate for their flight to Tel Aviv. They passed huge crowds of Arabs on their way to Mecca, the men wearing bright orange garments. In the Neubergers' overtired imaginations, they pictured long curved scimitars hiding beneath those orange robes just waiting to be used on the infidels. (Their fears were not unfounded, since there was an attack on an Israeli *mashgiach* in Istanbul Airport at around that time.)

While the plane from Baku to Istanbul was new, the plane from Istanbul to Tel Aviv was quite rundown. Something caught Yisroel's attention on the Baku-Istanbul flight: the State of Israel was missing from the map of the Middle East. The land mass was there, but there was no name to indicate what that land was. Lebanon was in the north, Jordan in the east, Egypt to the south, but no Israel.

Ironically, on the Istanbul–Tel Aviv flight, there had to be an Israel on the map, because that was where they were going.

And guess what: there was.

All of a sudden, there was an Israel in the world.

They thanked Hashem with heartfelt emotion when they reached home safely.

Chapter Twenty-Nine
The Belarus Disco

One day in 2013 the Neubergers' phone rang. The caller explained that he worked for Rabbi Moshe Fhima (pronounced "Feema"), who had established a Torah community in Pinsk, Belarus. He asked if the Neubergers would fly there to address students and adults for a three-day program.

Yisroel and Leah enthusiastically agreed.

They went to Tel Aviv to arrange for visas. There were a number of fees to pay, and they took care of everything, or at least that's what they thought. Then, visas in place, tickets were sent to them.

"When you travel to Belarus," Yisroel says, "you don't go empty-handed, because the people in Belarus don't have much. There's no kosher food, so everything has to be brought in. People give you lists of things they need, like ketchup and tuna, as well as assorted *sefarim*, tefillin, and so on."

Before they left, a van pulled up in front of their house in Jerusalem, and someone dropped off two duffel bags for them to shlep to Pinsk. At the airport, the representative of Belavia, the Belarusian airline, was upset when she saw all their baggage.

"I'm going to have to charge you a lot of money," she said.

"Yes, but this is for Rabbi Fhima," Yisroel replied.

The lady fairly snapped to attention.

"For Rabbi Fhima?"

Yisroel nodded.

"Oh! Rabbi Fhima! Why didn't you say so?"

Then, to her employee: "Send it through!"

Yisroel and Leah were beginning to understand just who Rabbi Fhima was...

♦ ♦ ♦

Soon they were boarding the plane.

The plane wasn't very up-to-date. The passengers also seemed to be having a little bit of a party on board. The Neubergers had a slightly uneasy feeling, but they kept in mind that they were going for the sake of a great mitzvah.

Eventually they landed. The terminal was somewhat primitive. Among other problems, there were no luggage carts, which made shlepping two duffel bags plus their own luggage a challenge. All their belongings had to be carried by hand from one side of the airport to the other.

Imagine the scene: It was Erev Shabbos at 2 a.m. The Belarus airport is in Minsk, four hours by car from Pinsk. Belarus can boast hundreds of years of Jewish history, but it's not advanced when it comes to material amenities. Before the war, Pinsk had been eighty percent Jewish. After the war, almost no Jewish presence was left. Rabbi Fhima was doing his best to change that.

Rav Chaim Volozhin, the Chafetz Chaim, and Rav Shach had all lived in Pinsk. The Steipler Gaon had learned in Novardok and later became rosh yeshivah of one of the yeshivah's branches in Pinsk. Rav Levi Yitzchak of Berditchev had served as the rav of Pinsk. And the Karlin-Stolin dynasty had been established in Pinsk. In fact, Yisroel and Leah spoke in the Karliner shul during the trip.

But first they had to get out of the airport, which was easier said than done.

The immigration officers in the Belarus airport asked for proof of health insurance.

Health insurance?

"Yes, you were supposed to get that together with your visa in Israel."

Yisroel now recalled a conversation he hadn't understood at the Belarus consulate.

Maybe that's what they were talking about.

In any case, they now had to get health insurance. They were directed upstairs.

They were told that health insurance costs the equivalent of $1.25 for each of them for each day in the country.

No problem.

"Do you take credit cards?"

"No."

"Well, do you take Israeli shekels?"

"No, only rubles or American dollars."

Whoops.

"We don't have either."

"In that case, you cannot be admitted to Belarus."

They had flown in to be the main speakers for a major event, and they couldn't get into the country because of a problem that amounted to less than ten dollars. They had no food, and Shabbos was little more than twelve hours away.

Suddenly they caught sight of a *frum* Russian couple who had been with them on their flight from Israel. They were the other speakers who had flown in for Shabbos. Maybe they had US dollars.

They did, and they were more than happy to bail out the Neubergers.

◆ ◆ ◆

When they emerged from the terminal, a driver was waiting for them, and they joined the Russian couple for the four-hour car ride from Minsk to Pinsk. It was a long trip, but Yisroel and Leah had a feeling that it was going to be worth it.

On the way to Pinsk, they passed small villages consisting of wooden houses, their walls painted in bright colors and surrounded by white picket fences. They saw timeless faces going about their business as horse-drawn wagons leisurely clip-clopped down the streets and people got ready to start their day. It was as if someone was announcing in a sonorous voice, "Welcome to Eastern Europe, where nothing changes." Most of the people were actually very poor. One US dollar equaled ten thousand Belarus rubles.

Four hours later, they pulled up outside their hotel in Pinsk, a ten-story building with an impressive façade. Upon entering, they found themselves inside a magnificent lobby, complete with a platform upon which sat a gleaming white grand piano. They couldn't help but be impressed by the opulence.

"You are in room 647," said the girl behind the desk.

When they walked into the elevator, things began to look a little different. They waited for it to rise, which it did, but with an ominous creaky sound that contrasted mightily with the shiny majesty of the lobby. The doors slid open at the sixth floor.

They were in for a shock.

Lightbulbs were hanging from the ceiling by their wires. The walls hadn't been plastered, and you could literally see the pipes running through them.

"I wonder what our room is going to look like," Yisroel murmured.

Their stay in Belarus was certainly going to be interesting!

◆ ◆ ◆

The first person to welcome Yisroel and Leah at the yeshivah was a young Frenchman. Rabbi Fhima had met Claude* in France and realized that he would make a wonderful addition to the staff. Although Claude was young, Rabbi Fhima saw great potential in him.

Claude joined Rabbi Fhima's yeshivah and developed into a natural leader and wonderful *mechanech* who somehow knew exactly what to say to everyone he met. Claude sat Yisroel and Leah down and prepared a delicious breakfast for them, complete with an omelet. It was a lovely beginning to a beautiful trip.

Rabbi Fhima grew up in Manchester, England, and had taught himself Russian so he was able to serve as their translator. Since they had to pause every few lines so that their words could be translated, Yisroel and Leah were able to speak only for half the time they normally did. You might think that such an arrangement wouldn't be conducive to inspiring people, but the message came through beautifully. As they had found with audiences all over the world, words from the heart enter the heart. Their words penetrated hearts, and many people lined up afterward to ask questions and buy books.

During their visit, Rabbi Fhima gave Yisroel and Leah a personal guided tour of the empire he had built in Pinsk. His yeshivos and girls' schools were the most modern buildings in all of Belarus. In his home, they were particularly touched by his "*shidduch* garden," a beautifully landscaped area adjacent to his house, where couples could stroll and talk. In the center was a little house with chairs and a table.

"Since the purpose of the garden is for dating," he told Yisroel and Leah, "we had a potential *yichud* problem. "We solved this by constructing one side of the house out of glass."

Rabbi Fhima's *shidduch* wall

After giving them a tour of the garden, Rabbi Fhima showed them the results: his "*shidduch* wall," with pictures of all the couples he had brought under the *chuppah*. In addition to making *shidduchim* between his students, Rabbi Fhima also enabled couples who had been married for years to get remarried according to the halachah.

◆ ◆ ◆

Yisroel and Leah spoke and spoke, and the response was fantastic. On Motza'ei Shabbos they retired at a late hour, only to discover that there was an all-night disco that could clearly be heard throughout the hotel. The music was ear-splitting, although it was six floors below them. They considered leaving the building, but where would they go? They couldn't wander around Pinsk in the middle of the night. It was dark and cold, and they had no idea how to contact Rabbi Fhima at that hour. But there was also no way they could sleep, and the bone-jarring noise continued until six in the morning.

It was one tough night.

They were scheduled to speak at the closing event the next morning, but — no surprise — they overslept. Rabbi Fhima was concerned and sent out a search party to look for them all over Pinsk.

Closing program in Pinsk, with Rabbi Fhima on the left and the Russian couple who helped Yisroel and Leah at the airport

Yisroel and Leah arrived just in time for the final panel, to the relief of everyone present, who were happy to see that they were fine, if overtired.

It was a memorable trip, in which the spiritual rewards definitely outweighed the physical challenges.

Chapter Thirty
Flagpoles and Hurricanes

As of today, Yisroel and Leah have given hundreds — maybe thousands — of lectures in fifteen countries. But sometimes things don't work out quite the way you expect.

One evening, Yisroel and Leah walked into a huge *kiruv* center in Manhattan for a scheduled speech and found that they were just one of a multitude of programs that were being offered that night. When they finally located the room where they were supposed to speak, they saw that it was only large enough for a few people, and that was exactly who had come to hear them that night.

Five people.

"Was this event publicized?" Yisroel asked the person who had shown them into the room.

"Sure. We posted it on the electronic screen in the lobby."

But if Hashem had sent them five people, they were going to speak for five people. To be honest, it wasn't actually five people, because one of them fell asleep toward the beginning of their speech, so they really had an audience of four. They couldn't help but wonder why Hashem had sent them to this particular place to address this particular mini-crowd.

After the program, they found out.

The woman they thought was sleeping hadn't been sleeping. She had been crying. She was covering her face because she was trying to maintain her composure.

That speech changed her entire life. She ended up becoming religious and spent many Shabbosos at the Neuberger home. And not only did she adopt a Torah life, but so did her daughter. Eventually, she moved to Florida and remarried. A few years later, she called to ask Yisroel and Leah if they would come and speak at her home in the Sunshine State.

A stunning conclusion to the night the Neubergers spoke to an audience of five — "one of them asleep."

♦ ♦ ♦

Another speech they gave in the New York area was at a unique yeshivah for teenage boys who were struggling with their *Yiddishkeit*. The yeshivah was located in a nondescript house in the Bronx, and the rosh yeshivah was a man by the name of Rabbi Yehoshua Danese. Rabbi Danese had been a frequent Shabbos guest of the Neuberger family when he still went by Josh.

Yisroel speaking at the yeshivah of Rabbi Yehoshua Danese (far right)

He had a very inspiring story himself: After he found his way to a life of Torah and mitzvos, he became a close *talmid* of Rav Avigdor Miller. He would memorize Rav Miller's Shabbos *derashos* and write them down after Shabbos, preserving these brilliant speeches for all time. Later, he compiled the *derashos* into book form. He went on to establish a yeshivah for teens who needed lots of love and attention.

Rabbi Danese's yeshivah was different from other venues, because here Yisroel and Leah were speaking at the yeshivah of someone who had spent so much time with them. It felt like they had come full circle, from those long-ago Shabbos meals to a yeshivah where lives were saved and sparks reignited.

◆ ◆ ◆

Saginaw, Michigan, is located about ninety minutes northwest of Detroit, in the middle of soybean and wheat fields. This is the Midwest, where the land seems to stretch onward forever and the winters can be brutal.

When you're in Saginaw, it seems as if you're far from everything. Yet Saginaw is home to a number of large companies that are part of the General Motors and Ford families, companies that make car batteries, tires, windows, and other components for the auto industry.

How did Yisroel and Leah wind up in Saginaw?

On a trip to Eretz Yisrael, they found themselves sitting next to a very special woman named Frumeth, who had become *frum* through Chabad. She was married to a lawyer named Frank Polasky, and they lived in Saginaw. The three spoke through much of the flight. When they landed, they parted as friends.

A few years later, remarkably, the same thing happened. Again they found themselves sitting next to Frumeth Polasky on a flight to Israel. This was too coincidental to be coincidental.

Frumeth attended the Neubergers' family *simchah* while in Jerusalem. While there, she told Yisroel and Leah that she wanted them to speak at her home in Saginaw the next time they came to the University of Michigan.

Yisroel speaking in Saginaw at the Polasky home

Pulling up in front of the Polaskys' house, they were amazed to see two giant, 150-foot flagpoles sitting in the middle of their spacious front yard, one flying an American flag and one an Israeli flag. Remember, this is Saginaw, where one doesn't expect to see Israeli flags, especially 150 feet in the air. But Frumeth was a unique woman, displaying her love of Israel proudly and without embarrassment.

Frank and Frumeth Polasky were the only *shomer Shabbos*, *chalav Yisrael* couple for an hour and a half in any direction, so they obviously didn't have much of a problem being different. Frumeth studied Judaism on her own and had become quite knowledgeable. Eventually she gathered a group of Jewish friends who were also interested in discovering more about their heritage. About thirty people gathered at the Polasky home to hear Yisroel and Leah speak.

Leah with Frumeth

"As soon as we entered the Polaskys' beautiful home, we immediately felt comfortable," Yisroel says. "It wasn't just the fine people and the Polaskys' courage and love of their Jewish heritage, but there was obvious *mesirus nefesh*. All their dairy products were *chalav Yisrael* and their meat was *glatt kosher*."

Incredibly, one woman who came that night had attended the Fieldston school, where Yisroel and Leah had met. Her husband was the CEO of a major corporation in the area.

Being in the company of such people as Frank and Frumeth Polasky is inspirational. They are Jewish heroes. They have since passed on to the World of Truth, where they are surely receiving the reward allotted to loyal and courageous Jewish souls.

◆ ◆ ◆

Yisroel and Leah are *mechutanim* with Rabbi Avigdor Slatus, legendary rav of the Jewish community in Savannah, Georgia, and a *talmid* of Rav Shmuel Berenbaum, the late rosh yeshivah of the Mirrer Yeshivah in Brooklyn. Rabbi Slatus was recruited by members of the Savannah *kehillah* decades ago, and today he leads a huge shul.

A few hundred people came to hear Yisroel and Leah speak at Rabbi Slatus's shul. They responded warmly and stayed to chat and have Yisroel sign his books.

"Standing there in the shul," Yisroel says, "I recalled Shabbos *sheva berachos* in Savannah, when our daughter Nechami married the rav's son Yaakov in August 1999."

That Shabbos was hot, even for Georgia. When they walked out of *sheva berachos* Friday night, it was ninety-seven degrees and humid even though it was after eleven p.m. Yisroel was walking with Reb Nosson Garfunkel, a *talmid* of Sh'or Yoshuv and descendant of a family that had been proudly *frum* in Savannah for two hundred years.

Yisroel remarked on the heat.

"It's going to be a big hurricane season," Reb Nosson replied. "When the weather is this hot, it means that the water in the Atlantic is hot, and that means hurricanes."

Reb Nosson went on to recount an amazing story.

"This weather reminds me of hurricane season ten years ago.

It was also incredibly hot, and there was no question that we could anticipate big hurricanes. Soon we learned that Savannah was in the path of Hurricane Hugo, which was expected to hit on Erev Rosh Hashanah. The authorities issued a mandatory evacuation order. The police turned all eight lanes of the interstate to Atlanta to go in one direction — away from Savannah — and everyone was ordered to get out.

"The problem was that it was Erev Rosh Hashanah. Before I fled from my house, I needed to make sure I was doing the right thing. So I called my rebbi, Rav Shlomo Freifeld, the rosh yeshivah of Sh'or Yoshuv, and asked him what to do.

"'Reb Nosson,' my rebbi said, 'you stay right where you are. That hurricane isn't going to strike within a hundred miles of Savannah.'

"Following my rebbi's counsel, I stayed home. At four in the afternoon on Erev Rosh Hashanah, the storm changed course, making landfall one hundred seven miles from Savannah.

"Just as my rebbi had said."

◆ ◆ ◆

Then there was Project Encounter in Manchester, England, where hundreds of Jews from all backgrounds gathered for an uplifting annual experience, whose goal was to foster *achdus* within the community and connect Jews to their roots. This event was so big that it took place in the Conference Center at the Manchester United Soccer Stadium, which is comparable to Yankee Stadium in New York.

Shortly after *From Central Park to Sinai* was published, a very special Jew from Manchester read the book and was so inspired that he personally undertook to fly Yisroel and Leah to England. One day they opened their mailbox and found an envelope containing two tickets to Manchester.

Nine hundred people attended their featured event. Unlike other events, where they would come and deliver a speech, this time a *frum* television personality named John Blaskey served as host and interviewed them. The three of them sat on high stools

Onstage at the Encounter conference

on a stage, with Mr. Blaskey asking questions, running the event seamlessly and with plenty of humor. The crowd loved everything that took place on the stage.

At the end of the program many people approached them. One was a high school girl from a totally assimilated family who attended a public school located very close to a Bais Yaakov. She had admired the modest and friendly girls she saw going to school there every day and became friendly with them. Then she started keeping mitzvos.

"I started dressing more like them," she said, "but this really bothered my mother. She would attack me and say, 'What's wrong with you? Why do you look so frumpy?'"

Yisroel and Leah spent an hour with this girl after the program, giving her *chizuk* as she poured out her heart. Afterward, they remained in touch, exchanging emails. Eventually she married a religious boy and today lives in Israel.

Think about it: If it hadn't been for the friendliness of those

Yisroel signing books at the Encounter conference

Bais Yaakov girls, this young lady would never have adopted *Yiddishkeit*. Someday in *Shamayim*, these girls will reap mountains of reward for their role in bringing her close to Torah.

◆ ◆ ◆

One afternoon the Neubergers spoke at a seminary in Yerushalayim geared to women who were in the process of becoming religious. On the day they were supposed to speak, one of the young women informed the dean that she had decided to leave the school and return to her old life. He couldn't convince her to stay.

As she left the dean's office, she glanced at the listing for the afternoon program and decided to go hear Yisroel and Leah speak before packing her belongings. After the speech, she informed the dean that she had changed her mind.

She would be staying, after all.

Another time they spent a Shabbos in Rockville, Maryland. As they walked into the home of Rabbi Shlomo and Rebbetzin

Devorah Buxbaum, where they were scheduled to speak, they were confronted by a hopping scene, with students and guests everywhere. As Leah sat down with the rebbetzin, the other woman said, "Do you know who I am?"

Leah looked at her, trying to remember where she had met her before.

"We met when I was in the eleventh grade at Bais Yaakov of Denver. Something you said changed my life."

"What did I say?"

"You spoke about how the small things we do can make a difference in other people's lives, a difference that can literally affect generations. And you brought home your point with an example.

"Let's say a girl walks into shul one Shabbos, you said. She's never been there before, and she's a complete stranger. It could be that this girl is trying to figure out if the Jewish way of life is for her. Imagine if no one greets her. She's gone. That's it. Finished!

"Now what if you say hello to her? What if you give her a warm welcome? Maybe even invite her for a Shabbos meal? This could change her entire life and the life of her descendants for generations forever!

Yisroel with Rabbi Shlomo Buxbaum
at Aish of Greater Washington

"I was so inspired by your message that after that every time a newcomer would walk into the shul where my father was the rav, I would approach her and give her a warm welcome, doing my best to help her feel at home."

Now, years later, the high school girl had grown up to become a very successful *kiruv* rebbetzin. She and her husband ran a flourishing program, and countless individuals passed through their doors. And she credits her lifework to the message she'd heard in high school from Leah Neuberger.

◆ ◆ ◆

One Erev Shavuos Yisroel and Leah flew to San Diego to spend Yom Tov as scholars in residence at the shul of Rabbi Avraham Bogopulsky. Yisroel was scheduled to speak on the topic of *Megillas Rus* at three in the morning on the night of *Kabbalas HaTorah*. During the flight, he was working on the *shiur* that he planned to deliver, a particularly beloved piece from the commentary of the Ben Ish Chai.

The Ben Ish Chai describes how Boaz is on the threshing floor. Rus comes in the middle of the night. Boaz awakens and sees someone there. He discovers her identity. He tells her that actually Ploni Almoni is next in line to serve as redeemer, but if Ploni Almoni refuses to redeem her, then "*chai Hashem*" — Boaz makes an oath — "I will redeem you. Meanwhile, stay through the night."

The Ben Ish Chai suggests that this conversation between Boaz and Rus is not just Boaz speaking with Rus, but also Hashem speaking to *Bnei Yisrael*.

"Stay through the night" is Hashem encouraging *Bnei Yisrael* to stay with Him through the long night of exile.

"In the morning," Boaz continues, "I will speak to Ploni Almoni."

Hashem is telling *Am Yisrael*, "When the end of *galus* — 'the morning' — comes, let us see if your own merits, your mitzvos and good deeds, are sufficient to redeem you. But even if you don't have the mitzvos and good deeds you need to redeem yourself, but you have stayed close to Me throughout the exile, then I Myself will redeem you!"

In other words, at the end of history, there will be two ways we can be redeemed.

Yisroel was excited about presenting this message. As he sat there, savoring the beautiful thought and planning his presentation, a stewardess approached and asked if he wanted a drink.

"I'd like a Coke, please."

You can learn a lesson, even from a can of Coke

She brought a can of Coke.

Yisroel still has that can. On it is a big note in Yisroel's writing, "Do not throw out!"

What's so special about this can of Coke?

"I was sitting in my seat, drinking the Coke, and idly reading the writing on the can. There was a promotion being offered for various theme parks. You needed to present the Coke can. Then a little further down, it said, 'Two ways to redeem... Present can at ticket booth...'"

Yisroel almost jumped out of his seat.

Two ways to redeem...

He couldn't believe it.

Suddenly he let loose with a yell. "That's my speech! Two ways to redeem, the exact words Boaz spoke to Rus! Either Ploni Almoni will redeem you or I will redeem you."

At that moment, Yisroel realized that Hashem speaks to us everywhere at every moment through every medium — even a can of Coke!

◆ ◆ ◆

Yisroel and Leah were on their way to Detroit and had to switch planes in Philadelphia. The gate through which they were directed was manned by a quiet man from the West Indies. Several people were waiting to board and, annoyed by various delays, were taking it out on the hapless airline officer.

When it was their turn to pass through the gate, Yisroel turned to the man. "Thank you so much," he said sincerely. "I really appreciate your help."

The man looked at him. "Did you say 'thank you'? Nobody ever says 'thank you' to me!"

The man came around the counter and took Yisroel's hand. He was overcome with emotion at being treated with such kindness. Bowing, he opened the door for them and accompanied them to the bus. Suddenly, he was standing straighter; he seemed to have grown a couple of inches.

As they walked through the gate, they heard him say, "You respect me. G-d bless you!"

♦   ♦   ♦

When Yisroel and Leah visited Cleveland, they stayed at the home of Dr. and Mrs. Bill Wieder, who own a beautiful African grey parrot named Suzie.

Suzie loved to say things in her high-pitched parrot voice, and the house was filled with her renditions of "hello," "good morning," "good Shabbos," and "time to *bentch*."

She never forgot what she heard and might repeat it anytime. Beware — you might hear from Suzie something you said twenty years earlier. You had to guard your tongue in Suzie's presence. You had to weigh every word. Suzie kept everyone honest.

Dr. Wieder told the Neubergers an amazing story. Suzie is not so young these days. The average life span of an African grey is about twenty-three years, and Suzie is about that age today. She has had two strokes and can no longer climb up to her perch in the bird cage.

On the occasion of her first stroke, Dr. Wieder took her to the veterinarian. Suzie was lying down after having had a seizure. She was in the bird hospital for a week and, because she refused

Suzie the parrot

to eat, the vet said there was little hope. But the Wieders refused to part with Suzie, and they brought her home.

As soon as she saw her familiar surroundings and the family whom she knew so well, she came back to life. She began to eat; she rose to her feet with great effort. Although she was suffering from the effects of the stroke, she struggled to climb up the bars of her cage and sit on her perch, and she wouldn't let anyone help her.

Dr. Wieder says that Suzie inspired the entire family. "She was an example for us of what to do in a crisis."

Between her *mussar* messages and her passion for living, Suzie is indeed the "*mussar* bird"!

♦ ♦ ♦

Many years had passed since the Master of the world had taken their lives in a whole new direction, and now they enjoyed returning to their alma mater, the University of Michigan, on a different mission, because that was where Rabbi Avraham Jacobovitz had established a ground-breaking *kiruv* program to bring university students close to Torah. When Rabbi Jacobovitz handed responsibility for the program to the supertalented Rabbi Fully Eisenberger, Yisroel and Leah continued to speak in Ann Arbor each semester and did so for twelve consecutive years.

One year Yisroel and Leah had plane reservations to travel to Ann Arbor on a certain Sunday in February, but the weather forecast for that day was predicting a major storm with winds up to seventy miles per hour. On Sunday morning, they received a phone call from American Airlines informing them that their flight had been canceled.

"We rescheduled you for tomorrow morning," the airline rep said.

Since they were supposed to speak on Monday evening, this wasn't the end of the world, although it would make everything tighter and more complicated.

When they awoke Monday morning, the storm was still going strong. Another call came in from American Airlines, telling them that their Monday flight had also been canceled.

Now they had a problem. It seemed that there was no way for them to make that evening's program.

But the Neubergers don't concede so easily. Knowing how much their speech meant to the students, and realizing that packed schedules made it impossible to reschedule, they decided that they were going to do their best to make it to Ann Arbor, storm or no storm.

The only question was how.

"Leah," Yisroel said, "are you ready to drive to Michigan?"

It would mean a twelve-hour drive. But Leah responded like Rivkah Imeinu: *"Eileich... I'm ready to go!"*

They left the house at eight in the morning. The drive would take them through Queens and over the Whitestone Bridge to the George Washington Bridge and on to New Jersey and the Interstate, which they would take all the way to Michigan.

At least, that was the plan.

They were approaching the Whitestone Bridge when traffic came to a dead halt. Yisroel turned on the radio, and they learned that the police were barring trucks from crossing the Whitestone Bridge because of gale-force winds. They were afraid the wind would blow the trucks off the bridge. The process of filtering out trucks had traffic backed up for miles.

Under normal circumstances, this would have been annoying, but they would have waited it out. That day, however, they were on a tight schedule. They had a limited amount of time to reach Ann Arbor, and now they had been handed a major setback.

Yisroel got off the highway at the next exit and began taking side streets, hoping to approach the bridge from the east instead of the west. Soon enough, they discovered that traffic was just as bad from the other direction.

Yisroel took advantage of the opportunity to duck into a gas station and fill up the tank. He was about to start pumping gas when he noticed that everyone around him was running like crazy.

It took him a second to realize that a truck at one of the pumps had caught fire. Flames were shooting out, and it looked like it was about to explode. Jumping back into the car, he raced out of there before the whole place went up in flames.

Hashem, what's going on? Why is everything blocked when we're trying to get to Ann Arbor to do a mitzvah?

Yisroel and Leah weren't ready to give up. Eventually, Yisroel found a side street that led straight to the bridge. Suddenly they were moving.

Soon they were over the bridge and in the Bronx. They made it to New Jersey, with the road wide open: Pennsylvania, Ohio, and then Michigan lay ahead.

Thank you, Hashem!

The road remained clear the entire way to Ann Arbor. They reached their destination at 8:20 that evening, giving them a grand total of twenty-five minutes to catch their breath before their speech was scheduled to commence.

Yisroel and Leah arriving in Michigan against all odds

"They almost fainted when we drove in," Leah says. "They couldn't believe we had driven all the way from New York."

Neither could Yisroel and Leah.

That night, the speech, the atmosphere, the intensity, was even more beautiful than usual. Afterward, the students lined up so that Yisroel and

Leah speaking in Ann Arbor after the long drive

Leah could sign books and write a blessing for them. (Rabbi Eisenberger gives each student a book as a graduation present.) They talked with many students, and the evening ended with blessings, hugs, and even invitations for Shabbos.

Hashem had been testing their resolve, but they hadn't given up. They kept going until Hashem had finally put the wind at their backs. They reached their destination just in time to make a difference to the lives of many young Jews who would hopefully never forget this special night so that they themselves would go on to become great people and inspire others.

PART 6

*"I'm also a person.
Can you please pray for me?"*

NYPD officer

Chapter Thirty-One
More Books

In the wake of the publication of *From Central Park to Sinai*, Yisroel unexpectedly found that he and his wife had become quasi-celebrities. Suddenly people were stopping him in the street to tell him that they had read his book. Yisroel and Leah were being asked to deliver speeches all over the world. Letters arrived from people telling him that they had begun keeping Shabbos because of his book. Not only that, but his father was proud of his son's achievements, and that meant the world to him.

Finally, Yisroel felt he was doing what he was meant to do.

The question became, what next?

First he wrote another book that he called *Worldstorm: Finding Meaning and Direction Amidst Today's World Crisis*, a spiritual history of the world from Gan Eden until Mashiach. It was significantly more intellectual than Yisroel's first book, containing original insights backed up by sources in Chazal and classic rabbinical works.

As with his first book, Yisroel arose at four in the morning to do his writing. Then he would place the finished pages on Leah's desk and go to daven Shacharis. She would do the first round of editing, marking up what he had written before giving it back.

Yisroel spent about a year writing the book, and when he

was done, he sought *haskamos* from a number of *gedolim*. One *haskamah* in particular stands out: the one he received from Rav Avigdor Nebenzahl, rav of the Old City of Yerushalayim, who read every word of the manuscript. The reason Yisroel knew that he had read every word was because Rav Nebenzahl gave him a detailed list of fifty passages that needed to be changed if he wanted his *haskamah*. After the changes were made, Yisroel's distinguished friend, Rabbi Yeshaya Klor, accompanied Yisroel to Rav Nebenzahl's home, along with Yisroel's son-in-law Avi Hess, helping to facilitate Rabbi Nebenzahl's agreement to write the approbation. When everything was agreed upon, Rav Nebenzahl took out paper and penned the *haskamah* that is in the book.

◆ ◆ ◆

Yisroel and Leah's first encounter with Rabbi Klor wasn't as auspicious. They had met him in 1998 when Rabbi Yehoshua Kalish, rav of Bais Medrash of Harborview, where Yisroel davened after they moved from North Woodmere to Lawrence, informed him that a *rosh kollel* from Israel would be visiting that Shabbos. Could the Neubergers host him for a meal?

Rabbi Klor, originally from Brooklyn, is a longtime *rosh kollel* from Bnei Brak, with a *kollel* comprised of over one hundred fifty *yungeleit*. That Shabbos, Rabbi Klor accompanied Yisroel home after shul on Shabbos morning for the *seudah*, and after a few minutes, everyone sat down at the table for Kiddush and *hamotzi*.

Leah noticed that their guest wasn't eating. She took the initiative and decided to serve him so that he would feel comfortable taking what he wished. She lifted the serving platter filled with an array of about eight different salads in order to offer it to her guest.

Now you have to know something: Leah Neuberger is a very put-together person, not the type to spill anything and certainly not on a guest. She is definitely not the type of hostess who spills a vast array of salads on distinguished rabbis from Bnei Brak. But on that Shabbos morning, somehow the entire tray containing the aforementioned vast array of salads tipped over, and the *rosh kollel* from Bnei Brak was covered with every kind of salad she'd prepared. Rabbi Klor was suddenly looking very colorful indeed, as the mustard combined with the cabbage, the mayonnaise with the rich hue of the Russian dressing.

Had the rabbi brought a few extra articles of clothing with him, it would have been one thing. But he had just the one Shabbos garment. What's more, he was scheduled to speak at one of the big local shuls after the *seudah*.

For Leah Neuberger, it was one of the most embarrassing moments in her life. She profoundly wished that she could sink through the floor to escape from planet Earth.

Sometimes it's possible to find the silver lining in the midst of a difficult predicament, but in this case it seemed as if this was an unmitigated disaster with no redeeming factors at all.

Rabbi Klor reacted like a superstar, reassuring his hosts that it was really not a big deal, even as he left the house to give his *derashah* looking like the circus had just come to town. After Shabbos, Leah told Yisroel that whatever donation he had been planning on giving the *kollel*, he should increase it and in addition they should pay for the rabbi's clothing to be professionally dry cleaned.

And so the traumatic incident came to an end.

Except that, in truth, it was just the beginning.

Somehow spilling the salads on Rabbi Klor caused him and the Neubergers to bond in a totally unexpected way. When they next visited Israel, Rabbi Klor took Yisroel to Rav Aharon Leib Shteinman for a private meeting that lasted half an hour. No doubt the fact that Rabbi Klor learned with Rav Shteinman every Erev Shabbos made it easier to arrange such a special visit. Rabbi Klor took him to Rav Shach as well and to other *gedolim* around the country.

And every year since they met (until Yisroel and Leah made aliyah), Rabbi Klor asked to spend Shabbos at the home of his great friends Yisroel and Leah whenever he visited America. Inevitably, after everyone washed their hands and took that first bite of challah, Rabbi Klor would jokingly suggest that the time had

Yisroel with Rav Klor and Rav Aharon Leib Shteinman, *zt"l,* in Bnei Brak

come to spill some more salad on him, since the outcome of that accident was so good for everyone involved.

◆ ◆ ◆

After *Worldstorm,* Yisroel decided to move in a different direction, and in 2008 he began work on a novel containing Torah insights set in the year 2020.

In a fascinating turn of events, many of the scenes depicted in *2020 Vision* came true in the year 2020, when Covid struck the world. That year, many people stopped Yisroel on the street and asked him how he knew that 2020 would be such a chaotic year. In a sense, it all went back to the *Malbim* commentary that provides the setting for the story. This *Malbim* is particularly special to Yisroel, since it was shown to him by his dear friend Amos Bunim, son of the legendary activist Irving Bunim.

Of course, there's a story here.

When Yisroel first began writing *2020 Vision,* and the story was taking shape in his mind, he received an unexpected gift. He was driving through the streets of Lawrence when his phone rang. It was Amos Bunim.

"Yisroel, can you please come over to my house? I want to show you something."

"Sure, I'll be right there."

When he got there, Mr. Bunim told him, "I want to show you an amazing *Malbim* that I think you'll find very interesting. It's on chapter 32 of *Yechezkel*."

It turned out that the entire book, *2020 Vision*, would coalesce around that *Malbim*. This quote, displayed at the front of the book, became the backdrop for *2020 Vision*. This is what it says:

2020 Vision

At the End of Days, after the Children of Israel have returned to their land, the children of Yishmael and the children of Esav will unite to attack Jerusalem. They will form a world coalition against the tiny nation of Israel. But something will go wrong with their plan. The religious beliefs of the children of Yishmael and the children of Esav will clash, and the two nations will collide and destroy each other. This is what is referred to as the War of Gog and Magog. Following this cataclysmic conflict, the final redemption of the Jewish people will occur, with the coming of Mashiach, a descendant of King David.

♦ ♦ ♦

Yisroel and Leah had first met Mr. Bunim when they moved to Lawrence from North Woodmere in 1998, and he became their neighbor. They came to learn that he was the kind of person who would do anything for a friend, and this was borne out when they once went to speak at a state university in the western United States. After a successful evening program, Yisroel found out that there was one minyan in the city and planned to head there for Shacharis.

"How far away is it?" he inquired.

"On the other side of town," he was told. "About half an hour by car."

The next morning, Yisroel rose early. After a half hour's drive, he found the shul, which was in an attractive building with an interior courtyard. He introduced himself to the rabbi, who had moved there decades earlier.

After Shacharis, the rabbi asked where Yisroel was from.

"Lawrence, New York," he replied.

"Do you know Amos Bunim?"

"Do I know Amos Bunim! Sure, I do! He's my neighbor. He lives a few houses away."

"I want to tell you a story."

Here is what the rabbi told Yisroel:

"I received *semichah* around thirty-five years ago. Afterward, a *kiruv* organization sent me out to bring Torah to this corner of the world. There was a shul here, but it was leaderless. It was a challenging time for my wife and me, and it wasn't long before I was faced with a major halachic *shailah* regarding the *mechitzah*, and I was hit with serious opposition from some of the members. Half the *kehillah* told me that I was too religious, and half the *kehillah* told me I wasn't religious enough. I felt like the *shmatte* squeezed between two rollers in one of those old-fashioned washing machines. I didn't know what to do.

"I needed advice, and a name flew into my mind: Amos Bunim. I called him and told him my story. 'Rabbi,' he said, 'hang in there. I'll be right over.' Then he hung up.

"At the time of that conversation, Amos Bunim was literally thousands of miles away, but he didn't let that stop him. The next morning he was standing on my doorstep. He had taken the first flight out of New York.

"'Don't worry about what anyone is saying,' he reassured me after I'd ushered him into the house. 'Do what you know is right, and you will see that everything will fall into place.'

"His visit gave me tremendous *chizuk*, and I followed his advice. It's been decades now, and Amos Bunim has come to visit me fourteen times — fourteen times! — right here in the 'wilderness.' He kept giving me *chizuk* so that I would be able to survive and thrive.

"And I'm still here!"

The first thing Yisroel did after leaving the shul was to call Amos Bunim back in Lawrence.

"Reb Amos," he said, "you will never guess where I am right now. You have a grateful

Reb Amos Bunim (left) with
Rabbi Aryeh Malkiel Kotler

rabbi here who attributes his success to the advice and encouragement you've given him all these years. He says that you're the reason that he's still here."

Reb Amos was thrilled to hear it.

◆ ◆ ◆

Ever since Yisroel and Leah have become religious, Yisroel continuously thinks about the need to bring Mashiach. His fourth book, *Working Toward Mashiach*, is a compilation of selected articles arranged according to the *parashah* or Yom Tov from Roy's weekly column, which ran in the *Yated Ne'eman* for twelve years.

The conviction that the events of our times are leading inexorably to the healing days of Mashiach motivated him to write a fifth book, this one entitled *Hold On: Surviving the Days Before Mashiach.*

Why "Hold On"?

As the Chafetz Chaim stated, "Before Mashiach comes, Hashem will stretch a rope from one end of the world to the other and shake it vigorously. Those who hold on tight will survive. Those who let go won't. These turbulent times are testing us in our faith in Hashem. We must hold on tightly until the end."

Yisroel's books inspire the *frum* as well as the non-*frum* world.

Here is a letter from Rebbetzin Blimi Cohen:

My feelings about Yisroel and Leah Neuberger are very similar to only one other person that I knew, namely my late father, Rabbi Chaim Yisroel Belsky *zt"l*. They have an ability to understand something that few people understand, namely that there is no such thing as saying, *"This person is very chashuv and that person is not so chashuv, but rather that everybody has chashivus."*

At the end of my father's life, as he was walking with one of my brothers, he said, *"You know who's such a special person..."* And he was going on with high praise and then he named someone who came over as such a surprise! It looks as if this person is very simple, but my father saw something great in him. I get that feeling when I'm with the Neubergers.

I remember when Mr. Neuberger introduced someone with such high praise and I couldn't believe whom he was speaking about. He has an ability to see to the *neshamah*.

Rabbi Belsky, the late rosh yeshivah of Torah Vodaath, commented in regard to Yisroel's books, "Mr. Neuberger brings awareness to us of what the days of Mashiach will be like and, more importantly, what is incumbent upon us to do in preparation for those lofty days."

Yisroel felt that the world needed to be inspired by the unfolding scenario of what he feels is the imminent final redemption. Shortly after *2020 Vision* was published, he met a very serious *avreich* in Jerusalem, who told him, "I've read a lot of books purporting to portray the steps leading up to the advent of Mashiach ben David. Frankly, I didn't believe one of them. But then I read *2020 Vision*, and I believe it could really happen that way."

Chapter Thirty-Two
Acadia Man 1 and Acadia Man 2

When Roy was in the third grade at the Ethical Culture School, his gym teacher used to take the class to Central Park every afternoon for recess. One day Roy had been kept back from the park since he had misbehaved in class. His teacher, Mrs. Eakright, said, "You will remain in the classroom and write the words 'I will be a good boy' on the board one hundred times."

Recess arrived. The rest of the class went to the park while Roy remained behind. When Mrs. Eakright returned to the classroom, she found that he had written only one sentence on the board: "I will be a good boy one hundred times."

Mrs. Eakright could be scary, and she seemed very angry about that little prank. (In fact, she was inwardly amused. Years later, they would laugh together over this incident.)

In truth, this was an indication of Roy's out-of-the-box imagination. While it may have gotten him in trouble then, it would come in handy later in life — such as when he sat down to write a book that would prove to be uncanny in its portrayal of future world events.

◆ ◆ ◆

While writing *2020 Vision* in 2007, Yisroel did the kind of research few authors do anymore. Knowing the route that he wanted his protagonists to take, he traced their journey on a map all the way from southern New Jersey to Portland, Maine. Then Yisroel and Leah got into their car and drove the actual route that the fictional Yisroel and Leah Neuberger took in the book. Every milepost and road sign mentioned in *2020 Vision* is accurate, from Long Island to the Hudson Valley to the Berkshires and onward to Maine. Wherever Yisroel wrote that people were camping out in a forest, he made sure that there actually was a forest there, and he calculated the distance the people in the book would be able to cover on foot every day.

At the conclusion of their research trip, Yisroel and Leah spent a few days at Acadia National Park in Maine. The park is situated on property that was donated to the United States by the Rockefeller family in order to preserve it in its pristine form. Carriage trails through the forest are still beautifully maintained from the days when the Rockefellers were driven through the stately forest in luxurious horse-drawn carriages.

One day, as Yisroel and Leah were walking on one of the carriage trails, they saw a man approaching from the distance. As the man drew closer, they were amazed to see that he appeared to be a *frum* Jew, a Yid with a beard in the wilds of Maine. When they were standing a short distance from one another, they greeted each other with a warm *"shalom aleichem"* that led to the standard list of questions that two Yidden ask when they meet.

(l to r) Reb Peretz Chaim Levin (a.k.a. "Acadia Man") and Tsemach Glenn

"What's your name?"

"Peretz Chaim Levin," the man told Yisroel. "And yours?"

"Yisroel Neuberger."

Leah interjected, "From his books and articles people know him as Roy."

The man started yelling at the top of his lungs.

"Roy Neuberger! I just finished your book last night!"

It turned out that Reb Peretz Chaim Levin was active in Vaad L'Hatzolas Nidchei Yisroel, the legendary organization founded in 1976 by Rabbi Mordechai Neustadt that was dedicated to reviving Torah life in the Soviet Union. Of course, after that auspicious meeting, they had no choice but to become close friends. To this day, they refer to one another as "Acadia Man 1" and "Acadia Man 2."

The Acadia friendship eventually led to an invitation to Yisroel to serve as the keynote speaker at the Vaad's annual dinner, which was appropriate given the Neubergers' experiences speaking in the former Soviet Union and the translation of *From Central Park to Sinai* and *2020 Vision* into Russian and Georgian. This dinner proved to be an emotional experience because Yisroel could bring first-hand testimony to the power of the rebirth that was taking place in those distant lands.

Yisroel at the Vaad L'Hatzolas Nidchei Yisroel dinner with
Rabbi Chaim Yisroel Belsky, *zt"l*, and Rabbi Matisyahu Salomon, *shlita*

As soon as he received *2020 Vision* from the publisher, Yisroel brought his father a copy, not sure how he would react since he generally didn't read books on Jewish topics. He left it on a table next to his father's chair, then went downstairs and drove home, doubtful that his father would read it. Besides, he was already 105 years old, and it wasn't so easy for him to read.

When Yisroel returned the next day, he found his father immersed in *2020 Vision*.

"Hi, Dad, how're you doing?"

His father put his finger on his lips. "Don't disturb me. I'm reading my son's book!"

"My father liked the book so much," Yisroel says, "that he read it four times, with his own 105-year-old eyes!"

It seemed that the book had a far-reaching impact on everyone who read it (just as Yisroel had hoped). The first email Yisroel and Leah received after the publication of *2020 Vision* came from an American medical student who is today a well-known physician living in Israel. Years later, Yisroel and Leah met him in Israel, and he told them that his family made aliyah because they were inspired by *2020 Vision*.

Many other enthusiastic letters followed.

On July 3, 2008, Yisroel was in the middle of a PR campaign for *2020 Vision*. He walked into a bookstore on Avenue M in Brooklyn called Judaica Place and got into a conversation with the owner, explaining the background and theme of the book and

Speaking at Barnes & Noble in northern New Jersey

People lining up to buy books and speak to Yisroel and Leah

adding that he would be happy to do a book signing in the store. In the middle of the conversation, the phone rang, and one of the store's employees called out to the owner, "Avrumi, it's for you."

Yisroel couldn't help but overhear the owner's conversation with the person on the other end of the line.

"Oh, Rabbi Zlotowitz, how are you? You want to send your driver over for a book? Of course! Which book would you like?"

It turned out the order was for Yisroel's book, *2020 Vision*.

"Wait a minute!" the store owner cried. "The author is standing right here with me now. I'll have him sign it for you!"

Two minutes later, Rabbi Meir Zlotowitz's driver walked in and received a signed copy of *2020 Vision* to bring to the founder and president of ArtScroll Publications.

That was a nice day for Yisroel Neuberger.

◆ ◆ ◆

In the month of Adar in the year 2013, Yisroel spoke on a Friday morning for the Jerusalem Kollel, founded and headed by Rabbi Yitzchok Berkovits. In this program Yisroel conveyed the perspective of a *baal teshuvah* and gave the *kollel* members insights into how to reach the hearts of people who had grown up without Torah. The program was well received, and Yisroel was extremely upbeat as he went out on the street to find a taxi. It was about twelve noon.

Somehow taxi hunting wasn't so easy that day, although it was a busy street. The taxis all had passengers, and Yisroel didn't feel like phoning for a cab. It was a warm spring day, and he was enjoying the sunshine, so he just stood there and waited. Finally, after about fifteen minutes, an empty taxi passed by going in the other direction.

Yisroel signaled and the driver yelled across the street, "Where are you going?" He started to make a U-turn but changed his mind: maybe the taxi driver was in a hurry to get home for Shabbos. He noticed another passing taxi, and the second taxi did make the U-turn.

Yisroel loaded his briefcase in the trunk and entered the cab. The driver, a friendly Bukharan named Menashe, wanted to talk. He asked Yisroel what he did, and Yisroel told him that he was

Yisroel with Menashe the cabdriver holding a copy of *2020 Vision* in Hebrew

a writer of books and articles and, together with his wife, went around speaking to Jewish groups around the world. Menashe asked what books Yisroel had written, so Yisroel handed him his business card, which shows pictures of his books.

Menashe gave a yell and said, "Turn around."

Needless to say, Yisroel was taken aback.

"Take a look at the back of the taxi."

Yisroel turned around in his seat, and there, on the shelf behind the seat, was a copy of his book, *2020 Vision*, in Hebrew.

The driver loved the book so much that he carried it around in his cab.

Yisroel had waited and waited for a taxi. Dozens passed by, but they were full. He almost got one, but then that driver handed Yisroel off to another driver, and this guy is carrying Yisroel's book in his taxi.

When the taxi pulled up in front of his house, Yisroel called Leah to come outside to take a picture of the two of them with Menashe holding the book.

For Yisroel, it was a testament to how far-reaching one's message can be when you find the right medium.

Chapter Thirty-Three
The Movie

There are books that create a storm when they're released. That's what occurred with *2020 Vision*, Yisroel's only novel, which features a dramatic story line on an epic scale. Seeing the readers' reactions, Yisroel and Leah began to consider the idea of turning the book into a movie.

From 2010 until 2017, Yisroel and Leah put immense effort into that dream. This would lead to dozens of conversations with movie professionals from the East Coast to Hollywood to Israel, until they hired a talented team to help carry out the dream.

Before he began working on the movie, Yisroel turned to rabbanim asking for their guidance. Rabbi Naftali Jaeger asked Yisroel, "What would happen if, after you're already deeply involved, you come to understand that there is no way of making this in a kosher manner? Would you be willing to drop it?"

"Yes," Yisroel answered simply.

"Then you have my *haskamah*," Rabbi Jaeger said.

After the *haskamos* were in place, the question became "Now what?"

How does one produce a movie?

Enter Ron Parnes.*

Ron had been working with Yisroel and Leah for years, handling PR for their many projects. He was an old-time New York PR pro who, among other coups, had placed the Neubergers onto numerous late-night radio shows that were broadcast to millions of people.

Naturally, when the idea came up to make his book into a move, Yisroel called Ron. "You've done a great job handling our PR for years," he said, "and now we want to take things to the next level."

"What do you mean?"

"We want to make a movie out of one of my books."

"Yisroel," Ron replied, "I'm ready to retire. Making a movie right now isn't for me."

"So what should we do?"

"I'm going to introduce you to my son-in-law. He'll help you."

Which is how Yisroel and Leah came to meet Ken Devine.

◆ ◆ ◆

Ken is a very talented individual who became inspired by Yisroel's vision for the film. He told Yisroel from the beginning that it was an "impossible" dream, but he was willing to help him try to achieve the impossible.

"To whom do you want to pitch the movie?" Ken asked. "What's your niche?"

"Everybody! The entire world is looking for hope! It's universal."

(This was Yisroel being Yisroel.)

"But you need a target audience."

(This was Ken being Ken.)

"The whole world is the target audience," Yisroel insisted.

During the next five years, Yisroel and Ken would speak to dozens of people in their attempt to produce the movie. The first step was to find a screenwriter and investors.

The first screenwriter they found was a young *baal teshuvah* who was in the film business. Yisroel sent him a copy of *2020*. He loved the book, was inspired by the message, and wanted to give it a shot. Yisroel and Leah were very excited by his response. But when they read his screenplay, their disappointment grew with every page. Yisroel had been very clear about his vision for the film, which basically meant being true to the narrative of the book. The screenplay was not that.

◆ ◆ ◆

In the wake of attempt number one, Yisroel and Ken followed up on every idea that came their way, to no avail. No one had good leads on a screenwriter, and no one was willing to commit to funding the project.

There is a specialty in the film industry called a line producer, whose job is to review a screenplay and tell you how many actors the movie needs for every scene and the projected costs for the entire project. The estimate Yisroel was given was in the range of fifty to one hundred million dollars if they made the breathtaking epic Yisroel had in mind.

A breathtaking epic that carried a breathtaking price tag.

But Yisroel is not one to give up. Someone suggested that he meet with a savvy woman named Julia Davis,* a wealthy widow who had produced some famous movies. The team hoped she would see the potential in *2020 Vision*.

Julia was cautiously interested and was impressed by Yisroel and Leah's sincerity. At the same time she did have a concern.

"Who is the audience for this film?"

Yisroel gave his usual reply. "Everyone!"

We've already learned that the professionals would shake their heads and smile at this answer, and she was no different.

And there were other problems.

Yisroel and Leah insisted that the movie be done completely in accordance with the halachah. Everyone had to dress modestly and act according to the highest standards. The professionals wanted more leeway in their mode of dress, less character development, and more violence.

◆ ◆ ◆

They met another filmmaker through Hineni. This woman, whose daughter attended the Ethical Culture Schools, was so inspired after reading *From Central Park to Sinai* that she decided her family was going to become strictly kosher. She called the school and informed them that from now on her daughter needed kosher food. But the school wouldn't hear of it. The reaction to her request prompted the mother to switch her daughter to a Jewish school instead. She came to love and value the Neubergers, but she still didn't feel that *2020 Vision* would be viable as a movie.

Then, finally, after years of searching, they were introduced to two *frum* professional screenwriters who believed in the project. They were smart, funny, idealistic, and wrote beautifully.

Yisroel and Leah thought this might actually work.

But in the end, the purity of the story as told in the book didn't survive the transition to a screenplay, and not through any fault of the screenwriters. Leah feels that it's because the medium — movies in general — is not a pure way of transmitting Torah values. Ironically, this point of view was echoed by one of the Neubergers' biggest fans, Steven Hill, who had been a Hollywood star. After he quit Hollywood, Steven Hill strongly opposed filmmaking and said that it was an inherently impure medium from which one should stay away.

There was a meeting with a religious Jew with a top-level job

Yisroel's movie team meets with Rabbi Naftali Jaeger, *shlita*

in Hollywood. He came to their house one morning, and the team shared breakfast and conversation. He had a few ideas, but that was where it ended.

They had put an incredible amount of time, energy, and resources into the project, but for whatever reason Hashem apparently didn't want it to happen.

In the end, after the project had occupied Yisroel and Leah for over ten years, another opportunity arose in Israel to make the film. The Israeli professionals were real believers and saw eye to eye with Yisroel and Leah. But then the rabbanim they consulted told them that the movie couldn't have women in it. Yisroel and Leah had no argument with the *psak*, but they felt strongly that the story depended on the family interactions that were depicted in the book. If there couldn't be women, then it wouldn't be true to the reality of a story that was written to be realistic.

And so they dropped the movie idea. That was it. It was finished.

Our job is to keep our eye on the goal and to do our best.

The rest is up to Hashem.

Chapter Thirty-Four
The NYPD and the NFL

After Yisroel and Leah became *frum*, Yisroel made a point of regularly meeting each of his parents for dinner in the city, usually on separate nights so that he would be able to spend quality personal time with each of them. It was an opportunity to honor his parents and maintain a close relationship with them even though they led a different lifestyle from his. These dinners also gave his parents the opportunity to discover the world of elegant kosher restaurants that existed in Manhattan, which made Yisroel and Leah's new life seem more normal. (His parents were at times surprised to encounter their own friends at these places.)

Yisroel would pick up his father after work at the City Athletic Club, and from there they would go out to dinner. One midwinter afternoon, he was on West Fifty-Third Street, in front of the Museum of Modern Art around the corner from the club. It was rush hour, and thousands of people were streaming out of the city on their way home. Those were the days when Edward Koch was mayor, and the street signs reflected his Jewish sense of humor, with slogans like "Don't even *think* of parking here!"

Suddenly, Yisroel realized that he had neglected to daven Minchah.

It was almost sunset. With no choice, he pulled out of the traffic, parked his car, and got out. Standing beside the car in a "No Standing" zone, with traffic streaming past and crowds rushing down the street, he turned to face east and began reciting *Ashrei*.

No sooner had the first syllable left his lips when he heard a loud and authoritative voice barking, "What are you doing stopping on this street? Move that car!"

Yisroel looked up to see a man in blue.

"I'm sorry, Officer," Yisroel said, "but sundown is in a few minutes, and I wanted to say my prayers before I miss my chance."

"You want to pray?" the cop responded. "You want to pray!"

Yisroel got nervous hearing the officer repeating his words. He figured he was really in for it now.

But no.

"You want to pray?" he said to Yisroel again. "That's a different story! You just stay here as long as you want. And don't forget — pray for me, too!"

When we do what we're supposed to do, people admire and appreciate us, and know that we are their connection to the Creator of the world.

Through the years, in his occasional interactions with members of the law enforcement community, Yisroel has found many cops with a strong spiritual side that can be very touching. Some would have told him to get back in his car, Minchah or no Minchah. But not this cop.

◆ ◆ ◆

One Erev Rosh Hashanah, Yisroel was on his way to daven at his mother's grave in Cypress Hills, Queens. On Jamaica Avenue, he made a left turn and realized there was a police car behind him, lights flashing. It was clear to him that the cop had been assigned to that spot, waiting for someone to make some technical infraction, because Yisroel couldn't figure out any obvious reason for being pulled over.

The cop approached the car. His first words were "What happened to your mirror?"

Yisroel's car had folding side mirrors that closed when the ignition was turned off, which made the cop think there were no mirrors. Yisroel showed the cop how, by turning on the ignition, the mirrors resumed their normal positions.

This deflated him a little, but not much.

"Where are you going?" was his next question.

"Tomorrow is Rosh Hashanah, Officer," Yisroel replied. "The Jewish New Year. I'm on my way to the cemetery to visit my mother's grave."

"You're going to your mother's grave?"

With those words, the most amazing thing happened.

The police officer literally began to shake. Yisroel had never seen anything like it. His gaze softened, and it seemed to Yisroel that he could see tears welling in the corners of his eyes.

"When you go to the grave, you're going to pray there, right?"

"Yes, Officer."

"Can you please pray for me?"

Yisroel drove off, leaving behind a New York police officer with tears rolling down his cheeks.

♦ ♦ ♦

Yisroel was walking home from shul one Motza'ei Shabbos in Lawrence. When he reached his street corner, he saw police cars, lights flashing in the darkness. The police had erected barricades and closed off the street.

Approaching a cop, Yisroel said, "Excuse me, Officer. May I ask you what's going on?"

"Do you live here?"

"Yes."

"There was a problem with an electrical line and a transformer exploded."

The next thing they knew, they were having a conversation and Yisroel was telling him his life story. The officer was intrigued.

"So you decided to become religious? Wow, that's amazing! And what do you do now?"

"Well, actually, I'm an author."

"That's great. What kind of books do you write?"

"The first book is my life story and the journey my wife and I took to become religious."

"How did it sell?"

"Thank G-d, people really like it."

"I'm glad for you."

Then: "May I please have a copy of your book? I'd love to read your story!"

Yisroel was more than happy to go home, get a copy of *From Central Park to Sinai*, and give it to the police officer.

◆ ◆ ◆

Yisroel was once entering the Cross Island Parkway when a highway patrol car, lights flashing, suddenly shifted into reverse and began backing up the entrance ramp, closing it off just as Yisroel was entering. Getting out of his car, Yisroel approached the officer to ask what the problem was.

"There's a 'package' coming through," came the terse reply.

"What do you mean, a 'package'?"

"A bomb."

"Really?"

"Someone reported a suspicious object, and the bomb squad is bringing it to Rodman's Neck in the Bronx, where we explode suspicious objects."

Meanwhile, dozens of police officers were closing off every entrance to the highway so that the bomb squad could get through. Everyone had to wait until the "package" had reached its destination. As they waited, Yisroel's conversation with the highway cop resumed.

"You look like a doctor to me," the highway cop said.

"Actually I once thought about becoming a doctor, but then I found out that I can't stand the sight of blood."

"Okay, so you're not a doctor. What line are you in?"

"I'm an author. I write books."

The cop's interest was piqued. "May I have a copy of one of your books?"

"I don't know if you're going to be able to relate to the book," Yisroel said. "It's the story of a Jew's journey back to his religion."

"On the contrary," the cop replied, "it sounds fascinating."

Yisroel happened to have a copy of *Central Park* in his trunk, which he handed over to the police officer.

"Oh, man," the cop said. "I'm really happy about this. Thank you."

The highway opened up soon afterward and they said good-bye.

◆ ◆ ◆

One Friday in the middle of the summer, Yisroel and Leah left their home for the drive to Lakewood to spend Shabbos with their children. As they approached the Goethals Bridge, which links New Jersey with Staten Island, traffic was very slow. It seemed that half of New York had chosen that afternoon to drive to the Jersey shore. Suddenly Yisroel caught sight of a low-slung sports car weaving in and out between cars as if it were a race car. If there was a small gap between cars, the driver would manipulate his vehicle into it and then push on to the next gap. Yisroel was hoping to see a cop who would put a stop to this dangerous game.

A few minutes later, lo and behold, he noticed a Port Authority police car parked beside the highway. He pulled over in front of the patrol car and walked back.

"Officer, did you see that guy weaving between all the cars?"

"What about him?"

"That was so dangerous!"

"Did you just move to New York?"

"Officer, I've lived here my entire life, but this guy was over the top!"

"Do you know how many guys like that I see every day?"

"Yes, Officer, but the way he was driving was just crazy!"

The cop looked at Yisroel.

"I want to tell you something," he said, and Yisroel never forgot these words: "Today, crazy is the norm."

Yisroel would reflect on that statement for many years to come.

"Today, crazy is the norm."

Yisroel liked this cop and said, "Officer, I want to give you a blessing."

The policeman smiled. "Go ahead."

"I want to give you a blessing that you meet only nice 'customers.'"

"I have news for you," he said to Yisroel.

"What's that?"

"I met a very nice person today."

"Who was that?"

"You!"

It had turned into a touching and beautiful conversation. More, Yisroel felt that it had been a *kiddush Hashem*.

◆ ◆ ◆

Sometimes you just have a bad day. Everything seems to go wrong, and you can't help but wonder what's coming next. That's what happened one day when Yisroel and Leah had an appointment in the city. One thing after another kept going wrong, culminating with their boiler exploding, which caused a flood and a massive mess. By the time they left the house, their nerves were stretched to the breaking point and it was extremely late.

The cherry on top of the cake was when Yisroel inadvertently drove in a bicycle-only lane in the Rockaway Peninsula. A minute later, they heard a siren behind them and were pulled over by two policemen in an unmarked car.

"You were driving in a bike lane," the cop said.

"I didn't realize it," Yisroel said.

There must have been something about the look on Yisroel's face.

The cop gave a commiserating smile. "Having a bad day?"

"Officer," Yisroel replied, "I'm having an incredibly difficult day, and, to top it off, my hot-water heater just exploded."

"Get out of here," the cop said.

Cops are human, too.

◆ ◆ ◆

An unexpected request for a copy of *Central Park* came during a particularly memorable flight.

Waiting in the lounge for their flight to Israel to be announced, Yisroel and Leah caught sight of a group of about fifteen very large men. They appeared to be a sports team on their way to a game. Since it was an El Al flight, the Neubergers couldn't help wondering if the group had come to the wrong lounge, but the men settled down into their seats and waited to board. Clearly, they too were going to Israel.

On the plane, Yisroel found himself sitting across the aisle from two of these men. It wasn't long before they were all engaged in conversation. It turned out that they were NFL players on a mission to bring joy and excitement to disabled kids in Israel. Yisroel's two neighbors had many questions about what it means to be Jewish and were fascinated by the story of how he and Leah had become religious. Since they had plenty of time, Yisroel gave them the long version.

Meanwhile, Leah kept glancing at the woman beside her, who was engrossed in her *Tehillim*. Eventually Leah found a moment to introduce herself. Then she asked the woman's name.

"Leah Finkel," she replied.

"Are you related to Rav Nosson Tzvi Finkel?" Leah asked her.

"He was my husband," the noble-looking woman replied matter-of-factly.

A beautiful conversation ensued. Leah told Rebbetzin Finkel their life story, mentioning in the process her son-in-law and several grandchildren who had been learning in the Mir for years. The conversation culminated with an invitation by Rebbetzin Finkel for Leah to visit her. Leah, of course, took her up on the invitation and brought her daughter Miriam with her. Leah also brought along copies of Yisroel's books, which Rebbetzin Finkel appreciated, and the two developed a warm relationship.

A few hours into the flight, Leah took a walk in the aisle, and Yisroel introduced her to the two football players. They responded as many people do and wanted to shake hands.

Leah wasn't fazed.

Yisroel on the plane with NFL players
Renaldo Wynn and Michael Pierce

"I can't shake hands with you," she said. "Jewish law states that physical contact between a man and a woman is reserved for a woman and her husband and close family members, such as children and grandchildren."

She went on to explain the holiness and sanctity of marriage and why the Torah's rules about physical contact are as relevant today as they were thousands of years earlier.

The football players were deeply affected.

"That's awesome! Could we have copies of your book?"

"We have books in our luggage. As soon as we land, we'll get them for you."

"We'll wait."

They waited patiently at the baggage area until Yisroel found the books. Thanking them profusely, they asked Yisroel to sign the books and give them a blessing. Then they went off to visit the disabled children who were waiting to meet them, books clutched tightly in their hands.

It had been an interesting flight, with Rebbetzin Leah Finkel on one side and two NFL players on the other, two different worlds. Somehow, Yisroel and Leah had managed to connect with both.

Chapter Thirty-Five
Back on the Home Front

For many years now, Yisroel and Leah had been living in Lawrence. They had moved there in 1998, a few years after Rabbi Meshulem Jungreis passed away. For both the Jungreises and the Neubergers, it was the end of an era, and it was time to move on. Hineni was flourishing, with the Rebbetzin's work extending far beyond North Woodmere. And so, a year after her husband's passing, the Rebbetzin moved to Lawrence and Barbara Janov, Hineni's executive director and the Rebbetzin's closest friend, followed suit. The Neubergers, too, felt that they needed a fresh start, and the Rebbetzin was, after all, family. They, too, made the decision to move to Lawrence.

When Yeshiva Sh'or Yoshuv moved from Far Rockaway to Lawrence in 2003, Yisroel began davening there regularly. Having spent the first thirty years of his life without opening a siddur — not even knowing what a siddur is — he has never gotten the hang of davening at the speed of sound. He likes to concentrate on every word, and consequently he loves a good yeshivah davening.

Yisroel was davening Minchah at Sh'or Yoshuv one day when he suddenly heard violent rattling. All the metal supports inside the walls and ceiling were vibrating. When the rattling finally ended, the shaking began, and Yisroel felt the floor moving beneath his feet. The effect of all this was magnified since the yeshivah was in the middle of *Shemoneh Esrei*, and there was total silence in the packed room. Remarkably, not one person moved from his place. There was no mass exodus of hysterical *bachurim*.

A good yeshivah davening, indeed.

It was, nevertheless, frightening.

After Minchah, Yisroel turned on his car radio, where he heard that an earthquake had just occurred in Virginia, almost four hundred miles away.

Sh'or Yoshuv was blessed with the presence of a special Yid named Rabbi Moshe Dov Stein, who was an inspiration to countless *talmidim*. Sadly, he passed away at a relatively young age. At the *levayah*, Yisroel heard words that he thinks about often.

"I called my father about two weeks ago," one of the sons said, "and I asked him, 'Tatty, how are you today?'"

"He answered, '*Baruch Hashem*, worse.'"

Rabbi Stein knew that he was dying. He knew exactly what was happening, and he had said, "*Baruch Hashem*, worse."

Sometimes three words can serve as a life lesson of epic proportions.

◆ ◆ ◆

Once he entered the halls of Sh'or Yoshuv, Yisroel found it hard to daven anywhere else, but occasionally he could be found at the Yeshiva of Far Rockaway, whose rosh yeshivah is Rabbi Yechiel Perr. (He was the one who had directed him to Jonathan David Publishers when he wrote his first book.)

One day Rav Nosson Tzvi Finkel, the legendary rosh yeshivah of the Mir in Yerushalayim, visited the Yeshiva of Far Rockaway. After Shacharis, Rabbi Finkel addressed the yeshivah. He stood at the podium, shaking from his illness. Yisroel would never forget a word he learned that day, a word he had never heard before: *teshukah*. Having a passionate desire for something.

Rav Nosson Tzvi said, "You have to have a *teshukah* for Torah!"

Every time he uttered the word *teshukah*, his arm would hit the *shtender*, an apparently involuntary movement caused by Parkinson's, but the arm always came down with a bang at the exact moment he uttered that word — *teshukah*.

It was an unforgettable encounter, even though Yisroel didn't even know what *teshukah* meant at the time; seeing Rav Nosson Tzvi's

Yisroel with Rabbi Nosson Tzvi Finkel, *zt"l*

face when he said the word and hearing that *BANG* was enough.

◆ ◆ ◆

Yisroel saw a similar look of *teshukah* on the face of a young man named Aleksey.

In the early nineties, a family of four named Chernobelskiy left Russia, along with many others, and immigrated to the United States. Though their roots in *Yiddishkeit* were strong, they had lost the *mesorah* due to oppression by the Soviet government. Both parents were engineers, and they had two young sons. The four suitcases they brought with them contained all their worldly possessions, so it was devastating when they discovered that someone had stolen one of their suitcases at JFK Airport. Unfortunately, that one contained their academic degrees and documentation, proving that they were qualified to work in their chosen field. The organization that had brought them to America found them a home in Tucson, Arizona, but was unable to find jobs for them since their academic credentials were missing. Thus, they were unable to support their family.

Their sons were resourceful and brilliant, and they decided that they would support their family. The older son found work in the field of computers — yes, even though he was still in high school — and he started earning money. The younger son,

Aleksey, was an expert ping-pong player who went on to become the ping-pong champion of Arizona. He made money not only from tournaments but also from endorsements from major companies.

Aleksey went on to attend the University of Arizona, where he had a quadruple major. In 2008, Aleksey, who at the age of nineteen had never met an Orthodox Jew who wasn't a rabbi, first heard Yisroel and Leah speak at a *kiruv* program in Brooklyn. Their story touched a deep part of him and contributed to his journey back to his roots years later.

Yisroel met Aleksey again a few years later when he was learning at Machon Yaakov, a yeshivah for *baalei teshuvah* in Yerushalayim. He didn't even know the *alef-beis* when he arrived, but he was so motivated that he and his *chavrusa* made a *siyum* on an entire *perek* of Gemara a mere six months after his arrival.

There was no doubt: he had a *teshukah* for learning!

Yisroel attended the *siyum*, where he heard Aleksey's *chavrusa* testify that the two of them had reviewed the *perek* 101 times. The *siyum* had taken place on the third *yahrtzeit* of Aleksey's father.

A week later, Yisroel took it upon himself to take Aleksey to Rav Chaim Kanievsky for a *berachah*. On the way back from their visit to Rav Chaim, the taxi driver asked them about their visit with

Aleksey (right) and his *chavrusa*, Mark Segal, as they make an emotional *siyum* on the sixth chapter of *Bava Metzia* with the rosh yeshivah of Machon Yaakov, Rabbi Berel Gershenfeld, looking on

the *gadol*, and Aleksey told him about the *siyum*, which he had made in honor of his father's *yahrtzeit*. The taxi driver asked what his father's name was. Then he said, "I'm assuming you learned the *perek* 101 times with your father in mind, because the *gematria* of his name is 101!"

Aleksey's *kallah* giving Leah a *berachah*

A Jewish taxi driver!

A few years later, Yisroel and Leah had the honor of attending Aleksey's wedding in Phoenix. When Leah gave the *kallah* a *berachah*, the *kallah* insisted on giving Leah one in return — a very long and memorable *berachah*.

◆　◆　◆

Gourmet Glatt is a popular supermarket. When the Neubergers moved to the Five Towns, Yisroel would often accompany his wife on her weekly pre-Shabbos shopping trips. Once, in the fruit section, Yisroel noticed an older couple nearby. Suddenly, the husband picked up some grapes and began eating them, followed by his wife.

Yisroel was shocked. Even if this couple had planned on buying the grapes, they still hadn't paid for them, and once they had eaten them, they wouldn't know how much money they owed. He decided to say something.

"Please don't," Leah told him. "The man is going to be angry and upset. Just leave it alone."

But Yisroel was determined.

Walking over to the couple, he said in a soft voice, "Excuse me, I'm sorry to bother you, but I want to point out that you just stole some grapes."

The woman looked down at the floor.

The man met Yisroel's eyes. Would he accept the reproof or get angry?

Grapes of *teshuvah* at Gourmet Glatt

The man replied in a soft voice, "You are absolutely right."

The Neubergers finished shopping and brought their cart to the checkout counter. Yisroel noticed that the other couple was also checking out. Suddenly the man made a bee-line toward them. Yisroel got nervous. Maybe he'd had second thoughts and was going to lash out?

Yisroel braced himself.

"Thank you," the man said. Then he repeated himself. "Thank you!"

He said the words fervently and sincerely.

Yisroel looked at him, utterly taken aback.

"I'm serious," the man replied. "I'm so grateful to you for having the courage to approach me. You gave me a wakeup call, and I'm truly grateful!"

Yisroel gave him a hug, and they parted as friends.

Yisroel left the store, excited. Here was a man who had not only accepted a *mussar shmuess* from someone he didn't know (and who likes receiving mussar?), but he even thanked Yisroel, and was now walking out of the store a new man.

"*Mi k'amcha Yisrael!*"

♦ ♦ ♦

There's a yeshivah in Queens called Stars of Israel Academy, which caters mainly to students of Russian and Bukharan background. The staff goes out of their way to convince nonreligious parents to transfer their children out of public school and into their yeshivah for junior high school. The yeshivah has an amazing way of reaching these boys and can usually bring them to the level where they are able to attend mainstream high school yeshivos.

"We don't usually speak to such young students," Yisroel says, "but the boys at Stars of Israel always ask so many questions. They're full of life and love of Torah. Every time we speak there, we leave even more inspired!"

"The first time we came," Leah says, "we were told that an hour was too long. The principal suggested that we speak for twenty minutes, but we wanted to give them a full program, and the kids loved it. Their comments and questions were focused and sharp. Not one boy became impatient."

Just after Chanukah in 2016, Yisroel and Leah pulled up outside the yeshivah for a speech. Leah got out first and started walking quickly toward the entrance because the program was starting soon. She didn't notice that a slab of pavement had been lifted by a tree root. The next thing she knew, she was lying on the sidewalk, her entire left side having hit the ground with shocking force. Her face and hands were bleeding and she was in pain.

Hatzolah arrived. Leah was examined, bandaged, cleaned up, and advised to go to the hospital. But by that time she was feeling better. She decided to recuperate in the yeshivah's office and told Yisroel to start the program by himself. The school secretary graciously made her a cup of tea.

Leah remembered the story of how Rebbetzin Jungreis's

Yisroel surrounded by the rebbeim and *talmidim* at Stars of Israel Academy

Leah inspiring the boys at Stars of Israel Academy

assistant, Barbara Janov, had once tripped over a metal bar at the entrance to a women's prison in Israel. She and her equipment, including expensive cameras. went flying in view of the prisoners. Like Leah, she picked herself up, bruised and banged up.

By the time Yisroel had reached the middle of his speech, Leah felt well enough to join her husband. The boys applauded loudly, since Yisroel had told them what had happened.

She didn't give her normal speech — she was still shaken — but rather, remembering the words of Rebbetzin Jungreis when Barbara fell, she said, "Boys, we all fall sometimes. I want you to remember that when we fall, Hashem helps us get up stronger than ever."

The boys burst into loud applause.

It would take Leah's bruises six months to heal. The inspiration she gave those boys, however, would last a lifetime.

PART 7

"I want my children to know that I am proud to be a Jew."

Dr. Stephen Trokel marking his "bar mitzvah"
at the age of eighty-three

Chapter Thirty-Six
The Journey of a Holy Soul

There was a restaurant called My Most Favorite Dessert Company, which was located on Madison Avenue between Eighty-Fifth and Eighty-Sixth Streets, essentially Neuberger territory. Yisroel was eating lunch with his mother there one day, when he took a deep breath and asked her a question.

"I know that you describe in your will the kind of burial that you want. Would you be willing to change your will and specify a Jewish burial?"

She answered him on the spot. One word. Direct.

"Yes."

He sat there, amazed and gratified.

When Leah later heard her mother-in-law's answer, she was certain that if they hadn't carefully nurtured their relationship with their parents after becoming observant, the answer would have been very different. Rebbetzin Jungreis never stopped stressing the importance of *kibbud av va'eim* and the debt of gratitude that people owe their parents. She always said that people need not only to respect their parents, but to be good to them as well. Yisroel and Leah went out of their way to work on their relationship with their parents. In fact, ironically enough, their relationship after becoming religious became even better than it had been before, not just with their parents, but with their siblings as well. After Yisroel became *frum*, Marie and Roy Senior generously donated significant sums to Torah institutions such as Beth Medrash Govoha in Lakewood. The fact that a couple like Roy Senior and Marie Neuberger contributed to religious organizations showed that they had learned to respect their children's decision to return to the ancient Torah way, and this was almost certainly a direct result of Yisroel and Leah's display of respect toward them.

As Leah's brother said to them, "You don't just talk the talk. You also walk the walk."

Coming from a close family member, that is high praise indeed.

Yisroel likes to retell a beautiful *vort* he heard from Rabbi Dr. Akiva Tatz. Rabbi Tatz said that *baalei teshuvah* often tend to disdain their parents because the parents are on a lower level of observance than they are.

This is a big mistake. Why, he asked, did these children become religious in the first place?

The answer is that they inherited something from their parents, certain sensitivities and values, a sense of searching, a desire to live by higher standards. Often the parents were not able to put their spiritual goals into practice, but the parents' spiritual goals were realized in the life of their children. So the children actually owe their parents the biggest debt of gratitude.

For this spiritual gift, they owe their parents even more respect and honor.

When they finished their meal, Marie Neuberger headed straight to her lawyer's office, where she instructed Jim Kaufman to write a new will incorporating her intention to have a Jewish burial. A religious Jew himself, Mr. Kaufman had been handling the family's legal affairs for decades and was a trusted adviser. Her dramatic decision had immediate ramifications, because shortly after her visit to the lawyer, Yisroel's father followed her lead and altered his own will as well.

How's that for a simple question tossed out over a piece of blueberry cheesecake?

♦ ♦ ♦

Rabbi Elchonon Zohn is the head of the *chevrah kaddisha* of Queens, as well as the founder of NASCK, National Association of Chevra Kadisha, an umbrella organization for the *chevrei kaddisha* of America. Yisroel first met him when Rabbi Zohn spoke at Congregation Ohr Torah in the 1990s.

"Following that speech, we developed a relationship," Yisroel says. "And if it weren't for him, I don't know if our parents would have had a kosher burial. It was *bashert*. We needed to meet Rabbi Zohn!"

Later Yisroel and Leah had the honor of visiting Rabbi Zohn's father, Rabbi Shachne Zohn, who lived in Yerushalayim. A former rosh yeshivah of Torah Vodaath and a *talmid* of some of the finest yeshivos of Europe, he also enjoyed the rare privilege of having been a *talmid* of the Chafetz Chaim. Yisroel brought a smile to

Yisroel with Rabbi Shachne Zohn in Yerushalayim

Rabbi Zohn's face when he described his son's outstanding work in helping countless Yidden successfully navigate the stressful moments of a loved one leaving this world.

In 2008, Rabbi Shachne Zohn had a dream that became famous in the Jewish world. In the dream, the Chafetz Chaim came to him and instructed him to tell the world that the final redemption was near and everyone should prepare for the arrival of Mashiach.

Reb Shachne, being a humble person, didn't mention the dream to others.

Then he had the dream a second time. In the dream, the Chafetz Chaim asked him, "Why didn't you announce publicly what I told you, that Mashiach is on his way and that they must prepare?"

This time, Rabbi Zohn followed his rebbi's instructions. At a family *simchah*, he recounted the dream, and the story was widely circulated. His son, Reb Elchonon, verified the authenticity of this incident.

◆　◆　◆

Three years before Yisroel's mother passed away, she became ill and had to be hospitalized. In the hospital, she was put into what is called a "medically induced coma." Yisroel, as her health care proxy, would repeatedly get calls from the hospital, who wanted to pull the plug on the respirator. He was under tremendous pressure, but he resisted.

Suddenly, after what seemed like an eternity, his mother woke up. She had been in a coma for weeks, but suddenly she was wide awake. Yisroel was vindicated for fighting so hard to keep her alive.

After she was discharged from the hospital, she was taken to Florival Farms, the family's summer estate, where she would be more comfortable. At Florival, the family needed a local physician to take on her care. Who could they call? Yisroel had an idea.

Yeshivas Ohr Hameir in Peekskill was located about ten minutes from the Neuberger country home. Yisroel spoke with

Rebbetzin Kanarek, the rosh yeshivah's wife, who told him that she had the perfect man.

"Call Dr. Melman."

Dr. Marty Melman told him — amazingly for the late twentieth century — that he would be happy to make a house call. The next Sunday morning he arrived at Florival. In the course of a pleasant conversation, Yisroel and Leah realized that Dr. Melman's own brother had spent many Shabbosos at their home!

Dr. Melman examined Yisroel's mother and then had a talk with the family. They sat on the screened porch. It was a beautiful spring day, but one of the family members was upset.

"Dr. Melman," he said, "we can't take it anymore. She's suffering so much. It can't go on like this!"

Dr. Melman had never met any of the family before, but he replied with direct and powerful words:

"I want to tell you something. Right now this woman isn't suffering at all. She has wonderful medical care and isn't in pain. *You* are the one who is suffering."

That lightning bolt changed everyone's perspective, and those words brought a new lease on life for Marie Neuberger. It was decided that she would be put into a nursing home where she would be given high-quality care.

In retrospect, the "high-quality care" wasn't good enough for Yisroel. If Yisroel has any regrets in life, it's that he didn't fight for the chance to take his mother into their home for the final years of her life. "Even the best nursing home is not like being at home surrounded by family," he says.

Of course, the family visited regularly, but Yisroel is still in pain because of this.

◆ ◆ ◆

Yisroel's mother lived for another year, her wits intact. Months later, Yisroel's siblings, Ann and Jimmy, went to visit her. During their visit, she made a statement that showed that she was well aware of her situation. People close to the Next World sometimes get flashes of what seems like *ruach hakodesh.*

She said, "It's time to cross me off the list."

Yisroel realized that his mother had experienced a premonition that her time in this world was drawing to an end. By the next morning — Erev Shabbos — her blood pressure was dangerously low, and she had edged into critical condition. She was rushed to the hospital, and Yisroel drove there to be with her.

After her condition was stabilized and the doctors felt it was safe for him to leave, he returned home for Shabbos.

"I returned to the hospital Sunday morning," Yisroel said. "When I arrived, I got a feeling this was it. I called Rabbi Zohn and he walked me through the steps. I recited *vidui* with Mother and asked her to repeat the words of the *Shema* after me, which she did."

Yisroel and Leah's dear friends David (who had come for so many Shabbosos when he was single) and Caroline Gabay joined Yisroel at the hospital. Meanwhile, Rabbi Zohn alerted the *chevrah kaddisha*, just in case. It was Mother's Day, and traffic jams were expected, so everyone was worried that the *chevrah kaddisha* might have difficulty reaching the hospital.

On the phone, Rabbi Zohn emphasized that in the event of her death, no tubes should be removed and she should not be moved to the morgue. Yisroel relayed these instructions to the nurse.

"I'm sorry, sir, but you're going to have to discuss this with the head nurse."

Shortly afterward, Terry Hyde, the head nurse, arrived.

"How can I help you, sir?"

Yisroel told her everything he had heard from Rabbi Zohn.

Terry started to cry.

Yisroel feels that she became emotional because she was a righteous woman who saw the *kedushah* in the way he was conducting his mother's ascent to the World of Truth.

"Just tell me what I can do for you," she said.

Yisroel's mother passed away between nine and ten Sunday evening. He was at her side during her final moments. Two men from the *chevrah kaddisha* dressed in suits and ties arrived, after navigating Mother's Day traffic, at 11:45 p.m. The nurses were impressed. Yisroel felt as if two angels had just entered the room.

♦ ♦ ♦

It was the end of an amazing life, which had begun in New York at the beginning of the twentieth century with her birth into a family who had forgotten their Jewishness. It ended with at least part of the family ensconced under the wings of Torah. Marie Salant Neuberger herself had tasted the beautiful fruit of Torah, had merited *frum* children and grandchildren, and had even traveled to Israel, where she had kept Pesach with her children.

And now she was about to merit a burial in accordance with Jewish law.

Discussions regarding burial arrangements would have to wait until the next morning. It was late at night and the rest of the family, including Yisroel's 94-year-old father, were far away in Manhattan. In the meantime, Yisroel's mother was in the care of the *chevrah kaddisha*, and that was a huge consolation.

After Shacharis, Yisroel drove into the city to meet with his father and siblings at the Pierre. He turned on the radio to hear the traffic report. Then came the weather forecast.

Something caught Yisroel's attention.

It was a beautiful spring day with a light breeze. The sun was shining, the sky was blue, and it was a perfect seventy-five degrees. "But," said the announcer, "there is a major weather change coming up. Starting tomorrow, a strong storm system will be moving in, with high winds and urban flooding expected until Friday."

Yisroel's brain clicked on those words.

Yisroel pulled up in front of the Pierre Hotel, where his father lived. Yuri the doorman greeted him with his usual warmth. Yisroel ran through the door, catching an elevator to the tenth floor.

The family was gathered in the living room, the atmosphere tense. They had already decided the funeral would be at the gravesite. The discussion turned to timing.

"We can't do it today," Yisroel's sister said. "My children in California need time to get here."

But there was a problem only Yisroel knew about: the weather.

"Dad," Yisroel said, "there are going to be severe storms every day this week, starting tomorrow. It will make the burial extremely difficult."

A long silence.

All of a sudden, Roy Senior slapped his knee. "That's it. We have to do it today!"

But could it be done? It was almost noon. And what about a minyan?

Yisroel called the cemetery, which closed at three.

"I'm sorry, we can't do it today," he was informed.

"Why?"

"There's an extra charge after three. We have to hold the workers overtime."

"What's the extra charge?"

"Four hundred and fifty dollars."

"We'll pay it."

Against all odds, the funeral of Marie Salant Neuberger was going to be that day. Yisroel started making calls to gather family and friends and organize a minyan. Jim Kaufman joined them. Jewish partners from Neuberger Berman agreed to come. The *chevrah kaddisha* was alerted, and they all made their way to the cemetery.

The *levayah* was well attended. Besides family and friends, there were those whose lives had been touched by Marie's kindness.

"When I was young and we were living on the Upper East Side, we lived in apartment buildings with doormen and elevator men," Yisroel says. "Most of the tenants never spoke a word to the building workers, but my mother knew every one of them and made a point of sending gifts to their children during the holiday season. When she died, all the Irish doormen and elevator men from 993 Fifth Avenue came to her memorial service and cried."

The funeral and burial took place as the shadows lengthened on a beautiful spring afternoon. Rabbi Osher Jungreis, Yisroel and Leah's son-in-law, presided.

"I was worried about how my father would react when he saw the casket," Yisroel says, "because it was so simple and unadorned. But he looked at the pine box and said, 'So unpretentious. Just like Mother!'"

Rabbi Osher Jungreis spoke to the assembled friends and family for about five minutes. Roy Senior was given a folding chair to sit on. When family members and close friends began shoveling the dirt into the grave, usually the most emotional moment, Yisroel's father, who had never seen this done before, rose from his chair and said, "This is how it should be."

He then delivered his own farewell to his wife of sixty-five years.

◆ ◆ ◆

The family wished to have an obituary in the *New York Times*, as befit such a great woman. Marie S. Neuberger had devoted herself to important causes in New York City and beyond.

Yisroel remembered a reporter named Wolfgang Saxon, who had written the obituary of Rabbi Meshulem Jungreis. He still had the contact information, so he called the *Times*. Saxon called back a few minutes later.

"No problem at all," he said. "Please call the obit assignment editor and tell them who it's for."

Saxon called back ten minutes later to tell Yisroel that he had been assigned the story. Later Yisroel would learn that the *Times* had obituaries prewritten on many famous and important people, ready to go to print when needed.

Saxon had only two questions:

"Does your father's art collection really include Jackson Pollock and de Kooning?" and "In which Westchester community is your parents' country home?"

Other than that, the paper had all the information it needed.

"What about a picture?" Yisroel asked the journalist.

"We have a picture of your mother in our files," he replied.

"Is it up-to-date?"

"Not very. Do you have something better?"

"Yes, I have a picture with me right now."

"Where are you?"

"At the Pierre Hotel."

"I'm sending someone right over."

A courier arrived ten minutes later. Early the next morning there was a beautifully written obituary in the *New York Times*, including a picture of Marie S. Neuberger.

♦ ♦ ♦

On his mother's first *yahrtzeit* in 1998, Yisroel visited her grave in Mount Neboh Cemetery in Queens. As he was leaving, he had a short conversation with Hashem.

"Hashem, I believe Mother is in the World of Truth with You, and if that's the case, I feel as if I had something to do with it. So I'm just wondering…if I could possibly receive a *shtickel* report about how she is doing…"

He didn't say a word to anyone about his conversation with the One above.

The next morning, his daughter Miriam said to him, "Abba, Grandma came to me in a dream last night. She was so happy!"

Yisroel sat there for a long time digesting this news.

Thank you, Hashem.

Chapter Thirty-Seven
Never Too Late

Roy's father had the habit of walking to work every day with several friends, even when he was in his nineties. His route took him through Central Park, starting at Seventy-Second Street and ending at Fifty-Ninth. His driver would be waiting for him, and the group of men would then be driven to their respective offices. After work, he would walk to the City Athletic Club on West Fifty-Fourth Street, where he enjoyed a daily massage, which was great for dealing with the various stresses of the day.

One day, on the way to the club, he was knocked down by a bicycle messenger as he crossed the street. Despite his advanced age, Roy Senior got up and continued walking. When he arrived at the club, a fellow member who happened to be an orthopedic surgeon said, "Roy, I don't like the way you're walking. What happened to you?"

"I just got knocked down by a bike."

"Roy, you have to go to the hospital right now," the doctor said emphatically.

Tests revealed a broken hip.

At the age of eighty-nine he had continued walking with a broken hip until his doctor friend made him go to the hospital.

It was a classic Roy Senior moment.

This shouldn't be such a surprise. Everything he had achieved in his life attested that Roy Senior had almost superhuman fortitude. Only a few years later, Yisroel was in his midtown office (during his Wall Street years) when his phone rang. Roy Senior's secretary was calling to say that there was a fire in the Neuberger Berman office building. Yisroel dropped everything and ran over. It was a five-alarm fire, and there were hundreds of firemen on the scene. (A battalion chief later told Roy that the fire was similar in scale to the first terrorist attack on the Twin Towers in 1993.) The entire building had been evacuated, except for one person: Yisroel's ninety-four-year-old father refused to leave.

"I'm busy," he told the firemen.

The firemen weren't quite sure what to do with this ninety-four-year-old gentleman. Finally, the battalion chief radioed the firemen on the scene and ordered him evacuated, even against his will. Four firemen strapped him in a "stair chair" and carried him down the forty-four flights to the ground floor.

As soon as Yisroel arrived at the scene, he tried to locate his father. There were two battalion chiefs in charge, one on Fortieth Street, the other on Thirty-Ninth. The first one had no patience for him, so Yisroel headed over to Thirty-Ninth Street, where the other battalion chief was happy to assist him and assigned a fireman to help Yisroel find his father.

The fire was under control by then, but smoke was everywhere. That was an education, as Roy learned firsthand about the dangers firemen regularly face and the physical stamina involved in the work they do. Since elevators are off-limits during a fire, firemen often have to walk up dozens of flights of stairs while carrying sixty pounds of gear on their backs. He came away with an appreciation for these heroes who put their lives in danger every day.

"We were already up to the thirty-fifth floor when we met my father being carried down," Yisroel says. "Under protest!"

Once the firemen had carried Roy Senior down to the street, a quick-thinking Neuberger Berman PR man handed him a copy

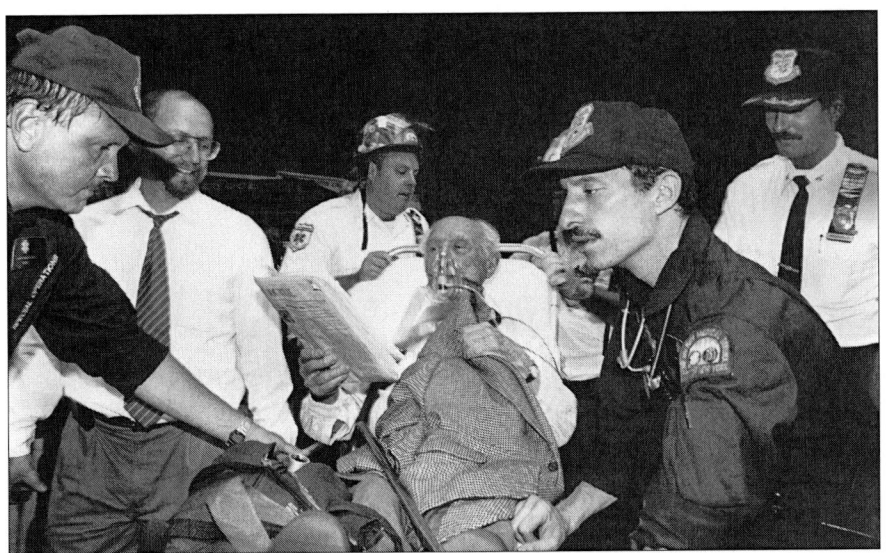

Roy R. Neuberger reading the *Wall Street Journal* after he was carried, under protest, away from the fire scene

of the *Wall Street Journal*. The founder of Neuberger Berman began reading the paper, still sitting on the "stair chair." An alert *New York Times* photographer promptly snapped the iconic image of Roy R. Neuberger surrounded by emergency personnel and calmly reading the *Wall Street Journal*. The picture appeared on the front page of the *New York Times* business section the next day.

It was another classic Roy Senior moment.

♦ ♦ ♦

At the age of ninety-nine, Roy Senior began having trouble walking to work every day because of a spinal condition. From then on, he was more or less confined to his suite at the Pierre Hotel, although he had a regular trainer and went out to the park across the street in a wheelchair.

Yisroel visited him every day, six days a week, until he passed away years later at the age of 107. It took Yisroel at least an hour to get there; he stayed for an hour and the drive back took another hour, which meant that his daily visits took over three hours out of every day. For Yisroel, it was an opportunity to perform the mitzvah of *kibbud av* and he grasped it with both hands.

Instead of riding the elevator up to his father's floor, he would take the stairs, walking up the ten flights to keep in shape. Since his father loved biographies and reading was getting more difficult, Yisroel would read to him, and they finished many books together.

Since he visited the hotel every day, Yisroel became friends with many of the hotel employees, including two Russian Jewish doormen, Yuri and Gregory.

Yuri was about six foot three and was so good at his job that he made it to the cover of a prominent New York magazine as "Doorman of the Year." The doormen at the Pierre wore long coats and top hats. The head of security at the hotel was a retired New York City detective. He and Yuri didn't get along, which was unfortunate, since he was Yuri's boss. But Yuri was one tough guy (with a soft heart beneath the hard exterior).

One day Yisroel was standing outside talking to Yuri when the head of security came out with one of the guards. In the middle of their conversation, he pointed at Yuri and said, "See that guy over there? He doesn't like me."

He said the line loud enough so that Yuri heard it nice and clear.

"I have news for you," Yuri replied. "Nobody likes you!"

As we said, Yuri was one tough guy!

When Yisroel left the hotel after his visits, Yuri would literally stop traffic for him. He would stand in the middle of the street and put both hands high up in the air like a traffic cop. It didn't matter who was

Yuri the doorman

Yisroel with Gregory

coming down the street. For his part, Yisroel always made sure to bring both Yuri and Gregory *mishlo'ach manos* for Purim and a package of *shemurah* hand matzah for Pesach.

Gregory is a quiet and wonderful man who loves Israel. Upon his retirement (he is now the most senior doorman at the Pierre), he and his family plan to go on aliyah. He loves nothing more than being Jewish. Gregory's face always shines with a big smile whenever Yisroel and Leah come to visit.

There is another remarkable story about a Pierre doorman, this one named Muhammed. No, he isn't Jewish, but he is a friend who shows Yisroel a great deal of respect. Whenever Yisroel would go to Israel, Muhammed would say to him, "Please remember to pray for me in the Holy Land."

One day Yisroel came downstairs and saw that Muhammed was upset. He said to Yisroel, "Someone told me that King David was a sinner. I told him, 'That is impossible. King David was a

Yisroel with Muhammed

holy man, the king of Israel!' Mr. Neuberger, tell me it's not true! Tell me that King David was not a sinner!"

"Muhammed, you are so right," Yisroel said. "G-d will bless you for saying that King David was a great man."

Every Yisroel and Muhammed should get along like this!

♦ ♦ ♦

When Yisroel's father was 103, he was told that he needed cataract surgery. There was no question in Yisroel's mind whom to consult: ophthalmologist Dr. Stephen Trokel at Columbia Presbyterian Hospital. Dr. Trokel knew his father and was familiar with his medical condition. With a patent on laser vision correction, Dr. Trokel is internationally known and respected.

Yisroel was sitting in the office of Jim Kaufman, the family's trusted lawyer and adviser, along with his sister and brother, discussing whether or not his father should have the cataract surgery.

"I have Dr. Trokel's cell number," Yisroel told them. "I'll give him a call and let's see what he says."

Dr. Trokel was vice chairman of the department at the hospital and extremely busy. Still, he answered the phone. (The busiest people usually do.)

"Dr. Trokel, this is Roy Neuberger. I'm sitting here at our lawyer's office with some members of my family, and we're trying to figure out if my father should have cataract surgery at the age of 103."

"I'll be right over."

Yisroel was taken aback. He hadn't expected Dr. Trokel to drop everything and come over in the middle of the day.

Dr. Trokel arrived a few minutes later.

"I want to tell you something," the doctor said. "Your father's whole life has revolved around art and his sense of sight. He has to be able to see. In my opinion, there is no choice but to perform the surgery."

Dr. Trokel arranged for the operation to be done by a famous cataract surgeon by the name of Dr. Richard J. Mackool, whose Long Island City clinic occupied an entire building. Before they knew it, the red carpet had been rolled out for Roy Senior. Dr. Mackool's sister, the administrator of the clinic, literally held Mr. Neuberger's hand during the procedure.

"Cataract surgery is quick, and my father returned home the same day," Yisroel recounted. "His first comment upon entering the apartment was 'Who cleaned the paintings?'" Obviously, the surgery had been successful.

The world was bright again.

♦ ♦ ♦

A few years later, Yisroel's phone rang. The caller identified himself as Rabbi Aharon Zuckerman from Lakewood, a patient of Dr. Trokel.

"To what do I owe this honor?" Yisroel asked.

It turned out that Dr. Trokel had just returned from a trip to Europe where he'd visited the cemetery where his grandfather was buried. He was now filled with questions about Judaism.

"Dr. Trokel told me that he has another religious patient — you — and I know that he likes and respects you," Rabbi Zuckerman said.

It seemed that Dr. Trokel, at the age of eighty-three, had decided the time had come to celebrate his bar mitzvah, a mere seventy years after he turned thirteen.

So it came about that Yisroel and Leah organized a beautiful bar mitzvah celebration for Dr. Trokel. By the time the day arrived, Rabbi Osher Jungreis had already provided intensive tefillin lessons for Dr. Trokel. The davening was held at The Beis (Rabbi Yonason Shippel's shul) on the Upper West Side of Manhattan with a large minyan in attendance. Since the bar mitzvah took place during Elul, Tsemach Glenn, who had also helped organize the celebration, not only *leined* the Torah but blew shofar as well. The davening was followed by a catered meal at which both Rabbi Zuckerman and Yisroel spoke, as well as the esteemed "bar mitzvah boy" himself.

"I'm eighty-three years old," Dr. Trokel said, "and I thought it

Yisroel with Dr. Trokel and Rabbi Aharon Zuckerman (right)

was time that I had a bar mitzvah celebration." He added another line, aimed at his entire family, who had gathered to celebrate with him: "I want my children to know that I'm proud to be a Jew."

◆ ◆ ◆

During their speeches, Leah always makes a point of telling listeners that it's never too late in life for a person to make important changes. She would tell the students how she and her husband, at the ages of thirty and thirty-one, married for eleven years with two children, completely changed their lives. This is true whether a person is thirty, fifty — or 105.

Years ago, Tsemach Glenn mentioned to Yisroel that Rabbi Shmuel Berenbaum, legendary rosh yeshivah of the Mirrer Yeshivah in Brooklyn, was experiencing severe back pain. Although he had never met the rosh yeshivah, Yisroel thought he might be able to help. He had a longtime connection with a famous neurologist and asked the doctor if he would consent to go to the Mir to examine the rosh yeshivah. Yisroel drove the doctor there, and when they arrived, they closed off a classroom and the doctor made his examination.

On the way to Brooklyn, the doctor, a Chinese American, mentioned that his father used to have a business in Shanghai selling fruits and vegetables. It happened to be that the Mir Yeshivah, which had fled to Shanghai to escape the Nazis, had bought their fruits and vegetables from him.

It brought new meaning to the saying, "It's a small world..."

It was through that interaction that Yisroel came to know Rav Shmuel, who eventually asked him to tell him his life story, which led to some questions about Yisroel's father.

"Did your father ever put on tefillin?" Rav Shmuel asked.

"I don't think so," Yisroel replied.

"Well, he needs to put on tefillin," said Rav Shmuel, quoting the Gemara in *Rosh Hashanah* 17a, which says, "Who are considered rebellious Jews who have sinned with their bodies? A head that never donned tefillin."

Yisroel with Rabbi Shmuel Berenbaum, *zt"l*

Now that Rav Shmuel had made that pronouncement, the question became how to make it happen.

While Yisroel wanted to do as Rav Shmuel had instructed, it was no simple matter. His father was over a hundred years old, and while they had a good relationship, he hadn't made any commitment to follow Yisroel's footsteps in returning to *Yiddishkeit*. Meanwhile, every few months Rav Shmuel's *gabbai*, Rabbi Pinchas Hecht, would call, telling Yisroel that the rosh yeshivah wanted to know if his father had put on tefillin yet. Besides, Yisroel couldn't stop thinking about Rav Shmuel's words and how he didn't want his father to leave this world without having performed this mitzvah. Yisroel and Leah felt the time was ripe after his father had been so inspired by Yisroel's book, *2020 Vision*.

◆ ◆ ◆

Yisroel asked Rabbi Naftali Jaeger for some advice as to how to proceed.

"Bring two pairs of tefillin with you next time you visit your father," Rabbi Jaeger said. "Help him put on the second pair. Then put on yours and say the *berachah* out loud. Have him answer amen to your *berachah*."

It would have been nice if Roy Senior would have been able to recite the *berachah* himself, but he was 105 years old and had no experience with making *berachos*. As it was, Yisroel was nervous and not sure how to explain all this to his father.

But in the end it worked out perfectly. Leah explained to her father-in-law that Jewish people have been putting on tefillin for thousands of years and that he would be joining a long chain of great people. Roy Senior not only agreed to put on tefillin but even raised the topic of traveling to Israel when he was speaking to his aide a few days later.

"How are we going to go to Israel?" the aide responded.

With complete confidence, his father said, "Roy knows. He'll take us."

Roy Senior had actually visited Israel back in 1993, over fifteen years earlier, when a Wall Street executive chartered an El Al 747 jet and flew a delegation of over one hundred businessmen to Paris and then to Israel, where they met with Prime Minister Yitzchak Rabin and Mayor Teddy Kollek. Roy's father was persuaded to join the group, and this became his first (and only) trip to Israel.

Each day, a different member of the group was asked to serve as the host. On the day they toured Yad Vashem, it was Roy Senior's turn.

"My father told me what an awakening that day was for him," Yisroel says. "He hadn't really understood what had transpired in Europe. That's how distant the Neuberger family was from anything Jewish, even something as momentous as the Holocaust."

It's not that he didn't know there was a Holocaust, but it had not penetrated his heart until he set foot in Israel's shrine to the six million.

♦ ♦ ♦

The year Yisroel's father put on tefillin, Yisroel spoke about it when he and Leah were back in Ann Arbor to speak to the students at their alma mater, University of Michigan. One of the participants that year was a premed student from Chicago by the name of Jared Spitz.

The morning after hearing Yisroel speak, Jared awoke with a jolt.

This man put on tefillin for the first time at the age of 105, he said to himself. *I'm twenty-one. Am I also going to wait until I'm 105?*

Jared called Rabbi Fully Eisenberger, the head of the *kiruv* program at the university.

"Rabbi, can you get me a pair of tefillin?"

"For sure! What's the question?"

The next time they returned to Ann Arbor, Yisroel and Leah learned that Jared had been putting on tefillin every day since their last visit. But it didn't end there, because Jared connected many other people to Torah and mitzvos as well, influencing many of them to put on tefillin.

So it was that the incredible story of Roy Senior putting on tefillin for the first time in his life at the age of 105 helped a

(l to r) Jared Spitz, Rabbi Jacobovitz, Yisroel, and Rabbi Fully Eisenberger
in Ann Arbor

young man named Jared become religious and make a positive impact on others as well.

It was a classic example of how one mitzvah leads to another, and sometimes to many, many more, not only for the person performing the mitzvah, but even for others in their orbit.

♦ ♦ ♦

Several years ago, Yisroel and Leah drove Rav Shmuel Kamenetsky home to Philly from a wedding in New York. It all began when Yisroel called the rosh yeshivah's *gabbai* and asked to discuss a personal issue with Rav Shmuel.

"The Rosh Yeshivah is going to be at a wedding in New York," he told them. "If you drive him back to Philadelphia, you can speak to him during the trip for as long as you need."

It seemed like a priceless opportunity, and they agreed. They made sure to stock the car with plenty of water for their guest. Rav Shmuel sat beside Yisroel, and during the long drive, Yisroel asked Reb Shmuel if he wanted a drink, but he declined.

It bothered Yisroel that Rav Shmuel had turned down the water. He thought about it a lot. In the end, he and Leah concluded that since they had forgotten to bring cups, Rav Shmuel wouldn't drink directly from a bottle.

They later had another opportunity to drive Rav Shmuel a second time. This time, they brought cups.

"I see you figured it out!" Rav Shmuel said with a warm smile.

At eleven p.m. Yisroel stopped at a rest area on the New Jersey Turnpike with Rav Shmuel sitting beside him. As they returned to the car, they

Rav Shmuel Kamenetsky looking over one of Yisroel's manuscripts passed a group of workmen laying floor tiles and creating an intricate mosaic design. Rav Shmuel stopped to look. Then he began questioning the men about their work.

"Can you explain to me how you lay the tiles? How do you manage to form the design so perfectly?"

The workers were flattered at the interest being shown in their work by the impressive rabbi, and they spent a good ten minutes explaining how they did their job. It was a beautiful scene, and Yisroel's only regret is that he forgot to take a picture, which he would have entitled "*Gadol HaDor* and the Tile Layers."

Chapter Thirty-Eight
A Meeting
With the President

In November 2008, President George W. Bush awarded Roy Senior the National Medal of the Arts at a White House ceremony. This medal is awarded to those who have made significant contributions to the arts.

Roy Senior certainly deserved this honor. He had gone out of his way to discover and nurture American artists, many of whom were unknown before he found them. Artists whose work he had purchased had gone on to take their place at the forefront of the American cultural scene. He had given numerous paintings and sculptures to museums around the country and had donated the bulk of his priceless collection to the state of New York.

Yisroel's father was one of twenty honorees, ten for contributions to the field of art and ten to the humanities. Every honoree was invited to bring along a number of family members and friends. The family was, of course, proud and excited about this momentous trip.

♦ ♦ ♦

On the appointed day, the entourage drove down to Washington D.C.: Roy Senior, Yisroel and Leah, Yisroel's sister Ann with her son Matthew, his brother Jimmy with his wife Helen, and one of the aides. The director of the Neuberger Museum also attended.

On the way, Yisroel had a conversation with Hashem.

"Ribbono shel Olam, I've been given the opportunity to meet the president of the United States, who I believe is the most powerful man in the world. Please allow me to utilize this opportunity to sanctify Your Name. Let the right words come to my lips, and let me speak the truth about Israel and the historical mission of the Jewish people."

Yisroel told his family that he hoped to have an opportunity to speak with the president.

No one thought there was a chance.

◆ ◆ ◆

There were around twelve hundred people at the White House that day, but only one wore a yarmulke on his head. The ceremony took place in a stately room, where rows of chairs had been set up for the honorees and their guests. Afterward a generous buffet was served in the State Dining Room. Separating the two rooms was a hallway nearly the size of a football field.

"The White House is like a palace," Yisroel says. "Looking through the grand windows, you can see the Washington Monument and many other landmarks. There was a sense of drama."

Yisroel later learned that those beautiful, clear windows were actually fourteen inches thick. And there were snipers on the roof...just in case.

President Bush struck him as a refined person. He had a short, personal conversation with each honoree, making him or her feel at home. Yisroel's father was in a wheelchair, being pushed by a young Navy officer wearing a black dress uniform with gold braids. Another honoree was also in a wheelchair. For some reason the officer pushing that wheelchair disappeared briefly, so President Bush himself took hold of the handles and pushed the wheelchair down the ramp. Yisroel was impressed with his self-effacement.

When the ceremony ended, the honorees and the president went into an adjoining room in order to be photographed, while the guests headed toward the buffet in the State Dining Room. Suddenly Yisroel had a hunch. He said to Leah, "I have a feeling that President Bush isn't going to come to the dining room."

He didn't know how he knew this, but he knew it.

"After the photos, he's going to his next appointment. Let's go back and see if we can find him."

◆ ◆ ◆

They headed back down the huge corridor toward the awards room.

Suddenly Yisroel saw a door opening in a wall maybe eighty feet away. President Bush emerged, surrounded by the Secret Service. It was obvious that he was leaving, heading for another door. It happened to be that Yisroel and Leah were standing in front of that door.

The president and his escort were moving very fast, and it seemed that Yisroel wouldn't have his opportunity to speak to him. But Hashem runs the show. Whatever He decrees will happen, no matter how unlikely.

Suddenly the president stopped. He had caught sight of someone with whom he wanted to speak, about six inches away from Yisroel.

"Ribbono shel Olam," Yisroel implored, "the president is standing beside me. Please place the right words in my mouth!"

When the president had finished his conversation, Yisroel spoke up in a quiet voice — he didn't need to raise it — and said, "Mr. President, may I give you a blessing?"

The president turned around. It looked to Yisroel as if the president really did want a blessing. (Didn't Hashem tell Avraham Avinu, "You shall be a blessing"?)

At that time, Bush was nearing the end of his second term. He was being lambasted for invading Iraq and failing to find "weapons of mass destruction." The press criticized the way he spoke. In fact, they criticized everything about him. This was the

Yisroel speaking with President Bush

backdrop as President Bush found himself face to face with a yarmulke-wearing Yid who wanted to give him a blessing, unlike so many others who only wanted to mock him.

It was a moment Yisroel would never forget. Hashem put the right words in his mouth, words that penetrated the heart of the president of the United States:

"Mr. President, I want to tell you why you're getting so much flak."

The president was listening. Yisroel had caught his attention.

"The reason you're getting so much flak is because you believe in G-d. You have moral standards. You believe in right and wrong. Most people out there aren't on your level. They don't believe in G-d and they don't believe in morality, and they want to pull you down to their level. That's why you're getting so much flak."

While he was speaking, Yisroel suddenly remembered that his camera was in his back pocket. He tried to pull it out, but it was stuck. It came loose abruptly, and Yisroel quickly handed it to Leah while he was talking.

"Mr. President, you are the most powerful person in the world at a time when the Children of Israel are returning to their land after two thousand years, as foreseen by the Biblical prophets. You have been given the opportunity to assist in the process of bringing about the return of our people to the Land of Israel.

"Mr. President, I bless you to be able to help G-d carry out His plans for our world. May He always be with you. May He put the right words in your mouth and guide you all your days. May He watch over you and your family, and may you have success in all that you do."

The president was looking at Yisroel intently. Clearly, his words resonated deeply with the Commander-in-Chief.

His words concluded, Yisroel asked, "Mr. President, would it be all right for my wife to take a picture of us?"

The president was more than happy to oblige. He put his arm around Yisroel, and the warmth between them was palpable. Leah snapped a memorable picture of her husband with the president of the United States. (Ironically, at the same time, the White House photographer was taking a picture of her taking a picture. The White House later sent it to Yisroel.)

Yisroel wanted to hand the president a signed copy of *From Central Park to Sinai*, which he had prepared in anticipation of their meeting. But a Secret Service agent grabbed it.

"No one is allowed to give the president anything," the official told him firmly. "We'll check it out and give it to him if it is fine."

Yisroel and Leah thought the chapter was closed, but there was a postscript to this beautiful conversation. A few minutes later, one of the president's aides came up to Yisroel and said something incredibly meaningful:

After the talk, a feeling of warmth

"Thank you for speaking to the president. He needs to know that he has friends."

♦ ♦ ♦

During the return journey, Yisroel's family was amazed to hear that he had actually had a deep one-on-one conversation with the president. Yisroel felt that it had been a great *kiddush Hashem*. President Bush later sent Yisroel and Leah a letter of thanks for the book. It was the perfect finale for what had been a truly monumental moment.

Chapter Thirty-Nine
Farewell in a Blizzard

Yisroel had just finished davening Shacharis at Sh'or Yoshuv on Friday, December 24, 2010, when his mobile phone rang.

It was Rosalinda, the nurse on call in his father's apartment at the Pierre. By that point, Roy Senior had an entire team looking after him. The head of this team was an experienced registered nurse named Lisa, and he had a nurse and an aide with him twenty-four hours a day.

"Your father isn't doing well," Rosalinda told him. "He's lost consciousness."

Yisroel told Rosalinda to call Hatzolah.

Yisroel stepped on the gas, but by the time he arrived, his remarkable father, at the age of 107, had already left this world. Hatzolah had tried to revive him, but his time had come.

♦ ♦ ♦

Yisroel spent that Shabbos at the Pierre. The *levayah* was scheduled for Sunday afternoon. On Sunday at midday, dark clouds descended over the city. Minutes later, the first snowflakes began to fall. A few snowflakes wouldn't have been a big deal — New Yorkers are accustomed to snow — but this wasn't a few snowflakes. The city was soon covered by a thick blanket of snow whipped around by sixty-mile-per-hour winds.

How would anyone be able to gather for the funeral on such a day?

Amazingly, despite the brutal conditions, there were three hundred people — including distinguished roshei yeshivah — at the funeral of Roy Rothschild Neuberger, which took place at a religious funeral home in Manhattan.

With Rabbi Elchonon Zohn's wonderful assistance, every detail was in place, so that when his father passed away, all Yisroel had to do was make a call to the *chevrah kaddisha*. For so long he had worried that he wouldn't be able to give his father the gift of Jewish burial, so he made sure to set everything up in advance.

The eulogies were moderated by Yisroel and Leah's son-in-law, Rabbi Osher Jungreis. The speakers included Yisroel, his sister, his brother, Yisroel and Leah's son Aharon Yaakov, his sister's

Rabbi Yechiel Perr, rosh yeshivah
of Yeshiva of Far Rockaway

son Matthew, a longtime Neuberger Berman partner, Marvin Schwartz, and the director of the Neuberger Museum.

After the *levayah*, Rabbi Yechiel Perr said, "Yisroel, you reminded me what a Jewish funeral is supposed to be like."

Yisroel believes that Rabbi Perr had in mind the unusual *shem tov* of Roy Senior, who was legendary in the world of big business for his righteousness and integrity, which was brought out at the *levayah* by the dignified *hespedim* offered by family members. Although Yisroel's father was not religiously observant, it was an astounding fact that he had

Rabbi Chaim Yisroel Belsky, *zt"l*, at the *shivah* for Yisroel's father

left behind a son who had come under the wings of the *Shechinah*. And the *hesped* delivered by Yisroel's son Aharon Yaakov demonstrated that the Torah had been passed down to the next generation. This was a huge *zechus* for the *niftar*. All this in the midst of a raging blizzard, which over three hundred people had braved to be there.

◆ ◆ ◆

Burial was a challenge. Yisroel would end up being an *onein* for four days.

The cemetery was a familiar place. It was where Yisroel's mother had been laid to rest, along with Roy Senior's parents and family, but getting there after the monster storm was another story. Driving in ordinary cars was unthinkable. It was only on Monday that Tsemach Glenn managed to get hold of several four-wheel-drive vehicles, and that was the only way they could reach the cemetery. Rabbi Zohn had had the foresight to order the grave dug on Erev Shabbos before the blizzard. Had they waited, there would have been no way to dig the grave, since the ground was frozen solid.

Burial in arctic conditions, with Rabbi Naftali Jaeger standing in the center

The burial took place under arctic conditions. A fierce wind whipped snow onto exposed skin. Looking at the pictures, one can see the pale and frozen faces of Rabbis Jaeger and Osher Jungreis. Despite these incredible challenges, Yisroel's father was buried with dignity, according to the halachah.

♦ ♦ ♦

When Roy Senior was about 106 years old, Yisroel and Leah brought a well-known rabbi to meet him. The rabbi wanted to understand how he had merited such a long life. His conclusion can be summed up in one word: *yashrus*. Honesty and integrity.

Roy R. Neuberger used to say, "I love to pay taxes." America had given him a good life and he wanted to give back.

Roy Senior was famed for his integrity, which was especially noticeable in the world of big business. Years later, Yisroel met the top New York surgeon who had operated on his father nearly twenty years earlier, when Roy Senior was ninety-nine years old. The surgeon was so impressed with Roy's father that when Roy

Yisroel with Rabbis Elchonon Zohn and Osher Jungreis
at Roy Senior's gravesite

Senior died in 2010, the surgeon and his wife braved the roaring blizzard to attend his funeral in Manhattan. The surgeon later told Yisroel, "Our only regret was that we didn't bring our teenage sons to the funeral to hear the words of praise for your father's integrity in the world of big business."

This surgeon isn't Jewish. But integrity is a statement to the whole world. It projects the message that "I fear G-d and I know that I must act scrupulously because I will have to account for all my actions in the World of Truth."

There are Jews who don't even know that they believe in Hashem, but their actions show that they do. This is the essence of the *pintele Yid.*

◆ ◆ ◆

In 2019, just after Succos, Roy's sister, Ann, visited Eretz Yisrael with one of her children, and the Neubergers spent a lot of time with her. Roy and Leah hired a guide and they spent one day touring Yerushalayim, another day in the Galil, and another at the Dead Sea. For Shabbos, the entire extended Neuberger family traveled up north to Kibbutz Lavi.

After the day meal, Roy enjoyed a Shabbos rest, but Leah went on a guided tour of the kibbutz with her sister-in-law and niece. Ann found herself walking beside a religious couple. Being fellow Americans, they started talking.

"Where did you grow up?" Ann asked.

"New York City."

"That's interesting. Where did you go to school?"

He laughed. "I'm sure you never heard of it."

Now she was intrigued. "Try me."

"Okay. It's called the Fieldston School."

He couldn't have shocked her more if he had told her that he'd gone to school on Mars. Her mouth dropped open. You have to understand: *frum* men with beards don't go to the Fieldston School. It's not the *minhag*...

"I also went to Fieldston!" she replied.

Now it was his turn to stare openmouthed. "What! I can't believe it!"

Roy, Leah and Ann with Fieldston graduate Rabbi Sholom Tzvi Brown and his wife at Kibbutz Lavi

"What do you do?" Ann asked.

"I'm a *sofer*," he told her. "I write Torah scrolls."

A religious Jew. Overtly *frum*. Long beard. A *sofer*. From Fieldston.

The whole scenario was incredible. Nobody could believe it. You could count on one hand (maybe two) the number of *frum* people who had been saved from the burning furnace that was Ethical Culture.

If the One Above wants a person to survive, he will.

Chapter Forty
The End of an Era

In August 2016, Yisroel and Leah traveled to Eretz Yisrael to be with their daughter Miriam, who was about to give birth. They had been in Yerushalayim for six days when they received a phone call from their daughter Yaffa, informing them that Rebbetzin Esther Jungreis had just passed away. It was difficult to believe. After all, this was the Rebbetzin they had been close to for decades and with whom they had become family. Their minds were filled with memories from their lifetime of interaction with the Rebbetzin.

They remembered the Rebbetzin standing in front of a shul in Newburgh about to speak, despite the fact that her assistant, Barbara Janov, had tried to convince her not to go, saying, "What's the point? Who will you speak to — two cows and a chicken?"

Speaking to a huge crowd in Madison Square Garden, her voice rising and falling, her emotions overwhelming her, making an impact on every individual who heard her message.

Giving *chizuk* to endless groups of people — singles and converts, children and soldiers.

Giving lectures at the Hineni center in Manhattan twice a week for years.

Leading trips to Israel, traveling on jeep trails to isolated military outposts to address the soldiers.

Adopting a young couple who had just moved to North Woodmere searching for truth so that their lives would never be the same again.

All this and more flashed through their minds when they heard the shocking news. They immediately called their travel agent to book the next flight to America in order to be at the funeral and pay their last respects to the woman who had filled their lives with Torah and hope.

"The next flight out is full," the travel agent informed them.

"When is the flight after that?" Yisroel asked.

"Tomorrow morning."

"But that's in another twelve hours!"

"Yes."

There was no choice. That was the only available flight.

"Please book us two seats."

◆ ◆ ◆

Yisroel had always been good at geography, which meant that he could look out of a plane window and know exactly where he was and what he was looking at.

"There are several approaches into JFK," he says. "We were coming in from the north. Leah and I were sitting on the left side of the plane, and as I looked out the window — we were pretty low by then — I saw that we were flying over Beth David Cemetery."

It was three in the afternoon.

"I remember looking up at the sky during my grandmother's burial," Yosef Dov Gertzulin later told Yisroel, "and seeing an El Al flight coming in literally right over our heads. Seeing the plane I commented, 'I'll bet Yisroel and Leah Neuberger are on that plane!'"

So it was that they were literally overhead as the funeral was taking place, even able to see it for a few moments. Of course, they remained in New York for the *shivah* and stayed with the Jungreis family throughout. After all, they were family.

When the *shivah* was over, they returned to JFK for their flight back to Eretz Yisroel. As soon as they landed, they took a taxi straight to the hospital to visit Miriam, who had just given birth to their new grandson.

As soon as one generation passes, another comes along to take its place.

Yisroel and Leah could have never asked for a better *nechamah*.

♦ ♦ ♦

With children and grandchildren living in Israel, Leah and Yisroel visited often. In February 2020, Yisroel and Leah traveled to Israel to attend their grandson's wedding. It was shortly before Purim and they planned to remain there until after Pesach. But Hashem had other plans, because this was when corona broke out and impacted the entire world. Planes were grounded and airports closed. They couldn't leave. Yisroel and Leah had always planned on making aliyah, and now they realized that this was the perfect time.

Yisroel said afterward that now he understood why it says in the Haggadah that Hashem took *Am Yisrael* out of Mitzrayim "*b'yad chazakah*," and then adds immediately, "*zu hadever*" — that this refers to the pestilence.

"Can you imagine?" Yisroel says. "The Haggadah predicted exactly how we would make aliyah! And if Hashem hadn't transplanted us to Israel like this without our even knowing what was happening, I don't think we would have had the fortitude to do it ourselves."

♦ ♦ ♦

Years earlier, on one of their regular trips to Israel, they arrived at their home in Yerushalayim and looked out the window. Leah did a double take.

"Yisroel, what is that thing in our backyard?"

"What thing?"

The "thing" was a rooster.

"Leah," Yisroel said before they turned in, "I'm so tired. I don't see how I'm going to be able to get up on time for Shacharis."

He needn't have worried.

The next morning at the crack of dawn their new pet rooster joyfully informed Yisroel that the time had come to rise and fulfill the will of his Creator. This experience brought new meaning to the *berachah asher nasan lasechvi vinah.*

The rooster in the backyard

Leah asked neighbors if they had lost a pet rooster. No one knew anything. They couldn't understand how the rooster had managed to enter their property, especially since the backyard was surrounded by high walls with no easy access. Since no one claimed ownership, they reached out to a *bachur* they knew who was learning at a yeshivah in a farm setting. He was happy to come to their home, where he cornered the rooster, placed it in a box, and took it back to the yeshivah — on a public bus.

Last they heard the rooster was living a very holy existence, waking up *yeshivah bachurim* for Shacharis every morning.

Only in Israel.

♦ ♦ ♦

In early 2020, just before their aliyah, Yisroel and Leah had an unforgettable experience when Rav Aryeh Malkiel Kotler, rosh hayeshivah of Beth Medrash Govoha, and his rebbetzin stayed at their home one Shabbos on a visit to the Five Towns. Yisroel felt quite anxious about hosting such a *gadol*, so he called in reinforcements in the form of his son, Aharon Yaakov, and his son-in-law, Yaakov Slatus. But Rabbi Malkiel is warm and approachable, and the family received firsthand experience of the delightful personality of this Torah giant.

One story sums it up:

Yisroel was davening Maariv on Motza'ei Shabbos at Sh'or

Yisroel with Rav Aryeh Malkiel Kotler and Rav Naftali Jaeger

Yoshuv, as was Rav Malkiel. When the davening ended, Yisroel's good friend Moshe Rubin, executive director of Sh'or Yoshuv, ran into his office to get his camera and take a picture of the two roshei yeshivah, Rabbi Naftali Jaeger and Rabbi Aryeh Malkiel Kotler. As Yisroel stood gazing at the majestic sight of these two great rabbis standing together, Rabbi Jaeger said to him, "Yisroel, get in the picture!"

"Rosh Yeshivah," he said, "I don't belong in this picture."

"Yisroel," Rabbi Jaeger insisted, "get in the picture."

Yisroel felt he had no choice, so he walked over and stood between the two roshei yeshivah, but he again repeated, "I really don't belong here!"

And then Rabbi Kotler made a remark that Yisroel will never forget, a remark that attested to his immense sensitivity to the feelings of every Yid and to his love of all of *Am Yisrael.*

"Yisroel, apparently you *do* belong here!"

Then Moshe Rubin snapped the picture.

Yisroel will never forget how these words touched his heart

and what they reveal about the great souls of the leaders of the world of Torah.

But perhaps even more, it is a testament to a years-long journey made in search of truth and the discovery of the place where one always belongs: living a life of Torah under the wings of the *Shechinah*.

Afterword

And so we arrive at the end of our current journey, though with Reb Yisroel and his *eishes chayil*, you surely know by now that they are already moving on to a whole new slew of wonderful and exciting projects.

What a life those two have had…so far!

From Roy's early days growing up on Fifth Avenue, his life was destined to take him along a highway that none of his family and friends had foreseen. From the moment Leah entered the picture, it was a perfect example of two halves of a *neshamah* finding one another. The two of them began a joint investigation into the purpose of life. Along the way, they spent months living in the wilderness as fire lookouts in an American National Park, years in Oxford studying and exploring Europe, years in Cornwall publishing a newspaper. And while it took them a very long time to discover the life of Torah, they got there in the end under the direction and tutelage of Rebbetzin Esther Jungreis, who would become their teacher, mentor, and friend, not to mention their *machateineste*.

Together with the Rebbetzin, they would travel to Eretz Yisrael and welcome thousands of people to numerous Hineni events, while hosting an endless parade of guests at their home for Shabbos, Yom Tov, and sometimes for months and even years at a time. Yisroel spent years working as the administrator of Yeshiva Ateres

Yisroel and Leah with their children, Sarah, Yaffa, Nechami, Ari, and Miriam

Yisroel, years on Wall Street, and finally years writing books and a long-running newspaper column in *Yated Ne'eman*, with Leah ever at his side, editing his work, hosting, and helping to share their story, all the while raising children who are themselves spreading the light of Torah.

Once *From Central Park to Sinai* was published, their life entered another stage. They started traveling around the world and addressing audiences who inevitably connected to their message and loved their words and Yisroel and Leah themselves.

From Mexico to Moscow, and from Manchester to Baku, Yisroel and Leah have never ceased conquering new frontiers, through their insightful words and personal story, and, more than that, with their delightful humor, warm smiles, and hugs or a shoulder to cry on.

Yet even now, after so many years of unceasing *avodas hakodesh*, they still wake up every morning and ask themselves the same question.

At home in Jerusalem

What kind of Jew are you?

And then they rise and prepare to be the kind of Jews that will make Hashem proud.

In a sense, their story is more than just their story. It is akin to the story of our nation, the story of a people who rises and falls, who knows the lows of suffering and torment and the joys of triumph and success. And it is their fervent dream and hope that all of us merit witnessing the real victory for our nation, so that they can one day write a book that will be titled *From Exile to the Beis HaMikdash*.

To contact Roy and Leah Neuberger:
email at roy@2020vision.co.il
or visit www.2020vision.co.il